D1271872

THE JOY OF FINANCIAL SECURITY

The art and science of becoming happier, managing your money wisely, and creating a secure financial future

Simplify

Prepare for Retirement

Nurture Creativity

Focus on Gratitude

Invest Wisely

Move Forward

DONNA SKEELS CYGAN, CFP® MBA

Sage Future Press ▪ Albuquerque, NM

Copyright ©2013 by Donna Skeels Cygan

SAGE FUTURE PRESS
4800 Juan Tabo NE, Suite D
Albuquerque, NM 87111
www.joyoffinancialsecurity.com
505.298.4040
Fax: 505.298.8080

Ordering Information:
Contact the publisher. Quantity discounts available.

Important Disclosure Information

Donna Skeels Cygan, CFP®, MBA is the founder of Sage Future Financial, LLC, a registered investment advisor located in Albuquerque, New Mexico. Please remember that different types of investments involve varying degrees of risk. Therefore, it should not be assumed that the future performance of any specific investment, investment product, or investment strategy (including the investment strategies referenced in this book), or any of the book's non-investment related content, will be profitable, prove successful, or be applicable to any individual's specific situation. No reader should assume that *The Joy of Financial Security* serves as the receipt of, or a substitute for, personalized advice from Ms. Cygan or from Sage Future Financial, LLC, or from any other investment or financial professional.

In addition to investment information, the book contains financial planning strategies, general tax information, insurance information, and estate planning information. This information is not intended as specific advice to any reader because financial planning strategies, taxes, estate planning principles, and insurance issues need to be customized for each individual person. The book also contains references to research by psychologists, neuroscientists, economists, and financial advisors. The author has used her best efforts in writing this book, and has attempted to give full credit to all of her sources. Citations appear in the end notes at the back of the book. Readers should be aware that internet websites offered in citations may change or disappear over time. The author makes no representations or warranties with respect to the accuracy or completeness of the contents of this book and specifically disclaims any implied warranties.

The advice and strategies contained herein may not be suitable for your situation. Should a reader have any questions regarding the applicability of any portion of the book content to his or her individual situation, the reader is encouraged to consult with the professional advisors of his or her choosing.

Certified Financial Planner Board of Standards Inc. owns the certification marks CFP®, Certified Financial Planner™, CFP® (with plaque design) and CFP® (with flame design) in the U.S., which it awards to individuals who successfully complete CFP Board's initial and ongoing certification requirements.

Blocks on cover are derived from a painting by Caitlin Dundon at *www.oneheartstudio.com.*

Printed in the United States of America
First Edition

For Randy, Kate, and Nora—
for reminding me that family is oh, so very important

■　■　■　■　■

TABLE OF
CONTENTS

■ ■ ■ ■ ■

PART THREE:
FINANCIAL STRATEGIES

▪ ▪ ▪ ▪

PART FOUR:
MOVING FORWARD

■ ■ ■ ■

INTRODUCTION

■ ■ ■ ■ ■

What value can you get from reading *The Joy of Financial Security*? Warren Buffett said: "Price is what you pay. Value is what you get." You should expect to receive value when you read a book. *The Joy of Sex* (from the 1970s) may have provided tremendous value, and *The Joy of Cooking* may have transformed some readers into gourmet cooks. The value and benefits offered by *The Joy of Financial Security* are immense—ranging from determining what will make you happier and creating a happier lifestyle, to taking control of your finances and attaining financial security.

You will learn how to combine happiness strategies and financial strategies so that your money is aligned with your values. Although the concepts of happiness and money may seem miles apart, they have many parallels. To attain financial security, it is essential to know what makes you happy. We will establish the premise that money does not *buy* happiness, but it certainly *impacts* our happiness. We will explore *how* it impacts our happiness, and what other factors may have a greater impact.

Many financial and investment topics are covered, and the great news is that managing your money wisely is not rocket science. Following the steps in the book to get your finances "in good order" will feel great.

The complex relationship between money and happiness has powerful ramifications. In my 15 years as a financial planner, I have seen firsthand the destruction and heartaches that money can cause, as well as the security and freedom it can provide. I have watched my clients evolve from being fearful that they may run out of money during retirement to having a sense of contentment when they realize their net worth is growing and their financial future is secure. No one wants to feel that their financial future is at the mercy of the next economic downturn.

The information in this book is grounded in research from the fields of psychology, neuroscience, and economics. There are a slew of practical strategies that can increase your happiness. The psychology research suggests that roughly 40 percent of our happiness is within our control. It is exhilarating to know that our choices (our behaviors and attitudes) have such an enormous impact on our happiness. (The remaining 60 percent is controlled by our genetics and our environment.) It would be a shame to miss such a wonderful opportunity to add more happiness to our lives.

Origins

I began investing personally in my mid-twenties while working in Chicago in corporate marketing. That was 30 years ago. When my husband and I moved to Albuquerque when I was 30, I knew my corporate marketing days were over. Albuquerque did not have corporate headquarters like Chicago, and the opportunities in marketing were limited. I spent a few years helping New Mexican artisans market their work to museum shops and galleries while my husband and I started our family.

I had been devouring financial books since my early twenties, and I knew that financial planning would be my second career. My father loved investing, and he purchased subscriptions to investment newsletters for me. I read books by Benjamin Graham, Warren Buffett, and Peter Lynch. In 1996 (when our youngest daughter was one year old), I began working on the coursework required for a Certified Financial Planner™ certification. After completing the CFP® certification requirements in 1998, I launched my fee-only financial planning firm. (Fee-only financial planning is described in Chapter Nine). Soon after, I had my first client. I built the firm gradually, and by 2001 it was growing quickly.

My financial planning clients hire me to help them manage their finances, and that usually requires focusing on their investments first. During the first year we also prepare retirement projections, and we cover estate planning issues, insurance issues, and tax planning. My focus is always on helping my clients achieve their goals. By the end of the first year, we have covered all the major financial topics. In subsequent years, my job is to keep everything running smoothly, which includes monitoring their investment portfolios, rebalancing them, and making changes as needed. Retirement projections and net worth statements are updated annually, tax planning is ongoing, and we respond to changes in estate laws as needed.

Within a few years of launching my firm, I realized I had a golden opportunity to help my clients with many issues that reach far beyond money. Our discussions often involve family issues, values, goals, and ways to become happier. Watching my clients become happier is incredibly rewarding, and we celebrate together when they achieve a goal. After all, a rich life is not contingent upon the size of a person's investment account. A truly rich life is based on strong relationships with friends and family, giving back to our community, expressing ourselves creatively, leading healthy yet simple lifestyles, and spending our money in a way that is in alignment with our values. Working with my clients is an honor, and I am grateful for the happiness they bring to my life.

The idea of writing a book about the relationship between money and happiness began percolating in my mind eight years ago, and I have spent the past six years writing the book.

How to Use This Book

My goal in writing *The Joy of Financial Security* is to provide you with *practical* strategies for becoming financially secure and happier. There are plenty of books that guarantee to make you rich. This is not one of them. There are scads of self-help books that promise to transform you into a different person. Not this book! (Plus, we all know that drastic changes don't work. I would much rather you be successful and reap the rewards). You will choose the strategies you want to try, and you will select the small changes you choose to make. Changes don't have to be large; making small changes can have a profound effect on your life and happiness.

You do not need to read this book from front to back. You can refer to the Table of Contents and go directly to the topics that resonate with you. I recommend you have a highlighter and pen handy when you are reading, as well as a journal or notebook. When you read something that appeals to you, highlight the text, and write notes in your journal. If you don't want to use a journal, write directly in the book and dog-ear the page so you can refer back to it later.

Throughout the book, you will find stories my clients have shared with me. I have received permission to use their stories, and their names have been changed. All personal stories are included out of tremendous respect for the people involved and the hope that you will learn from them. I also make comments throughout the book about the services I provide my clients. I have committed to keeping my financial planning firm small, and I am not accepting new clients. The book is intended to reach a larger population than I could ever reach through my financial planning firm, and to educate you on many financial topics.

Throughout the book you will find sections called "Invest in Yourself." These include tips and action items for you to try. Putting into action what you have learned will help you identify the small changes that may significantly increase your happiness. Look at this as a fun journey of self-exploration.

The worksheets provided throughout the book are available on the website www.joyoffinancialsecurity.com. A Resources section, providing useful website links and book titles, is available at the back of the book and also on the website.

The book is divided into four parts:

Part One reviews the research involving the relationship between money and happiness, specifically from the fields of psychology, neuroscience, and economics. How to develop a healthy relationship with money is addressed, and you will be encouraged to reflect back on the money messages you learned as a child.

Part Two delves into happiness strategies. Many are easy to implement in your daily life, and you will learn how powerful small changes can be. Some topics provide compound benefits, where happiness strategies have a parallel financial strategy.

Part Three covers all things financial. Many financial planning topics are discussed, including tax planning, investment planning, and retirement planning.

Part Four pulls it all together, encouraging you to look at what is working for you and what is not. You will be encouraged to create your wish list, and then select happiness strategies and financial strategies that you want to try during the next month. Chapter Twelve also focuses on celebrating your accomplishments.

The rewards for becoming more financially secure and for experiencing greater happiness are extensive. Financial security helps you sleep at night, knowing your financial future will be safe, regardless of what our economy throws your way. You will also experience the freedom that financial security provides—freedom to do many of the things that make you happy.

Becoming happier is more abstract and difficult to describe. Feeling more lighthearted and more content, having richer relationships with those you love, leading a simpler lifestyle (that does not include "keeping up with the Joneses"), having a sense of purpose, being more creative, and being healthier all provide extraordinary rewards.

So, to return to the question, What value can you get from reading *The Joy of Financial Security*? My goal is to help you become happier, manage your money wisely, and create a secure financial future. Accomplishing this will require that you make intentional, small changes; simply reading about the strategies is not enough. When you implement the happiness strategies that resonate most with you—and you weave those strategies together with your finances—you will experience *The Joy of Financial Security*.

Enjoy the journey!

I welcome your feedback on the book, as well as your comments about your experiences as you strive to increase your financial security and happiness. Please send your comments to:

dscygan@joyoffinancialsecurity.com

PART
ONE

■ ■ ■ ■ ■

Happiness Doesn't
Grow on Trees

 Did your parents ever say to you "Money doesn't grow on trees"? My dad said this quite often, and I catch myself saying it to my kids. Although it seems like an old-fashioned comment, it is packed with practical advice. It conveys "we worked hard for our money...it didn't come easily...we should not take it for granted...we should not spend it frivolously...we should manage it wisely."

Happiness doesn't grow on trees, either. We should not take it for granted, and we should not live our lives on autopilot. Our happiness can ebb and flow—changing drastically from month to month and even moment to moment. The exciting news is we can increase our happiness with intentional actions.

Chapters One and Two look closely at the complex relationship between money and happiness. Research from the fields of psychology and neuroscience suggests that each of us has significant control over our personal happiness and our financial security. The way our brains are "wired" impacts the way we make financial decisions (and we are each wired differently). Questions such as "Does money buy happiness?" are addressed, and strategies for developing a harmonious relationship between money and happiness are provided. Chapter Three helps you clarify your values and look back at the money messages you were taught as a child. These impact the way you live your life today and how you manage your money. Reviewing your values and looking back to the past are helpful as you prepare to move forward.

CHAPTER ONE

■ ■ ■ ■ ■

The Relationship Between Money and Happiness

*You will either step forward into growth
or you will step back into safety.*
—ABRAHAM MASLOW

oes it seem irrational to put money and happiness in the same sentence? The two topics often seem miles apart. Money has tremendous power in our society, and many people struggle with managing their money. Although the concept of financial security may sometimes feel out of reach, a healthy relationship with money *is* attainable, and the benefits are certainly worth the effort.

What about happiness, which often feels elusive? Our lifestyles are ingrained and habits are hard to break. We work too hard, we are driven, and there is very little time remaining for happiness or joy. Oftentimes, we feel like we are running on a proverbial treadmill—running faster and faster—but getting nowhere.

The relationship between money and happiness is not simple. Many people think the goal is to be rich and that being rich will make them happy. Yet there are many wealthy people who are very unhappy. My experience in working with clients throughout my financial planning career has convinced me that having plenty of money does not automatically lead to happiness and being happy does not lead to having money. The relationship is more complex. Yet money can definitely impact our happiness.

For example, having money may give us the freedom and the time to create a lifestyle that makes us happy. There is a common saying that "time is money." Having plenty of money may allow you to work fewer hours. You may choose to spend the extra time with family and friends, or to travel, pursue hobbies, or do volunteer work. Having money may give you the freedom to put your children or grandchildren through college, give generously to a cause for which you are passionate, or buy high-quality health care. The freedom and time that money can provide—much more than the size of our investment accounts—can make us happy.

Undoubtedly, nature and nurture play a role in our happiness and financial security. Research has shown that *nature* (our genetics) has a much greater impact on our happiness than *nurture* (our environment and the way we were raised). Conversely, nurture likely has a greater impact on our financial security than nature. Our parents' lifestyle, our education, and our careers all fall under the nurture category, and these impact our financial security.

We have limited control over the impact that nature and nurture have on our happiness and our financial security. Yet we can control a third component that plays a major role in determining how happy we are and whether we are financially secure. This third component is determined by the choices we make, our attitude, and our behavior.

This book focuses on the enormous impact our choices have on creating a lifestyle with more happiness and financial security. Choices that support a healthy lifestyle, nurture us emotionally, deepen our relationships, and strengthen our finances will likely require some intentional changes.

As you read this book, I encourage you to embrace change. Do not just accept it or allow it to happen. To embrace change is more emphatic. Changes allow you to move forward, reaping the benefits of new experiences along the way. If we drift through life—accepting our normal routines and not striving for improvement—then we know exactly what to expect. But why accept the status quo? As The Beatles' George Harrison wrote in the song, "Any Road," "If you don't know where you're going, any road will take you there."

Be open to new ideas. This book contains many strategies to increase your level of happiness and financial security. Rather than reading the book quickly, read it with a sense of wonder and curiosity. Approach it with an experimental attitude, knowing you can pick and choose whichever strategies appeal to you.

The Definitions

What Is Happiness?

Merriam-Webster defines happiness as the quality of being content; pleasure. Many English-language terms—such as joy, jubilation, euphoria, and bliss—refer to various forms of happiness and pleasure. These definitions are focused primarily on the present, with a goal of having a "pleasant life."

The definition I prefer is from psychologist Martin Seligman, in his book *Authentic Happiness*.

> *Happiness consists of positive emotions and activities relating to the past (satisfaction, contentment, pride, and serenity), the future (optimism, hope, confidence, trust, and faith), and the present (pleasure and gratification).*

Seligman's definition includes the past, present, and future. Because his definition for happiness offers more depth than only pleasure, it extends to the realm of well-being. Other psychologists also prefer a broader definition of happiness. Ed Diener and Robert Biswas-Diener state: "We refer to 'happiness' as 'subjective well-being' in scientific parlance, because it is about how people evaluate their lives and what is important to them." Throughout this book, a broad definition of happiness is used, encompassing many components of well-being, such as a having a sense of purpose, expressing gratitude and positive emotions, and enjoying meaningful relationships.

The concept of happiness is subjective, and the behaviors, feelings, and circumstances that make someone happy are different for each person. Playing in the rain may make you happy, but it may sound horrible to someone else. Sitting on my patio early in the morning, listening to the birds with my pets, a newspaper, and a cup of coffee makes me happy, but it may sound awful to someone who enjoys sleeping late. This diversity is what makes the concept of happiness so intriguing.

The pursuit of happiness requires intention. Developing healthy relationships with friends and family, practicing gratitude, and nurturing our creativity all require a conscious effort; these things don't happen automatically. But what if, like many people, you do not know what makes you happy? This is your chance to find out. Exploring what makes you happy—and what does not—could lead you down a new, exciting path. For example, you might discover that gardening makes you immensely happy, but if you never planted a garden and rejoiced as the flowers or vegetables grow, you would never know.

Happiness is not a destination. There is no finish line when you suddenly become happy for the rest of your life. Life is a journey with many hills and valleys. Making changes to increase your happiness will add memorable experiences throughout your journey.

What Is Money?

The definition of money is quite simple, but the concept of money is much more complex. *Merriam-Webster* defines it as "something generally accepted as a medium of exchange, a measure of value, or a means of payment." The most common form of money is currency, such as the American dollar, the euro, the peso, or the yen.

If money were only the coins or bills in our wallets, life would be much easier and less stressful. Money is much more. For people who have experienced periods with lots of money and other periods with very little money, it can trigger feelings of insecurity. For people who have experienced periods with lots of money and very little money, it can trigger feelings of insecurity. Money can also incite feelings of fear and anger, which occurred during the financial crisis in late 2008 when people watched their hard-earned investments decline in value as the stock market plummeted.

Many people have a love-hate relationship with money. People who come into "sudden money" due to an inheritance, winning a lottery, or a court settlement often experience a variety of emotions. We hear of wealthy dictators who are not willing to share their riches with their incredibly poor countrymen. But there are also celebrities and corporate executives who are generous with their money, feeling they have a responsibility to help those less fortunate. Money is the number-one cause of arguments among married couples and life partners. Olivia Mellan, psychotherapist and author, states: "Money is tied up with our deepest emotional needs: for love, power, security, independence, control, and self-worth. And since so many of us are unaware of the emotional load that money carries, we fight about it without understanding what the battles are about or how to settle them."

When not used wisely, money can be destructive. Sometimes people are negatively impacted by having large sums of money. Perhaps they have no ambition to work or contribute to society. They may become addicted to drugs, alcohol, or gambling. They may become too materialistic, allowing their desire for possessions, wealth, or status to become the dominant motivator in their lives.

If having lots of money can be destructive, then the goal must be something other than simply acquiring large sums of money. The goal is to use money wisely—as a tool—and to attain financial security.

What Is Financial Security?

Financial security is not a magic number. Assets totaling $50,000, $500,000, or even $5 million will not guarantee financial security. A random number is too nebulous. The practical definition used in this book is:

> *Financial security is the amount of money you need to feel confident that you can pay your bills, live the lifestyle you want, achieve your goals, and not run out of money before you die.*

The amount of money needed to attain financial security will be different for each person and will fluctuate over the course of your life. Career changes, losing a job, changes in health-care expenses, taxes, increasing or decreasing investments, getting married or divorced, and having children will all impact the amount of money you need to be financially secure.

Different lifestyles require vastly different amounts of money. You may live simply, spending very little money to maintain your lifestyle, while someone else who may love to travel to exotic and expensive places will need significantly more money. Another person may derive great joy from giving away large sums of money each year to charities, and this would be reflected in their annual expenses.

The term *wealth* is often used when discussing money. Wealth and money are not synonymous. Wealth has multiple definitions. A narrow definition may infer that someone has a lot of money; "they are very wealthy." In that instance, wealth pertains directly to money; it does not pertain to financial security or happiness. A broader definition includes having large sums of money, as well as other factors—such as close relationships with family and friends, good health, a job and a community you love, the ability to support worthwhile causes, status or power, and freedom to do what you choose. In this broader definition, one may say "she is *truly* wealthy," denoting a combination of financial security and well-being.

Attaining financial security provides many benefits, including peace of mind, a sense of fulfillment and accomplishment, and status in the community. Two of the most valuable benefits are time and freedom.

Time

In our society, the saying "time is money" is more than a cliché. As our lives become more hectic and stressful, we recognize how valuable our time is. If your parents or grandparents lived and worked on a farm when they were younger, you've probably heard about their long workdays tending to animals and crops.

A classic essay written by John Maynard Keynes in 1930 titled "Economic Possibilities for Our Grandchildren," predicted that American and British workers would only need to work 20 hours per week by 2010 and 15 hours per week by 2030. He also predicted that per capita income would increase by four to eight times because of continued capital investment. One of his predictions has proved accurate, as per capita income has increased approximately six times, and there are still 17 years remaining before 2030. However, his prediction for reduced work hours was inaccurate. Americans with full-time jobs worked an average of 42.5 hours per week during 2012. In today's tough economic climate, frequently both spouses are working full time, with many working more than one job just to make ends meet.

One of my clients—a high-level manager for a large technology company—explained recently that she has never worked harder or longer hours in her 25-year career than she is working now. The recession in 2008 and 2009 caused many companies to reduce their workforce, but often the amount of work did not decrease. Companies expected the remaining employees to accept the additional responsibilities. Working long hours leaves little time for family, relaxation, or fun. Furthermore, the added stress can severely affect our health.

Although it seems like we never have enough time, Laura Vanderkam, in her book *168 Hours*, emphasizes that we all have 168 hours every week. "The problem," she says, "is not that we're overworked and under-rested; it's that most of us have absolutely no idea how we spend our 168 hours. We don't think about how we want to spend our time, so we spend massive amounts of time on things—television, web surfing, housework, errands—that give a slight amount of pleasure or feeling of accomplishment, but do little for our careers, families, or personal lives."

She encourages us to consider our week as a blank slate and to choose the activities we want in our 168-hour week. If you are working full time, then the 8 am to 5 pm slot Monday through Friday is likely filled. However, after inserting all the non-negotiable responsibilities (getting ready for work, taking the kids to school, picking them up, making dinner, doing laundry, and sleeping), you will likely find there are still large amounts of time available in your 168 hours. This is where your choices come into play.

Do you want to sit in front of the TV for two hours each evening, or would you rather do a project with your kids, take a walk, enjoy a hot bath, or read a book? If your life is full of evening or weekend commitments, reviewing the way you spend your 168 hours gives you permission to get rid of some of them. It also helps you clarify your priorities. For example, rather than thinking you *must* do volunteer work eight hours a week, you may decide that you want to limit your volunteer work to four hours per week. This frees up four hours for other activities that may add more happiness to your life.

Time is a valuable resource, and financial security can provide you with more of it. For instance, you can afford to retire at a younger age, take a vacation with family and friends, take a month off without pay, or limit your work hours to 40 or less per week. Or you may choose to have more discretionary "free" time.

Freedom

In addition to time, money also provides freedom. Freedom allows you to choose how to spend your money and also to align it with your values and goals. Money can be used to pay for a nice house and a comfortable retirement, putting your kids or grandkids through college, supporting worthy causes, or travel. It can be saved for a rainy day, be given to your favorite charities, or be left to younger family members after your death.

The typical American family does not experience the freedom that financial security affords. Many people have adopted the modern lifestyle—bigger, better, more—which can lead them to live beyond their means. Sometimes, the individual investor or homeowner is not entirely to blame. For many years, the mortgage industry encouraged people to buy bigger houses and borrow more than ever before. The investment banking industry bundled mortgages into financial investments that were doomed to fail, then sold them to unsuspecting investors in the United States and foreign countries. Even government officials were telling us that everything was fine in mid-2008 when the economy was about to collapse like a house of cards.

The severity of the financial crisis in late 2008 and early 2009 was a jolt to the psyche of most Americans, especially those who had saved for many years. They were looking forward to a secure retirement, when they suddenly realized their financial security was at risk. They watched their retirement accounts and their home values plummet. Some people lost their jobs. Many have still not found jobs, or their careers have suffered.

My clients were also affected by the recent recession. Many of them were justifiably angry. They followed all the rules: They worked hard, contributed to their retirement accounts, and did not live beyond their means. They managed their household budgets responsibly. Yet their investment accounts and homes still lost value. This was a classic example of the importance of "Control the Controllables," which is discussed in Chapter Four. We didn't have control over many of the events that led to the economic downturn—such as the budget deficit, government spending, or the behavior of the mortgage and investment banking industries. But by focusing on the variables that we *can* control, we can secure our financial future and significantly increase our happiness.

The freedom that money provides can also reduce the need to worry about the next economic crisis. Having plenty of money provides some assurance that your investment account and your home may decline in value, but you will be just fine. Feeling a sense of contentment about the future leads us into the field of positive psychology.

The Research

Positive Psychology

Psychologists have been intrigued by the concept of happiness for many years. Yet from the end of World War II until the late 1990s, traditional psychology was focused on treating mental illness. Significant strides were made in treating depression, neurosis, anxiety, and delusions. The goal of practitioners was to bring patients from a negative, ailing state to a neutral normal, or, as University of Pennsylvania psychology professor Martin Seligman puts it, "from a minus five to a zero." Fortunately, a few psychologists were exploring new concepts that surpassed the limitations of traditional clinical psychology.

Humanistic psychologists, such as Abraham Maslow and Carl

Rogers, were in the forefront by the 1950s, with theories that focused on each individual's potential. Their research stressed the importance of growth and self-actualization, taking into account factors such as values, creativity, spirituality, love, grief, and caring. The work focused on a person's personality and on improving life satisfaction. The fundamental premise of humanistic psychology is that people are innately good. Humanistic psychology paved the way for positive psychology.

In 1998, Martin Seligman was elected president of the American Psychological Association (APA). Every incoming APA president was asked to choose a theme for his or her term in office; Seligman chose to direct his attention to research focusing on well-being, happiness, optimism, and positive emotions. He was not content with traditional psychology that focused on negative traits, and he wanted to emphasize the enormous potential that lies within each of us. "I realized my profession was half-baked. It wasn't enough for us to nullify disabling conditions and get to zero. We needed to ask, What are the enabling conditions that make human beings flourish? How do we get from zero to plus five?" Through his work and vision, the field of positive psychology was born.

Prior to 1998, several psychologists were focusing on topics related to positive psychology. Ed Diener of the University of Illinois had been researching "subjective well-being" for more than two decades. Mihaly Csikszentmihalyi (pronounced "cheeks sent me high"), professor at Claremont Graduate University, had been researching a happy state of mind called *flow*, which occurs when people experience deep enjoyment, creativity, and intense concentration in an activity. Robert Emmons, professor at the University of California at Davis, was researching the effects of gratitude, and Daniel Kahneman and Amos Tversky, professors at Princeton University, were researching how we make decisions. These research topics were outside the realm of mainstream psychology (which was still focused on mental illness), and the research often went unnoticed. When the field of positive psychology was established in 1998, the research gained credibility and the pendulum swung to focus on positive traits that can greatly improve the quality of our lives.

A few months after Seligman was elected APA president, he was in his garden weeding with his 5-year-old daughter, Nikki. Seligman tells the story:

I have to confess that even though I write books about children, I'm really not all that good with children. I am goal oriented and time urgent, and when I'm weeding in the garden, I'm actually trying to get the weeding done. Nikki, however, was throwing weeds into the air, singing, and dancing around. I yelled at her. She walked away, then came back and said, "Daddy, I want to talk to you."

Yes, Nikki?

"Daddy, do you remember before my fifth birthday? From the time I was three to the time I was five, I was a whiner. I whined every day. When I turned five, I decided not to whine anymore. That was the hardest thing I've ever done. And if I can stop whining, you can stop being such a grouch."

This was, for me, an epiphany, nothing less. I learned something about Nikki, about raising kids, about myself, and a great deal about my profession. First, I realized that raising Nikki was not about correcting whining. Nikki did that herself. Rather, I realized that raising Nikki is about taking this marvelous strength she has—I call it "seeing into her soul"—amplifying it, nurturing it, helping her to lead her life around it to buffer against her weaknesses and the storms of life. Raising children, I realized, is vastly more than fixing what is wrong with them. It is about identifying and nurturing their strongest qualities, what they own and are best at, and helping them find niches in which they can best live out these strengths.

As for my own life, Nikki hit the nail on the head. I was a grouch. I had spent fifty years mostly enduring wet weather in my soul, and the past ten years being a nimbus cloud in a household full of sunshine. Any good fortune I had was probably not due to my grumpiness, but in spite of it. In that moment, I resolved to change.

Although Seligman was already well known for his research in learned helplessness and learned optimism, his development of the positive psychology movement has been his greatest achievement. Positive psychology asks: What is working? What am I grateful for? How can I focus on the positive? What makes me happier?

Since its birth in 1998, the field of positive psychology has flourished. Seligman is now training students at the University of Pennsylvania Positive Psychology Center. The movement has spread on an international level, and there are now hundreds of psychologists, researchers, and professors in many countries working on concepts such as happiness, hope, wisdom, creativity, gratitude, relationships, spirituality, and positive emotions.

Beyond Nature and Nurture

Seligman's story about his daughter calling him a grouch is charming. Yet it leads to a critical question about happiness: How much ability do we have to increase our own happiness? Should we assume that our happiness is only controlled by our genetics and our environment?

Most of us assume that genetics (in other words, nature) plays a significant role in how happy we are. Some people seem to be born happy and optimistic, while others have a gloomier disposition. However, genetics is not the only factor. What about our environment (nurture)? This includes the country, state, or city where we live; the climate; our home; our access to food and good nutrition; our safety; our families; and our upbringing. Many would assume our environment also plays a large role in determining our level of happiness. If we assumed that our happiness is controlled only by genetics and environment (nature and nurture), trying to become happier would be futile. Fortunately, the research being conducted within the field of positive psychology has shown that we have a significant amount of control over our own happiness.

Studies are often conducted on twins due to the similarities caused by their genetic structure. Researchers at the University of Minnesota studied 4,000 sets of twins born in Minnesota between 1936 and 1955, both identical and fraternal. The findings, published in 1996 by David Lykken, showed that the similarities in happiness were strongest among identical twins, supporting the suspected genetic component of our happiness. The study concluded that about 50 percent of our happiness is a result of genetics.

Using the Minnesota twin study results as a starting point, Sonja Lyubomirsky, Ken Sheldon, and David Schkade collaborated to determine what makes up the remaining 50 percent of our happiness. Their research focused on what role environment plays and how much control we each have in determining our level of happiness. They concluded that our environment determines approximately 10 percent and our own actions (choices, attitude, behaviors) contribute roughly 40 percent. Their findings are reflected in Figure 1.1.

Knowing that we can control as much as 40 percent of our own happiness is exciting! So how do we apply this at a personal level and actually become happier? Chapters Four, Five and Six provide specific strategies for increasing our happiness. For now, we will explore some characteristics of happiness.

FIGURE 1.1 WHAT DETERMINES OUR HAPPINESS?

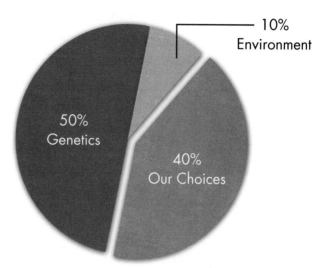

The Ebb and Flow of Happiness

We live our lives in seasons, and it is inevitable that we will experience some sad and painful seasons and some happy seasons. The level of happiness each of us feels at any time is on a continuum; it ebbs and flows throughout our lives, with changes occurring from month to month, day to day—even moment to moment. Also, our emotions are often intertwined. A wise friend said to me once, "There is a lot of sadness in happiness."

The goal in becoming happier is not to stay in a state of euphoria. People try this with drugs or alcohol, but it doesn't work. Our lives are enriched by positive and negative experiences. We strive for more positive experiences (hence our desire to become happier), but we need to realize that negative and painful experiences, such as grief and sadness, are also rich. The wide range of emotions is what makes us human. Accepting that your level of happiness is on a continuum and will ebb and flow during your lifetime is a healthy starting point.

We should not ask ourselves, "Am I happy?" That assumes that happiness is a finite destination and that we are either happy or not. If we accept that our happiness is on a continuum, a better question to ask is: "How can I become happier?"

A Happiness Baseline

Do we each have a happiness baseline that we tend to return to, even after a happy or sad event in our life? Let's assume you have a wonderful experience that makes you happy. Maybe you spend some special time with family or friends, you travel somewhere fabulous, you get a promotion or receive an award at work, or you move into a new home. Would you assume that shortly after that event is over, you would return to your prior level of happiness?

Conversely, let's assume you have a traumatic event happen in your life. Someone (or a pet) you love dies, you get a divorce, your house burns down, or you are in a car accident. Would you assume that within a certain amount of time following the traumatic experience, you would return to your prior level of happiness?

The answer to both questions is "yes," primarily because the 50 percent genetic component and the 10 percent environmental component tend to pull you back to your baseline.

Being pulled back to the baseline is called *adaptation*, a concept researched by psychologist Philip Brickman and colleagues in the 1970s. They developed a theory called the *hedonic treadmill*, which suggests that people quickly adjust to a positive event. (Hedonic is defined as the science of how we feel from moment to moment). Immediately after receiving a promotion or a raise, we are elated. However, very rapidly our expectations increase to reflect the improved situation (we *adapt*), leaving us no happier than before.

I've seen the adaptation principle many times in my financial planning clients, especially when clients decide to buy an expensive item. A few years ago, a couple close to retirement bought a new luxury car. I had recommended they keep their old car a few more years, because they said it was working well. Immediately after buying the car, the couple took it on a trip—and they enjoyed it. But when we updated their retirement projections a few months later, they had to add nearly $8,000 per year to their budget for the next four years for monthly car payments. Suddenly, the car no longer looked so appealing. Car payments had become a significant part of their annual budget. By then they had adapted to their previous level of happiness—only they were left with a car loan of $32,000.

The adaptation principle is often apparent after spending money on "things," such as cars, huge homes, expensive clothing, jewelry, and gadgets. These material goods provide pleasure for a short time, but the pleasure wears off quickly, leaving the owner with less money and less financial security. When the pursuit of happiness is misguided to include the acquisition of more and more possessions, it can feel like being on a treadmill running faster and faster, just to stay in the same place; hence the hedonic treadmill.

This translates to teaching our children to always expect the latest electronic gadget. Several years ago (as young teenagers), my daughters wanted an iPod. New iPod models were released every few months, and they wanted the newest version; the same thing happened with the latest smartphone. Laptops are replaced sooner than necessary in our home, and the bad habits are reinforced. The adaptation principle applies in two ways. First, the new gadget loses its appeal within a few weeks of purchase so the buyer reverts to their happiness baseline. Second, the buyer's expectations rise, leading them to crave the next gadget. A third factor is that these gadgets cost money that could be used for other purposes, such as saving for college.

Spending money on nonessential things is a prime example of a concept called *opportunity cost*. In the example above of the couple who bought the expensive car, delaying buying a car for a few years would have meant they could have saved the money that is now going for their monthly car payments. That money ($32,000 over four years) could be growing and compounding in their investment accounts. This could have a significant impact on their retirement projections—conceivably the difference between feeling confident that their money will last until age 95 or will be depleted much sooner.

The concept of opportunity cost considers how the money could have been spent if it were not used for a new car. Certainly, it could go into the couple's retirement nest egg. It could also be used to fund a family reunion, which would provide rich experiences and memories. It could also pay for several nice vacations or help fund a grandchild's education. Recognizing that spending money on unnecessary things has an opportunity cost (in terms of the lost opportunity if that money were saved for the future or spent in other ways) may help improve your financial security.

If we were to assess our happiness level each day over many years and keep a journal of various events and feelings each day, it would be fascinating to plot our happiness on a graph. We would see spikes in happiness on some days and valleys on others. Ed Diener and Robert Biswas-Diener did a similar experiment with a young man who was undergoing cancer treatment for Hodgkin's disease. They asked him to gauge his happiness for 80 days, including the day he learned that the treatment was effective in eliminating his cancer. The adaptation principle was clearly evident; he showed a huge spike in happiness on Day 38, which was the day he learned the treatment had been successful. Surprisingly, within one or two days, his euphoria had declined and his level of happiness had returned to more typical levels. But, for the remainder of the study, he experienced fewer days of sadness, and his happiness baseline rose following the good news.

This leads us to an exciting phenomenon. Although we tend to return to our happiness baseline, we can permanently raise our baseline to a higher level.

An Update on Adaptation Theory

The adaptation theory (originally proposed in the 1970s) has far-reaching ramifications, because it presumes that individuals return to a neutral baseline (also termed a set point) after an emotionally positive or negative experience. This could lead to a conclusion that individual and societal efforts to increase happiness may be doomed to failure. It also contradicts the idea that we can raise our happiness baseline with intentional actions.

Psychologists Ed Diener, Richard Lucas, and Christie Napa Scollon have been studying adaptation theory in recent years, and have determined that revisions to the original theory are needed. Specifically, their research suggests that most individuals have a positive rather than neutral set point (most people are happy most of the time), a person may have multiple set points because different components of well-being can move in different directions, and well-being set points can change under certain conditions. In addition, their research has shown that individuals differ in how they react to external events.

Their research has raised new issues involving adaptation, such as: Can people slow adaptation following good events and speed recovery from bad events? Or, which strategies can help us recover most quickly after a negative experience? Their findings support the beliefs of other psychologists who have concluded that we have significant latitude in increasing our level of happiness. As you make changes to increase your happiness, you can determine for yourself which strategies work best for you.

Raising Your Happiness Baseline

Most people have baselines in the "mildly positive" range, and research shows the baselines can be moved up to a higher level through intentional actions. The 40 percent of our happiness within our control is significant, providing an excellent opportunity to increase our level of happiness. David Lykken (the lead researcher in the Minnesota twin study) stated, "It's clear that we can change our happiness levels widely, up or down."

The key to becoming happier (and shifting our happiness baseline to a higher level) lies in our choices and our intentional behavior. If we do not make intentional changes to increase our happiness, we will slip back to our baseline. Csikszentmihalyi emphasized the importance of intention when he said a vital ingredient of happiness is "the knowledge that one is responsible for having achieved it. Happiness is not something that happens to people, but something that they make happen."

Maslow's Hierarchy of Needs

How does money impact our happiness? One of the first theories that addressed human motivation is still widely accepted today. Maslow's Hierarchy of Needs, developed by psychologist Abraham Maslow, was introduced in 1954. It states that a person must meet needs at the bottom of the pyramid before they can consider moving up to the higher levels. For example, in Figure 1.2, the bottom sections include basic needs such as food, shelter, and safety.

Victims of famine are focused on finding food. Victims of a devastating earthquake are focused on finding shelter. People in a war-torn country are focused on their safety. If you don't know how you will get food for today's meals, it is difficult to think about concepts like self-esteem or self-actualization, which are much higher on the pyramid.

FIGURE 1.2 ABRAHAM MASLOW'S
HIERARCHY OF NEEDS DIAGRAM

Many psychologists and economists embrace Maslow's Hierarchy of Needs theory, and it makes sense intuitively. Likewise, there is widespread agreement that money or income has an *impact* on happiness. However, there is less agreement on *how* money impacts happiness or whether other factors may have a greater impact.

Economic Research

Richard Easterlin, professor of economics at the University of Southern California, found that the average self-reported happiness level did not increase in Japan during the almost 30 years between 1958 and 1987, although real per capita income increased fivefold. He found similar results in China and the United States. After researching 37 countries over many years, he concluded that increases in economic growth (real per capita income) have almost no detectable effects on life satisfaction or happiness.

Before we jump to the conclusion that income does not have an impact on our happiness, we need to look more closely at Easterlin's research. He was examining the impact of happiness over a period of time from 12 years to more than 30 years. He calls this *time-series evidence*. When he looked at a specific point in time (which he terms *cross-section evidence*), he found that happiness and income *are* positively related. In other words, people who have higher incomes report being happier than people with lower incomes. The fact that societies do not seem to become happier *over time* as they become richer is why Easterlin's body of research was named the Easterlin paradox.

The Gallup organization has been researching happiness for many years—both internationally and in the United States. The research includes annual samples of more than 1,000 respondents in 150 countries. The data collected between 2005 and 2011 was summarized in the *World Happiness Report* in 2012. Let's look first at the international studies.

In earlier research, gross national product per capita (also called household income or per capita income, and referred to as GNP) was typically measured for each country, with an assumption that higher household income may result in greater happiness. Consistent with Maslow's Hierarchy of Needs theory, inhabitants of the countries near the bottom of the list (the poorest countries) are often concerned with basic needs such as food, shelter, and safety. Researchers have agreed that the impact of income on happiness should be viewed by using percentage changes in income rather than absolute changes. (They term this the *logarithm of income*.) For example, if a poor family in the West African country of Togo has a household income of $1,000 per year, increasing their income by $1,000 would be a 100 percent increase. While referencing the countries with extreme poverty, the *World Happiness Report* states:

Even small gains in a household's income can result in a child's survival, the end of hunger pangs, improved nutrition, better learning opportunities, safe childbirth, and prospects for ongoing improvements and opportunities in schooling, job training, and gainful employment.

The fact that relatively small amounts of money can have a major impact on raising the GNP in very poor countries supports the efforts underway (by the United Nations and many others) that focus on ending extreme poverty.

Conversely, if a person in the United States has an annual household income of $50,000, increasing their income by $1,000 will have a negligible effect on their happiness. However, increasing their income by 100 percent (from $50,000 to $100,000) may have a significant effect.

The international research ranked over 150 countries on life satisfaction. The top 15 countries and the bottom 15 countries are shown in Figure 1.3 on the following page. Note that the United States is ranked number 11 and that the top four countries are all in Scandinavia (northern Europe). The majority of the bottom 15 countries are in sub-Saharan Africa. Countries that ranked highest on the life satisfaction scale tended to be more advanced in economic development and higher in freedom and human rights. Conversely, countries that ranked lowest tended to be extremely poor, with unstable governments and frequent conflict with nearby countries.

Recent studies were designed to measure *subjective well-being* (the research term often used for happiness) through two aspects. One aspect is *emotional well-being*, which refers to the emotional quality of a person's everyday experience. Respondents are asked whether they experienced various emotions yesterday, such as enjoyment, happiness, anger, sadness, stress, and worry. Sometimes called *affective happiness*, this pertains to whether a person perceives his life as pleasant or unpleasant based on day-to-day emotions.

FIGURE 1.3 HAPPIEST COUNTRIES AND LEAST-HAPPY COUNTRIES

Top 15 Countries Based on Life Satisfaction	Bottom 15 Countries Based on Life Satisfaction
1. Denmark	156. Togo
2. Finland	155. Benin
3. Norway	154. Central African Republic
4. Netherlands	153. Sierra Leone
5. Canada	152. Burundi
6. Switzerland	151. Comoros
7. Sweden	150. Haiti
8. New Zealand	149. Tanzania
9. Australia	148. Congo (Brazzaville)
10. Ireland	147. Bulgaria
11. United States	146. Georgia
12. Costa Rica	145. Chad
13. Austria	144. Burkina Faso
14. Israel	143. Mali
15. Belgium	142. Zimbabwe

The other aspect of subjective well-being that the *Gallup World Poll* is attempting to measure is called *life evaluation*. It is a long-term view of how satisfied a person is with their life. Life evaluation is sometimes called *evaluative happiness*, and the question is typically "How satisfied are you with your life as a whole these days?" Respondents are asked to answer the question using a scale of 0 (worst possible life) to 10 (best possible life).

The results show a clear correlation between per capita income and happiness on measurements for emotional well-being as well as life evaluation. Within any society, richer people are on average happier than poorer people.

However, income has a much higher correlation on the life evaluation questions than on the emotional well-being questions. In other words, income has a greater impact on how you evaluate your life (the question "How satisfied are you with your life as a whole these days?") than on questions pertaining to the emotions you experienced yesterday. The research also suggests that although income definitely impacts life evaluation, many other factors—such as health, education, social support, freedom, and the strength of our family life—play a major role in our happiness.

The Gallup Organization has also conducted research on subjective well-being (happiness) specifically in the United States. Like the international studies, the U.S. study focused on the same two aspects of happiness (emotional well-being and life evaluation). Called the *Gallup-Healthways Well-Being Index*, it surveyed 450,000 U.S. residents in 2008 and 2009. Psychologists Daniel Kahneman and Angus Deaton analyzed the findings and concluded that higher logarithm income impacts both emotional well-being and life evaluation, but in different ways. They found that increased income led to higher life evaluation for incomes "well over $120,000." However, the satiation point for emotional well-being (the emotions that respondents reported they experienced yesterday) was at an income of approximately $75,000. In other words, for incomes up to approximately $75,000, a higher income resulted in higher reported emotional well-being. Once income reached approximately $75,000, emotional well-being did not increase with higher incomes.

We all know that $75,000 is not a magic number, but the researchers saw it as the point at which there are diminishing returns. People with household incomes below $75,000 gave lower responses to both life evaluation and emotional well-being questions. Those with household incomes above $75,000 did not rank any higher on emotional well-being (the positive and negative emotions from everyday experiences) than those who earned $75,000, but their life evaluation rankings (the long-term view of how satisfied one is with their life) continued to increase as their income increased.

There are many theories as to why emotional well-being does not increase when household income is above $75,000. One plausible explanation is that $75,000 allows us to live comfortably and to afford social experiences. Deaton states: "No matter where you live, your emotional well-being is as good as it's going to get at $75,000, and money's not going to make it any better beyond that point. It's like you hit some sort of ceiling, and you can't get emotional well-being much higher just by having more money."

U.S. research suggests that different variables impact our emotional well-being and our life evaluation. Recognizing that emotional well-being is a short-term view that reflects the positive and negative emotions participants experience with everyday experiences, a high score in emotional well-being often originates from social interactions. Kahneman states: "Emotional happiness is primarily social. The best thing that can happen to people is to spend time with other people they like. That is when they are happiest." Kahneman and Deaton also suggest that poor health, being a caregiver for an adult, and loneliness can have a significant negative impact on our emotional well-being.

The highest life evaluation scores came from people who went to college, were married, and had good jobs. Accomplishing goals and feeling financially secure impact life evaluation, as do a person's health, family, friends, and freedom.

Based on the research, many economists believe that gross domestic product is not an adequate measure of happiness. Maybe our happiness has very little to do with the country's average income per person. Perhaps other factors have a much greater impact on our happiness. Countries such as France measure well-being through employment levels, health care, vacation, household assets and income, consumption, and education. Great Britain is studying well-being, and Bhutan has developed a *National Happiness Index*.

In his summary of recent research, Adam Davidson (writer and co-host of NPR's *Planet Money*) states that one explanation for the fact that Americans are not any happier now than they were 40 years ago—in spite of the United States being three times as rich as it was in 1973—is because "many Americans have not shared in the increased wealth. With the disappearance of pensions and the increased volatility of labor markets, many workers face more uncertainty than ever before."

Another factor that may be reflected in the happiness data is income inequality. In the United States, people in the top 1 percent for annual income (defined in 2012 as those earning over $367,000) have doubled their share of the nation's collective income from about 10 percent to about 20 percent since 1979. A Pew Research Center study concluded that the top 7 percent of Americans saw their average net worth increase by 28 percent between 2009 and 2011, while the remaining 93 percent experienced a loss in their net worth of 4 percent. There is no doubt that the rich are getting richer.

Income inequality is not just a problem for the United States; it is a problem in many countries. Richard Easterlin wrote an essay for the *New York Times* in 2012 summarizing the impact of income inequality in China. The Chinese government began moving toward a free-market economy in 1990, and real per capita income has quadrupled since then. Yet there is no indication that the Chinese people are any happier. If anything, the bottom third of the population in wealth is more *un*happy. Easterlin believes this is because the safety net that the government once provided has been taken away. Previously, the government provided people in urban areas permanent jobs, subsidized food, housing, health care, child care, pensions, and jobs for their grown children. Due to the shift to a more private economy, many urban workers were laid off. Rural migrants took city jobs without benefits. Workers are concerned about job security and benefits, and Easterlin observed that life satisfaction in urban areas has declined significantly.

Why Are Those Danes So Happy?

There are many possible reasons why Denmark is the world's happiest country, according to the *World Happiness Report*. Low taxes is not one of them. The tax rate in Denmark is considered the highest in the world, reportedly slightly below 50 percent for most Danes and roughly 60 percent for people earning over $70,000 per year. However, they are not complaining. They receive free health care, job training, child care, a college education, and elder care. All citizens have equal rights to Social Security, and the average Dane retires on 87 percent of what he or she made while working. Danes have the lowest poverty level in the world and the smallest income disparity between rich and poor. This is not happenstance; Denmark devotes about half its annual budget to smoothing out society's inequalities.

Denmark has what it terms a "flexicurity" system where employers can dismiss workers with relative ease, and the workers have access to up to four years of unemployment benefits. Roughly 30 percent of Danes change jobs annually, mostly to pursue more interesting work or to attain higher pay. Yet the unemployment rate for Denmark has been as low as 2 percent. Most Danes work 37 hours per week and have six weeks of vacation. They have a strong work ethic, with the attitude that they need to get their work done so they can pursue other things they enjoy.

Danes place a high priority on living a socially balanced life, with time for their families and friends. Many Danes ride bicycles as their primary mode of transportation, so they get lots of fresh air and exercise. The country prides itself on its green energy goals, striving for 50 percent clean energy use by 2020 and becoming independent of fossil fuels by 2050. It is well on its way: Wind power provided

continued...

30 percent of the country's electricity in 2012.

When compared to American values, the Danes' attitude about money is unique. Modesty is a virtue, and showing off is looked down upon. This eliminates the pressure to "keep up with the Joneses" so there is no need to pursue bigger homes, nicer cars, and more fashionable clothes. Danes are very tolerant of other races and lifestyles, and they are very trusting of others.

The United States and many European countries would benefit from studying the lifestyle of the Danish people. Although it may not be feasible to emulate every facet of the Danish culture, it seems clear that happiness can be increased through government policies.

The Responsibility of Government

What are the implications of the happiness research on an international basis and for the United States? The research has far-reaching implications for government policymakers trying to determine how to spend limited resources.

Is it government's responsibility to ensure everyone is employed? President Franklin Roosevelt's New Deal program of the 1930s attempted to end the Great Depression by providing jobs. Should the government provide the resources so everyone can feed their family, afford health insurance, and send their children to college? Should there be entitlement programs that provide secure income for retirees? Should government provide programs to help those in poverty move into the middle class? Or should the government strive to be smaller, forcing individuals to provide their own benefits? Would any of these government programs impact a society's happiness? Or would programs that provide more free time for cit-

Limitations of Research

Research results should always be questioned. Do not assume that $75,000 is a magic number, and people with incomes below it will become happier if their incomes increase, but those earning $75,500 will not. The $75,000 figure is only a guideline. Similarly, the roughly 50 percent of our happiness that is assumed to be controlled by genetics is also a guideline. Other U.S. research studies involving identical and fraternal twins report that genetics determines 33 to 50 percent of our variance in happiness. If genetics represents only 33 percent (rather than 50 percent), then the amount of control we have over our happiness (through our choices, attitude, and behaviors) may be significantly over 40 percent.

Psychologists are accustomed to being criticized for their research. After all, humans cannot be placed in a petri dish, and there are inevitable biases in how we answer questions about happiness. Cognitive scientist Hal Pashler of the University of California at San Diego states, "The field is suffering a 'crisis of confidence'… thanks to a glut of neat results that are long on mass appeal but short on scientific confirmation." Good scientific studies should lend themselves to being replicated (with very similar results), but they often are not. In response to this concern, a group of psychologists established the Reproducibility Project in 2012, which is reproducing major studies by a different set of researchers. The objective is to make sure the basic tenets of science—transparency, skepticism, and self-correction—are reflected in psychological research.

izens and more parks and recreational areas have a greater impact on happiness?

It is important to remember that research shows that at any point in time, richer people tend to report being happier than poorer people. However, research has also shown that increasing per capita income *over time* does not necessarily increase happiness for wealthier countries such as the United States. These findings are consistent with Easterlin's research. Why is this? Wouldn't one assume that increasing per capita income over time would increase happiness? Researchers suggest many possible reasons, ranging from the possibility that people in wealthier countries are more materialistic, to adaptation, income inequality, and uncertainty about the future (employment, health care, and retirement).

Economists' views vary widely on these issues. Easterlin's research has been challenged in recent years, so the debate continues. Easterlin believes strongly that factors other than money and per capita income have a greater impact on a society's happiness. In response to a researcher challenging his conclusions, Easterlin stated:

> *Instead of straining to feed the illusion that a focus on economic growth will create happiness, an approach is needed that explores the impact on national trends in life satisfaction, not just of material goods but also of family life, health, work utility, and the like.*

Other researchers agree that we should not assume that more money would make us happier. When discussing the correlation between money and happiness, Daniel Kahneman, psychology professor at Princeton University and a Nobel Laureate, wrote: "Standard of living has increased dramatically and happiness has increased not at all, and in some cases, has diminished slightly. There is a lot of evidence that being richer ... isn't making us happier."

CHAPTER
TWO
■ ■ ■ ■ ■

How Your Brain
is Wired

*October is one of the peculiarly dangerous
months to speculate in stocks.*

*The others are July, January, September, April, November,
May, March, June, December, August and February.*

—MARK TWAIN

Neuroscience and
Financial Decisions

n the previous chapter we reviewed psychological research that indicates we have a tremendous amount of control over our own happiness. By making intentional choices about our attitude and behavior, we can choose to become happier. We also looked at economic research (international and within the United States) that attempts to measure the impact that earning more money will have on our happiness. Another body of research that is very pertinent to the way we make financial decisions is from the field of neuroscience.

Neuroscience is defined by *Merriam-Webster* as "a branch of the life sciences that deals with the anatomy, physiology, biochemistry, or molecular biology of nerves and nervous tissue and especially with their relation to behavior and learning." Although most people tend to think of neuroscience as simply the study of the brain, it pertains to the nervous system, which includes the brain and spinal cord, as well as nerves and ganglia outside the brain and spinal cord. Although neuroscience originally resided within the field of biology, it now includes researchers from psychology, medicine, chemistry, philosophy, and education. In addition, new fields, such as neuroeconomics and behavioral finance, have evolved as a way to interpret how we make financial decisions.

Neuroscientist and professor of psychology Richard Davidson has developed the field of *affective neuroscience*, which he defines as "the study of the brain mechanisms that underlie our emotions and the search for ways to enhance people's sense of well-being and promote positive qualities of mind." He and his colleagues at the University of Wisconsin at Madison have been using brain imaging equipment to study the brain. Loosely called *brain mapping*, researchers can see different parts of the brain "light up" based on various activities or emotions.

Davidson focuses his research on the unique emotional *styles* each human possesses and the underlying brain activity that determines that emotional style. He researches traits such as resilience, outlook, and self-awareness. These traits (and the ways our brains are "wired") clearly impact our level of happiness. To understand how it may also impact the financial decisions we make, we need a brief overview of two parts of the brain.

There are many different parts of the brain, but two distinct parts are involved in financial decisions. The first part involves the amygdala. It lies within the limbic system, which is often called the *reflexive* brain, the *reptilian* brain, or the *lizard* brain. It is in the core of the brain, and it processes information very rapidly and often subconsciously. The amygdala is considered a major center within the brain where our intuition, emotions, perception of risk or reward, and first impressions originate. The amygdala causes us to seek rewards (sometimes crave rewards) such as sex, money, alcohol, and drugs. Impulsive behavior originates in the amygdala, along with anger, fear, and greed. All mammals have an amygdala, and it plays a crucial role in our survival. When you are about to step on a snake, when a dog runs in front of your car, or when you see an object coming toward your face, it is the amygdala that causes you to avoid the snake, hit the brakes, or duck.

In addition to the amygdala, other parts of the brain are involved in our emotions and intuitions, and most brain functions are widely distributed. Neuroscientists have discovered that the brain is *dynamic*, meaning it responds differently to the same events at different times and under different circumstances. Most brain areas can also multitask, which is evident when studying people with brain injuries. Although a portion of the brain that typically controls certain functions may be damaged, other parts of the brain can sometimes take over that function.

The second part of our brain involved in financial decisions is the prefrontal cortex, which lies behind the forehead and is often called the "reflective" brain. This is where analysis, weighing the pros and cons of an idea, and formulating a plan originate. The human brain has evolved with a larger prefrontal cortex than animals, which is what allows humans to think rationally. Psychologist Kelly McGonigal states in her book *The Willpower Instinct* that this is "one reason you'll never see your dog saving kibble for retirement."

Researchers are learning that the prefrontal cortex is also involved in controlling a person's emotional resilience. Davidson defines resilience as how slowly or quickly one recovers from adversity. Specifically, his research has shown that greater activation in the left prefrontal cortex indicates that a person will recover quickly from adversity. Taking this a step further, he determined that the left prefrontal cortex sends inhibitory signals via the white matter (axons that connect one neuron to another) to the amygdala. These inhibitory signals tell the amygdala to "quiet down," allowing the brain to recover from an upsetting or emotional experience. His research showed that some people have more white matter between their prefrontal cortex and their amygdala than others, and those people are more resilient. A diagram of the brain which shows the prefrontal cortex and the amygdala is provided in Figure 2.1.

FIGURE 2.1

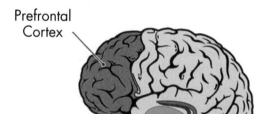

You may be thinking this is all rather interesting, but how does it impact your decisions involving money? In a huge way! Your amygdala is what causes you to panic if the stock market goes into a downward spiral. If you are likely to be impulsive and sell your investments in a panic, then your amygdala is being dominant in your decision-making process. If you tend to overanalyze your investments to the point where you feel paralyzed and cannot make a decision, then your prefrontal cortex is being dominant. Yet Davidson's research shows that the prefrontal cortex can calm down your emotions and allow rational thinking to prevail. A person would want plenty of white matter between their prefrontal cortex and amygdala so the calming down can occur. Not everyone has a significant amount of white matter (which may be apparent by how impulsive or fearful a person is), but Davidson's research shows that people can actually increase their amount of white matter.

Jason Zweig, in his book *Your Money and Your Brain,* questions whether wise investing involves rational thinking or emotions. His answer is that it involves both. "Pure rationality with no feelings can be as bad for your portfolio as sheer emotion unchecked by reason."

When making financial decisions, a wise approach is to be aware that the amygdala and prefrontal cortex portions of your brain may be in conflict with each other. If you suspect your amygdala is dominant and you have a tendency to make impulsive financial decisions that are detrimental to your financial security, try some of the strategies shown in "A Balanced Approach."

Conversely, if you tend to overanalyze your financial decisions, ask yourself occasionally what your gut feeling is regarding a decision, and pay attention to your intuition. The amygdala and prefrontal cortex can both be helpful for making wise financial decisions. You just need to keep them in check and not allow one or the other to be overly dominant.

Over the years, I have had a few clients who were impulsive (a dominant amygdala) and several clients who overanalyzed their financial decisions (dominant prefrontal cortex). The impulsive clients were often their own worst enemy. I considered it my job to provide a disciplined investment strategy, help them stay committed to their long-term financial plan, and prevent them from jumping in and out of the stock market based on fear. I encouraged them to call me when they became fearful due to stock market volatility or frightening economic news. I suspect I've had very few impulsive clients because people with this personality type would not typically hire a financial planner. However, if you know you tend to be impulsive, a financial advisor can be a valuable "voice of reason" to counter your impulsive tendencies and help you follow your plan.

A Balanced Approach

Try the following 10 strategies to neutralize the harmful emotional signals (such as fear, greed, and impulsive behavior) that originate in the amygdala:

1. Have a long-term financial plan that includes specific goals. Your plan will provide discipline when you are tempted to react emotionally to the gyrations of the stock market.

2. Review your goals often and stay focused.

3. Establish some investing guidelines. In the financial industry, we call this an Investment Policy Statement (IPS). In the simplest form, your IPS should state your investment objective—such as aggressive growth, long-term growth, balanced growth, conservative growth and income, or capital preservation and income. You may also want to include the asset allocation you have chosen for your investments. Chapter Ten is devoted to investment topics, including asset allocation.

4. Set a limit for yourself, such as committing to wait at least one day before buying a financial product. Deciding you are going to "sleep on" a financial decision before taking any action may allow you to tap into your prefrontal cortex to gain logical, rational thinking about the decision.

5. Get a second opinion before buying a financial product.

6. Understand your loss tolerance. If your tolerance is low, keep your investments conservative so the losses in your accounts will be less than the overall stock market when it drops significantly.

continued...

7. Be aware that fear and greed are the worst enemies to your financial security.

8. Turn off the TV and the computer if the "noise" from a stock market correction gets too loud. Go for a walk, ride your bike, or play tourist for a day.

9. Remind yourself that you have a long-term plan that will serve you well. Statistics from the U.S. stock market have been collected since 1926. During those 86-plus years, there have been many frightening events, and the stock market has nosedived many times. But it has always recovered.

10. Stay in control of your finances by implementing the strategies in Chapters Seven through Eleven. Prepare your net worth statement, manage your saving and spending, build three tax buckets, know your tolerance for risk, monitor your investment accounts, and don't neglect your finances.

Many of the clients who overanalyzed their financial decisions were engineers and scientists. I often joked with them that I could line the walls of our conference room with spreadsheets if that would satisfy their need to "analyze the issue." However, their financial decisions frequently came down to reviewing the statistical analysis I provided, followed by a discussion during which we applied the analysis to their goals and personal situation. The statistical analysis was required so they would know their decisions were not being made on a whim, which would be very uncomfortable for them. Yet the statistical analysis was only one piece of the puzzle, and it was most beneficial when it was discussed in the context of their personal lives and goals.

Fortunately, the majority of my clients use a balanced approach to investing. They are logical thinkers, so they don't make impulsive financial decisions. They also do not overanalyze to the point they cannot make a decision. Good investors use both parts of their brain when making financial decisions.

There is a fascinating story in Jason Zweig's book about Harry M. Markowitz. Markowitz is well known in the financial industry for his theories on risk and return and "Modern Portfolio Theory," which he created and which led to a Nobel Prize in economics in 1990. Zwieg tells the story:

> *In the 1950s, a young researcher at the RAND Corporation was pondering how much of his retirement fund to allocate to stocks and how much to bonds. An expert in linear programming, he knew that "I should have computed the historical co-variances of the asset classes and drawn an efficient frontier. Instead, I visualized my grief if the stock market went way up and I wasn't in it or if it went way down and I was completely in it. My intention was to minimize my future regret. So I split my contributions 50/50 between bonds and equities.*

Why would Harry Markowitz set aside theories and statistical analysis when working with his own portfolio? One would assume that his rational thinking (his prefrontal cortex) was dominant due to the fact that he was an economist who spent his career analyzing financial statistics. Yet he realized that measuring risk and return was only a portion of the solution. The bigger issue was recognizing that human behavior (and the way we respond to stock market fluctuations) cannot be predicted or controlled by theories and statistics. This emotional reaction to stock market swings originates in the amygdala, and Markowitz understood how powerful this emotional behavior can be. In this sense, he was way ahead of his time.

Training Your Brain

Neuroscientists have learned that our brains are constantly changing, from the time we are born until the time we die. Our brain can build new neural pathways when we replace an old habit with a new habit, or change our attitude or lifestyle. The brain's ability to build new neural pathways is termed *neuroplasticity*.

Malcolm Gladwell explained the importance of practicing an activity 10,000 hours in his book *Outliers*. Although the traditional thinking was that reaching a high level of achievement required extensive talent plus preparation, a classic experiment by psychologist K. Anders Ericsson and two colleagues at Berlin's elite Academy of Music showed that innate talent (genetics) played a very minor role in achievement. Instead, studies have shown that practicing at least 10,000 hours typically causes a person to become an expert at a skill. Studies have shown this to be true for basketball players, ice skaters, tennis players, and musicians. It also applies to technology experts, such as Bill Gates, Paul Allen, and Steve Jobs, who all spent thousands of hours tinkering with technology when they were teenagers.

Research in recent years has shown that practicing for long periods actually alters the brain due to the brain's plasticity. According to neuroscientist Richard Davidson:

> The brains of virtuoso violinists show a measurable increase in the size and activity of areas that control the fingers, and the brains of London taxicab drivers, who learn to navigate the insanely complicated network of streets in that city, show a significant growth in the hippocampus, an area associated with context and spatial memory.

continued...

What are the implications of neuroplasticity to you and me? Our brains can change based on our actions and our thoughts. Just like it is very exciting that small, intentional changes in our behaviors can significantly increase our happiness, we now know that our actions and thoughts can also change our brains. The way our brains function is not limited to genetics or experience. We are far more malleable than previously believed. If you consider yourself grumpy, you can change. If you consider yourself to be set in your ways in terms of bad habits, you can change. If you consider yourself not to be creative, you can become more creative through practice. So practice really does make perfect!

System 1 and System 2

Cognitive psychologist Daniel Kahneman has devoted his entire career to researching how we make decisions, and he has shown that our decisions are often irrational. Kahneman won a Nobel Prize in Economics in 2002 for his work with Amos Tversky.

Kahneman's book *Thinking, Fast and Slow* summarizes his many years of research on how we make decisions. For the sake of simplicity, he named the two ways we make decisions as System 1 and System 2. He describes System 1 as being fast, intuitive, and emotional. System 1 runs automatically and cannot be turned off. System 1 is what allows us to complete the phrase "bread and …," to go into a restaurant and know that we will sit in a chair at a table, and to drive the same route each day to our office. It allows us to know what a clock is for, to understand simple sentences, and to solve the equation $2 + 2 = ?$

In contrast, System 2 is required in complex computations and analysis. Kahneman provides examples such as filling out a tax form, counting the occurrences of a single letter in a page of text, or comparing two washing machines for overall value. Only System 2 can follow rules. Yet System 2 is lazy. Kahneman states:

System 1 runs automatically, and System 2 is normally in a comfortable low-effort mode, in which only a fraction of its capacity is engaged. System 1 continuously generates suggestions for System 2: impressions, intuitions, intentions, and feelings. If endorsed by System 2, impressions and intuitions turn into beliefs, and most of the time, System 2 adopts the suggestions of System 1 with little or no modification. You generally believe your impressions and act on your desires, and that is fine—usually.

However, accepting the quick answers provided by System 1 can lead to irrational decisions. Kahneman and Tversky conducted many experiments over their careers, and one involved what Kahneman terms *emotional framing*. Physicians at Harvard Medical School were given statistics about the outcomes of two potential treatments for lung cancer: surgery and radiation. The five-year survival rates clearly favored surgery, but in the short term, surgery was riskier than radiation. Half the participants were given statistics about survival rates; the remaining half received the same information in terms of mortality rates. The two descriptions of the short-term outcomes of surgery were:

- The one-month survival rate is 90 percent.
- There is 10 percent mortality in the first month.

You can predict the results. Surgery was much more popular when physicians were given the first statement (which Kahneman terms a *frame*). In fact, 84 percent of the physicians chose it. For the physicians who were given the second statement, 50 percent chose radiation.

Clearly, the physicians were not aware that they were being tricked or challenged. Their System 1 gave an automatic reply based upon intuition. If they had activated System 2 (which takes deliberate effort), they may have had a different response. The statements are identical in meaning. Yet depending on which statement the physicians were given, they responded very differently.

The advertising industry is full of similar examples. When you buy lunch meat at the grocery store, it may be described as "90 percent fat-free." Would you still buy it if it were described as "10 percent fat"?

Kahneman offers some wise advice on deciphering System 1 and System 2 when he says, "The way to block errors that originate in System 1 is simple in principle: Recognize the signs that you are in a cognitive minefield, slow down, and ask for reinforcement from System 2."

The Dangers

Relative Income

In our quest to have a healthy relationship with money, there are several dangers lurking in the financial landscape that we should try to avoid. The first is the theory of *relative income*. This theory states that we care more about how much we make *relative to others* around us, rather than what we actually make, which would be termed *absolute income*.

Let's assume Sally earns $50,000 a year. She lives in a modest home, and $50,000 pays her bills and supports a simple lifestyle that she enjoys. Overall, Sally considers herself to be happy and content. (See Figure 2.2)

FIGURE 2.2

SALLY:
Income = $50,000 per year;
Sally is happy!

Over the next few months Sally makes new friends or changes jobs or starts interacting with new neighbors. (See Figure 2.3) This is all good. But, at some point, she finds out that most of her neighbors earn $80,000 per year. Does Sally care what they earn?

FIGURE 2.3

SALLY'S NEW FRIENDS:
Income = $80,000 per year

According to the relative income theory, even though Sally *was* happy earning $50,000, she will now be less happy because her $50,000 income is much less *relative to* the people around her. In other words, the $50,000 that Sally earns is almost irrelevant to her level of happiness. (See Figure 2.4)

FIGURE 2.4

SALLY:
Impacted by theory of relative income;
Sally is unhappy!

Wouldn't it be nice if we could experience happiness only on our own terms? If Sally was happy earning $50,000, why should she have to worry about the relative income theory disrupting her happiness? Why should she (consciously or unconsciously) compare her income to anyone else? Some may say it is human nature. However, we have already established that roughly 40 percent of our happiness is impacted by our choices. Applying intentional behaviors can minimize or negate the relative income theory. One way to combat the relative income theory is by simplifying our lives. Going to live in a cabin in the woods seems a bit extreme, but reducing the amount of possessions we own and deliberately restricting the influence of materialism in our lives is a healthy step forward.

Keeping Up With the Joneses

If we do not defend against the relative income theory, it can lead us down a treacherous path, into a behavior pattern called "keeping up with the Joneses." This dynamic is pervasive in American culture, and it is dangerous. Figure 2.5 (provided by Carl Richards, founder of *BehaviorGap.com*) shows a behavior pattern that is common.

FIGURE 2.5

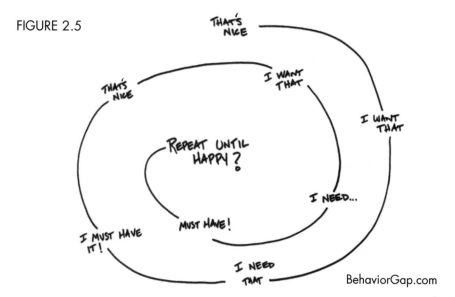

BehaviorGap.com

At the beginning of the pattern, you see something someone else has and you say, "That's nice." But as the behavior progresses, you say, "I want that." You then convince yourself that "I need that," and then you *must* have it. After that stage, the vicious cycle starts again.

Keeping up with the Joneses feeds on itself, much like an addiction. Working hard and striving to get ahead financially is not the problem. The problem is that we have become accustomed to always wanting more. But there are repercussions to this behavior: Buying a bigger house includes a higher monthly mortgage payment, an increase in property taxes, and a higher premium for homeowner's insurance. Then there is the added expense of purchasing the contents to fill the house (furniture, flat-screen TVs, appliances, and electronics). In addition to a bigger house, we convince ourselves that we need more cars and more gadgets.

Ed Diener and Robert Biswas-Diener found that the level of satisfaction with what we currently have is a key component of happiness. If you are satisfied with your current lifestyle and are not striving for more material possessions, you will be happier. If you strive to keep up with the Joneses and seek more possessions, you will be less happy. This suggests that it is not the *amount* of money that impacts our happiness, but our *attitude* toward it.

Jason Zweig, in his book *Your Money and Your Brain*, suggests that the urge to keep up with the Joneses (which he calls a "comparison complex") is a part of our biological makeup: "To envy is human," he says. Unfortunately, envy does not have many redeeming qualities and often negatively impacts our happiness. Zweig states:

Suffering a mild case of the "comparison complex" can be beneficial; it motivates you to work hard, gives you hope for the future, keeps you from being a total miser, and prompts you to clean up the house before visitors arrive. There is good reason, however, that the Ten Commandments close with a thundering inventory of all things that "Thou shalt not covet." While a secret pinch of envy is a positive motivator, a chronic comparison complex can ruin your life. If you cannot control the ancient urge to measure your success against that of your peers, your happiness will always depend less on how much money you have than on how much money they have. And that's something you will never have any control over. Always wanting more, in order to keep up with whoever has more, makes millions of people perennially unhappy.

The tug to keep up with the Joneses is pervasive in our society. However, it can be resisted. Most of my clients have investment assets ranging from $800,000 to $5 million. Someone with more than $1 million would be considered wealthy by most standards, but not in my clients' minds. The vast majority would describe themselves as being middle-income. They are extremely responsible with their money and have not forgotten the lessons they learned when they were younger and had far less money. They are aware of the dangers of keeping up with the Joneses.

For a few years, I worked with a married couple who were very different from my other clients. They were extremely materialistic. They "wore their wealth on their sleeve" and wanted everyone to know they were wealthy. Their ostentatious behavior led me to realize that the amount of money one has is definitely not a requirement for being wealthy; I would actually describe this couple as poor in other, more important ways. This experience helped solidify my view that people should consider money to be a tool; it is not to be worshipped. This couple was very unhappy, and their behavior demonstrated that striving for more and more material possessions can be toxic.

The American dream encourages us to work hard and aspire to move up in the world. Wanting a bigger paycheck, a better house, more extensive travel, or a high-quality education for your children are all worthy goals. It's OK to enjoy your wealth, and I am not suggesting that anyone should become overly frugal. The key is to keep in control of your finances and to align the way you spend money with your values and goals.

Loss Aversion

How do System 1 and System 2 impact our financial decisions? Kahneman's research showed that we often make irrational financial decisions. His work determined that loss aversion can impact our decisions. Behavioral finance experts have shown that the pain we get from losing $1,000 is far greater than the pleasure we get from gaining $1,000. Kahneman reports that the loss aversion ratio from several experiments is estimated to be 1.5 to 2.5. If we use an average of 2.0, this means that a person must have a potential gain of $2,000 to justify a risk of losing $1,000. This is not rational, but it is suspected this may be a function of evolution. According to Kahneman: "Organisms that treat threats as more urgent than opportunities have a better chance to survive and reproduce."

This aversion to loss becomes more predominant when the stock market is declining. Investors may be very hesitant to sell an asset that has declined in value, even though if they looked at the situation rationally, they should be selling.

Following the Herd

Another danger from irrational financial decisions is the tendency to "follow the herd." There is a feeling of urgency that we should do what everyone else is doing, or we will be left out of the action. When the stock market has gone up significantly, there often seems to be a frenzy of excitement, which encourages investors to buy equities. The media emboldens this irrational behavior, as articles and TV commentators go into an exuberant mode. Similarly, when the stock market seems to be in free fall, our emotional brains tend to shout "sell, sell, sell," as our amygdala floods our thoughts with fear. It is important that you are aware of the emotional messages that originate in your amygdala and you work to silence them with rational thinking from your prefrontal cortex.

The amygdala can lead investors to want to follow the herd, and greed (which originates in the amygdala) may play a role. Being vulnerable to scams and exclusive investments, such as the Ponzi schemes created by Bernie Madoff, Alan Stanford, and others probably originates in the amygdala. (Hint: If it seems too good to be true, it is.) The prefrontal cortex, which is where rational thinking originates, may lead an investor to ask, "How could Bernie Madoff report good returns year after year, even in years when the overall market is declining?" This rational thinking can help you avoid scams, which will also improve your financial security.

Overconfidence

The amygdala can lead to overconfidence. This is a serious problem when an investor chooses a stock or mutual fund that increases significantly in value. The amygdala will cause the investor to believe he or she is a talented stock-picker. This is evident with people who brag about an investment to their neighbor or at a social gathering. (When you meet these folks, run in the other direction. Their advice will almost always cause you to lose money.)

Excessive Risk Taking

Neuroscientists are researching how our brains react when we take risks. This is especially interesting when looking at traders at an investment bank. If you watched any of the documentaries that were produced about the 2008 financial crisis, you may have noticed that young male traders were the ones typically involved in the excessive risk taking. Scientists are now researching the impact that hormones have on increased risk taking. The findings suggest that testosterone (a hormone produced in significant quantities by young men and in much smaller quantities by women and older men) increases confidence and appetite for risk among traders. Adrenaline, cortisol, and dopamine are also being researched. One theory is that traders who are normally calm (and sometimes risk-averse) may become overconfident and take excessive risks due to the hormonal changes in their bodies following volatility in the financial markets. Physiologists are hoping that studying the biology of risk taking and irrational exuberance could help provide stability for the financial markets in the future.

Having the wrong attitude about money, or giving money too much power in our lives can be dangerous to our happiness. So what is a healthy approach?

A Healthy Approach

Realize that money, when used wisely, is a very practical tool. One of my clients said to me: "Having money allows me to volunteer for the Animal Humane Society, which brings me great joy." She is only 60 years old, and if she and her husband had not saved and invested wisely over the years, she would likely be working full time. Money is a good thing. It is definitely not "the root of all evil," as some would like us to believe. I encourage you to enjoy your money and never apologize for having it.

After reviewing the research from the fields of psychology, finance, and economics—and by working closely with clients over many years—I am convinced that money does not *buy* happiness. If you could buy happiness, then everyone with enough money would be happy. However, when used wisely, money can *impact* our happiness, and having money can lead to greater happiness. But it does *not* buy happiness. This is an important distinction. Many things, such as family and friends, laughter, a sense of purpose, and gratitude can have a much greater impact on our happiness than money.

Ways Money Can Impact Happiness

- working fewer hours
- retiring when you choose
- spending more time with friends and family
- finding a sense of purpose in what you do
- having more free time
- traveling more frequently
- being able to focus on education
- being spontaneous
- contributing to your children or grandchildren's education
- worrying less, sleeping better, and having peace of mind
- donating money to your favorite causes
- buying services such as a house cleaner or gardener
- purchasing better health care
- buying health club memberships or hiring a personal trainer
- enjoying massages
- pursuing hobbies
- launching a new career
- paying bills without stress
- helping family members financially
- volunteering
- having more time to focus on goals
- hiring a good financial planner, estate attorney, and accountant
- pursuing elaborate adventures

Each of us may have a different definition of happiness, but we each need to be an active participant in creating that happiness. We also need to remember that it is a journey, not a destination.

On the previous page is a partial list of the ways that money can impact our happiness. Some of the items will appeal to you, and others may not. That's OK. Some may not even require money. You will notice that many of them would fall under the categories of time and freedom, which, as you recall from Chapter One, are two of the greatest benefits money can provide. There are, no doubt, many items that are not on the list that may increase your happiness. I encourage you to ponder the items listed, circle the ones that appeal to you, and add to the list.

Invest in Yourself

- Make a conscious decision to avoid the comparison complex ("keeping up with the Joneses"). This will make you happier and help you manage your money wisely. You also will be teaching your children an important lesson through your actions.

- Make a game out of it. Ask yourself if you're willing to live in one the smallest houses and to drive one of the oldest cars in your neighborhood. Decide you don't need a super-sized television or a trendy wardrobe. Even better, strive to keep your car for 12 years. It's a good first step.

- The next time you are contemplating making a major purchase that is not essential, stop yourself. Avoid buying the item for at least three days. During those three days, think about whether the item is a *want* or a *need*. If you want to simplify your life and reduce the number of possessions you own, contemplate whether you really need another item.

- When you are faced with a financial decision, consider whether your amygdala seems to be dominant (you are feeling emotions such as fear, greed, or impulsivity) or your prefrontal cortex (rational thinking) is dominant. Or maybe both are engaged, helping you make a wise decision.

- Reward yourself after making smart decisions regarding your finances. The rewards may be a hike in the mountains, a picnic at the beach, making a nice meal with healthy fruits and vegetables, taking a hot bath, sleeping late on Saturday, or going to bed with a good book. You get the idea.

CHAPTER
THREE

■ ■ ■ ■ ■

Your Foundation

Sometimes a person has to go back, really back—
to have a sense, an understanding of all
that's gone to make them—
before they can go forward.
—PAULE MARSHALL, AUTHOR

n Chapter Two, the adage "embrace change" was introduced. Now, in Chapter Three, you will be encouraged to "ponder." Another word for pondering is daydreaming—a time that is not filled with anything and your mind is allowed to wander. Research has shown that daydreaming is very healthy. Psychologist Jonathan Schooler at the University of California at Santa Barbara, found that people who daydream are more creative. Slowing down our hectic lifestyles has many benefits, including reducing stress. It can also help provide clarity for the changes you want to make. Those changes will be discussed later in the book. For now, just give yourself permission to ponder as you think about your values, the money messages you learned as a child, and memories from your childhood. Our childhoods played an important role in molding us into the adults we are today.

Your Core Values

According to the *Oxford Dictionary*, values are "principles or standards of behavior; one's judgment of what is important in life." Values provide a strong foundation for the way we live our lives. When our actions are aligned with our values, we feel content and satisfied. We rarely think about our values, yet they deserve our attention. "Stay true to yourself" is an expression that touches on honoring our values with conviction. Your values are unique to you, and they may be very different from the values of your friends, family members, or coworkers. Values can also evolve and change over time.

To find which values are most important to you, complete the following Top 20 Core Values exercise. There are two boxes to the left of each value. Using the box immediately to the left of each word, go through the list, marking every value that is important to you. Do this quickly, and check as many as you wish. If you're unsure about some of the words on the list, use the following phrase in front of each word: "I value _____." It might also help to remember that some people refer to the words listed as character strengths, virtues, or personality traits.

After completing the first run-through, go back through the list of values you checked. Using the remaining box, place a checkmark next to the 20 values that you feel most strongly about. These are your *core* values.

The list is not all-inclusive. If you have a value that is not represented, write it down at the end of the list. Feel free to cross out values if you change your mind. There is no right or wrong way to identify your values. If you end up with only 10, that is fine. If you identify 25 values, that's OK too.

Your core values help define you as a person and make you unique. After completing the exercise, I recommend that you refer to the list of your 20 core values as you read through the book. The

small changes you decide to make later in Chapter Twelve will likely
pertain to honoring your core values. This exercise is also on the website (*www.joyoffinancialsecurity.com*).

Top 20 Core Values

❏ ❏	Achievement		❏ ❏	Education
❏ ❏	Adventure		❏ ❏	Empathy
❏ ❏	Affection		❏ ❏	Enthusiasm
❏ ❏	Ambition		❏ ❏	Environmental responsibility
❏ ❏	Appreciation of culture		❏ ❏	Equality
❏ ❏	Artistic expression		❏ ❏	Ethics
❏ ❏	Autonomy		❏ ❏	Excellence
❏ ❏	Beauty		❏ ❏	Fairness
❏ ❏	Challenge		❏ ❏	Faith
❏ ❏	Charitable giving		❏ ❏	Family
❏ ❏	Close relationships		❏ ❏	Flexibility
❏ ❏	Commitment		❏ ❏	Financial security
❏ ❏	Communication		❏ ❏	Forgiveness
❏ ❏	Community		❏ ❏	Freedom
❏ ❏	Compassion		❏ ❏	Friendship
❏ ❏	Competition		❏ ❏	Generosity
❏ ❏	Confidence		❏ ❏	Giving back
❏ ❏	Contentment		❏ ❏	Gratitude
❏ ❏	Cooperation		❏ ❏	Hard work
❏ ❏	Courage		❏ ❏	Harmony
❏ ❏	Creativity		❏ ❏	Having goals
❏ ❏	Curiosity		❏ ❏	Health
❏ ❏	Decisiveness		❏ ❏	Honesty
❏ ❏	Determination		❏ ❏	Hope
❏ ❏	Discipline		❏ ❏	Humility
❏ ❏	Diversity		❏ ❏	Idealism

❑ ❑ Inclusiveness   ❑ ❑ Practicality
❑ ❑ Independence   ❑ ❑ Preparation
❑ ❑ Innovation   ❑ ❑ Privacy
❑ ❑ Integrity   ❑ ❑ Public service
❑ ❑ Intelligence   ❑ ❑ Purpose
❑ ❑ Job satisfaction   ❑ ❑ Quality relationships
❑ ❑ Kindness   ❑ ❑ Quiet
❑ ❑ Knowledge   ❑ ❑ Recognition
❑ ❑ Laughter   ❑ ❑ Resiliency
❑ ❑ Leadership   ❑ ❑ Respect
❑ ❑ Listening   ❑ ❑ Responsibility
❑ ❑ Love   ❑ ❑ Sacrifice
❑ ❑ Love of country   ❑ ❑ Safety
❑ ❑ Love of learning   ❑ ❑ Security
❑ ❑ Loyalty   ❑ ❑ Self-respect
❑ ❑ Meaningful work   ❑ ❑ Sensitivity
❑ ❑ Mentoring   ❑ ❑ Serenity
❑ ❑ Motivation   ❑ ❑ Sharing
❑ ❑ Nature   ❑ ❑ Simplicity
❑ ❑ Nonviolence   ❑ ❑ Sincerity
❑ ❑ Open-mindedness   ❑ ❑ Social responsibility
❑ ❑ Opportunity   ❑ ❑ Solitude
❑ ❑ Optimism   ❑ ❑ Spirituality
❑ ❑ Organization   ❑ ❑ Sportsmanship
❑ ❑ Passion   ❑ ❑ Stability
❑ ❑ Patience   ❑ ❑ Status
❑ ❑ Perseverance   ❑ ❑ Strength
❑ ❑ Physical challenge   ❑ ❑ Strategic thinking
❑ ❑ Pleasure   ❑ ❑ Structure
❑ ❑ Positive attitude   ❑ ❑ Supervising others
❑ ❑ Power and authority   ❑ ❑ Teaching by example

❏ ❏	Teamwork		❏ ❏	Vision
❏ ❏	Time alone		❏ ❏	Volunteering
❏ ❏	Tolerance		❏ ❏	Wealth
❏ ❏	Trust		❏ ❏	Wisdom
❏ ❏	Truth		❏ ❏	Working alone
❏ ❏	Unity		❏ ❏	Working with others
❏ ❏	Variety			

Next Steps

Now that you have determined your 20 core values, what is next? Look through your list and think about whether each core value is represented in your life. If it is not, note that the core value may need to be a part of one of the small changes you will make in Chapter Twelve.

For example, assume that one of your core values is *adventure*. Adventure may mean you love to travel and you should be planning your next vacation to a destination where you have never been. Or maybe adventure means you love to take time to explore local areas on weekends. It may mean going to new restaurants, visiting museums, attending lectures, or hiking in the mountains nearby.

Once you identify what adventure means to you, make it a part of your lifestyle. If your idea of adventure is going on a vacation, schedule it and put it on your calendar—in ink. I have known many people who think they cannot take a vacation from their jobs, and they are kidding themselves. Vacations have been shown to rekindle our energy and creativity, as well as provide a relaxing change of routine. If your idea of adventure is exploring local areas, then free up a half day on the weekend to be adventurous. Do not work on weekends, and do not fill weekends with chores that feel like burdens. This may require intentional changes, but aligning your actions with your values can significantly increase your happiness.

What if one of your core values is *working alone?* You may be an introvert. Susan Cain, author of the book *Quiet*, points out the redeeming qualities of being an introvert. She estimates that of all the people you know, at least one-third are introverts. These are people who prefer listening rather than speaking and reading rather than partying. They prefer working on their own rather than brainstorming in teams, and they tend to be innovative and creative. Although the corporate world and our education system tend to reward extroverts, many great contributions originated from introverts, including Vincent van Gogh's sunflowers and the personal computer. Realizing that working alone allows you to be extremely productive and creative may encourage you to embrace this trait and consider it a strength.

Perhaps one of your core values is *creativity*, but you feel like your current routine does not include any expression of creativity. The topic "Nurture Your Creativity" in Chapter Five will provide ideas on how to build more creativity into your life. One of my clients, Dawn, knew she wanted to become an artist, so she began taking painting classes several years before she retired. As a speech therapist working for the local school district, she had summers off. She decided to go to France one summer to study with an artist for a month. The next summer she went again. She then retired from the school district and began painting frequently in the studio she had built in her garage. Dawn entered local art shows and continued to study with other artists. She is now an accomplished artist.

Money Messages
You Were Taught as a Child

During our childhood, we received messages about money, and they are deeply ingrained in our behavior as adults. Money is often a taboo topic among families. Most of us learned at a young age that it was not an acceptable topic at the dinner table. Yet even if money was not discussed openly, you received powerful messages from the behaviors of your parents and relatives.

The following exercise includes a list of questions that will help you identify your childhood money messages. You may find that this exercise brings up memories that you had forgotten. Increasing your awareness about how your parents and your family handled money while you were a child can help you understand why you treat money as you do today. Becoming aware will help if you want to change your behaviors or your feelings about money. This is an important step toward having a healthy attitude about money.

Money Messages You Learned as a Child

1. How did your mother address money issues as you were growing up?

   _____

   _____

   _____

   _____

2. How did your father address money issues as you were growing up?

   _____

   _____

   _____

   _____

3. How did your grandparents address money issues as you were growing up?

   _____

   _____

   _____

   _____

4. What is a happy memory from your childhood that is related
    to money?

    _____

    _____

    _____

    _____

    _____

5. What is an unhappy memory?

    _____

    _____

    _____

    _____

    _____

6. Do you remember any money "sayings" that your
    parents used?

    _____

    _____

    _____

    _____

    _____

7. Do you believe you developed a healthy attitude based
    on the money messages you received during your childhood,
    or an unhealthy attitude? Why?

    _____

    _____

    _____

    _____

    _____

8. Which of your parents' or relatives' money messages continue to
    affect you today?

    _____

    _____

    _____

    _____

9. How are those money messages (from #8 above) impacting your behavior or your feelings about money today?

_____

_____

_____

_____

10. After answering the above questions, are there money messages you would like to change? If yes, what are they?

_____

_____

_____

_____

Treasure the Memories

Our past holds many memories, and a wealth of emotions are tied to them. Living for the *now* is important, but we must not forget that our *now* was shaped largely by our past. William Faulkner said, "The past isn't dead and buried. In fact, it isn't even passed."

This book is about happiness and financial security. Happiness inevitably pulls on your heartstrings. Most people agree that when you start thinking about happiness and other emotions (sadness, anger, hope, frustration), you must let your guard down to experience the emotions. Most people may not think about money as being emotional, but it is loaded with emotion. If you completed the "Money Messages" questionnaire above, you may have noticed that just thinking about old memories regarding money made you feel emotional.

Below I share others' nostalgic stories as well as my own personal story. These are included to help you reflect on memories from your childhood. Some memories may be happy; some may be sad. Some may surprise you, as you look back over many years with a new perspective. As you plan your future, recognize that the lessons from your past may also be your road map for the future.

Reflections: Investing for the Future

My relationship with my parents directly impacted my feelings toward money. In my father's later years, he asked me to manage his investments for him. Although he was not wealthy, investing was his hobby. His time serving in the Korean War led to a lifelong love of Japan, where he spent his time on leave from his military duties. He invested in Japanese technology companies in their heyday during the 1980s. He passed his love for investing to me, and I am grateful for this.

While pursuing my first career in corporate marketing in Chicago, investing and financial planning became a hobby. After getting married and moving to Albuquerque, a career change was required; corporate marketing jobs did not exist in a relatively small city such as Albuquerque. When my youngest daughter turned one year old, I decided to pursue my dream of becoming a financial planner, and I began working on the required coursework to become a Certified Financial Planner™ professional. In 1998, after earning the CFP® certificate, I launched my independent, financial planning firm.

Money messages from my father had a positive impact on how I handle money today. While I was a child he often said, "Save for a rainy day." When I went to college, I did not have a credit card, but he told me to always keep an extra $20 hidden in my purse for emergencies. After he died, I helped clean out his home, which included sorting old paper files. I discovered that he and my mother had paid off their mortgage just three years after building their home in 1955. Clearly, he was opposed to having debt.

However, it was my grandparents on my father's side who had a greater impact on the money messages I received as a child. They

continued...

decided that my sister and I should go to college, and they wanted to pay for it. They began saving when we were children. When we were teenagers we learned that they had saved $20,000 for each of us. They did this quietly, without any fanfare. We were the first members of our family to attend college.

There is no doubt that saving $20,000 each for my sister and me was incredibly difficult; $20,000 was an enormous sum of money in the 1960s and '70s. My grandparents lived in a small house and led a frugal lifestyle. My grandfather worked at the local Whirlpool factory, climbing the corporate ladder over many years from the production line to a management position. He died at age 62 when I was 10 years old, but my grandmother continued to save.

I wonder what they gave up to save the money so my sister and I could go to college. The concept of *opportunity cost* addresses all the things they could have purchased if they had not been committed to saving the money. Maybe they would have purchased a bigger house, a newer car, more frequent vacations, or better clothes. Maybe they would have eaten out more often. I'll never know.

When my sister and I left for college, we were each given $20,000 and told to stretch it so it would pay for college and, hopefully, extend beyond college. Giving us control of the money all at once seemed very unorthodox and risky. Since I had never had any financial courses and did not know how to manage the money, I simply kept it in a savings account at a local bank.

In 1975, savings accounts earned a small amount of interest, and I managed the account carefully. It paid all my expenses for four years of undergraduate school at Indiana University, and I had enough remaining to move to Albuquerque after I graduated. When I decided to go to graduate school, I took out a student loan and worked part time. I paid the loan off within three years.

continued…

Looking back, I realize that my grandmother was indirectly teaching me about money. When I was in college, she asked me each spring to help her organize her tax documents. Like many people from that generation, she had multiple bank accounts scattered around town. Helping her was fun for me, and I did not realize that I was learning important financial skills.

A friend recently told her daughters that her gift to them is an education. What they choose to do with their education (future jobs, careers, interests) will be up to them. I suspect my grandparents would agree with her statement. They felt strongly that we should go to college, and they gave us a very generous gift.

My grandparents' gift of a college education, along with my father's entrepreneurial spirit and the investment books and newsletters he sent me, all shaped my career and attitudes toward money. I felt confident opening a financial planning firm, and I am fortunate that it has been successful.

Every Day Matters

We have all known people who did not live long lives. It seems like they were taken from us much too soon, and we don't understand why. People who have lived through cancer are often an inspiration to others. They treasure each day and have learned the lesson that every day matters. Yet it seems that many of us are too stubborn, too dense, or too busy to learn that every day matters. What will it take for us to slow down our lives, appreciate what we have, and enjoy each day?

Author Anne Lamott, in her book *Bird by Bird*, says that she wrote one of her first books as a present to her father, who had been diagnosed with brain cancer. She writes:

... all of a sudden I had a sad story to tell. It was a story rich with drama and humor, about a father and his three semi-grown children living in a tiny town filled with aging hippies, trust-fund radicals, artists, New Agers, and ordinary people, whatever that means. Out of nowhere, the rug was suddenly pulled out from under the family, when it looked as if the father had a terminal illness and was actually going to go ahead and die.

Lamott explains that she went to the library and asked a librarian if there were any "really funny books about cancer." The librarian said there were not. She decided to fill the void by writing:

... a book about our experience, showing one family's attempt to stay buoyant in the face of such a potentially flattening process, seemed like it might be a welcome present to other people with sick relatives. This is all I tried to do, to tell our family's story, because with an enormous amount of support from friends, there were laughter and joy folded into all that fear and loss. It helped my father have the best possible months before his death and the best possible death. I can actually say it was great.

Lamott finished her book (titled *Traveling Mercies*) before her father died, and she considered it to be a love story to him.

The excerpt above illustrates several issues. First is the realization that we can have the rug pulled out from under us at any time. This seems to occur most often with a diagnosis of a serious illness, but it can also happen suddenly with a car accident or a plane crash, or slowly and deceptively through a gradual progression of Alzheimer's disease. Or it may not involve an illness at all. You may create your idea of the perfect lifestyle—the perfect spouse, family, home, job, etc.—and it may change tomorrow. Life-changing events, such as a divorce or the loss of a job, often catch us by surprise. Life is not always fair or kind. It is important to realize that money does not buy happiness, and issues involving health and relationships supercede money issues.

Second, the excerpt illustrates Lamott's need to tell the story and to tell it with humor. Her writing is very expressive and brutally honest. She states that "there were laughter and joy folded into all that fear and loss." Our emotions are often jumbled, ranging from pure joy to horror, sadness, grief, and everything in between. This exemplifies the fact that happiness is not a destination. We cannot become permanently happy, although we can become *happier*. As stated earlier, there is a lot of sadness in happiness. We can accept the fact that we experience a wide variety of emotions, and that is perfectly natural.

Seeking to Understand

In an article in the *Wall Street Journal* titled "Over the Internet, Into My Mom's Heart," Katherine Rosman described her quest to understand her mother's hobby of buying Venetian antique glass on eBay. Her mother, Suzy, fought a long battle with cancer, and she became engrossed with her hobby during her cancer treatments. With $25,000, she built an impressive collection of vintage glass and made many friends. As her health rapidly declined, Suzy asked Katherine and her sister Lizzie to monitor her eBay account and "safeguard her eBay reputation."

Almost two years after her mother's death, Katherine decided to research her eBay hobby, and learn about the antique glass items she had purchased. She made contact with a friend of Suzy's named Carl Bellavia. Suzy had talked about him often, and described him as a "glass-world guru." Suzy had lived in Tucson, Arizona, and Carl lived in Greenwich Village in New York City. They had never met, but had forged a strong friendship over the internet. Katherine visited him in person, and the following is an excerpt from her article:

"Your mom was angry," Mr. Bellavia told me. "She was surprised. She was devastated. She had been dealt a very bad hand. At the same time, she was adamant about beating it."

Buying vintage glass—fragile but resilient—was her escape from a life that quickly became defined by disease. The glass "gave her focus," Mr. Bellavia told me. "It was a release. Something she could do. Something that she had power over. She said that to me. She said it gave her a sense of being normal."

I asked him if he felt uncomfortable in my mom's confiding in him. Was it surreal that some woman across the country whom he had never met was telling him about the emotional isolation brought by cancer? Was he burdened by her needs? "I went to church and lit candles for her," he said. Then he grabbed my hand and sobbed.

Katherine continued to learn about the vintage glass her mother had purchased, and discovered that her mother was purchasing sets to leave to her and her sister. She also discovered that her mother had purchased a little green vase described on the receipt as "mezza filigrana Venini Murano Scarpa" for $36 on the day she was diagnosed with cancer. She had written on her records "Katie's vase." She had given it to Katherine, but she did not tell Katherine anything about the vase or its significance.

The article ends after Katherine visits her stepfather's house in Tucson and spends a day alone admiring her mother's glass collection, with her newfound knowledge and appreciation for the pieces. She then returns home to New York, pulls the little green vase out of the top of the cabinet, places five pink roses in it, and sets it in her family room.

The story about Rosman exploring her mother's hobby of purchasing Venetian antique glass is rich with lessons. First, her research and visit with Bellavia honors her mother. She wants to know why her mother was attracted to buying Venetian glass.

What was the appeal? Why did she befriend Bellavia, and what was the story behind her hobby? One theory is that her mother wanted to leave her two daughters a legacy, and leaving them the Venetian glass she had so lovingly collected served as a part of her legacy. Continuing the hobby throughout her cancer treatments gave her something to do that she enjoyed and made her happy, rather than focusing on her illness. She may not have shared the details of her hobby with her daughters because she felt they may not understand. Or maybe they were so busy with their own lives that she didn't want to bother them.

The story about Suzy and her hobby of collecting Venetian glass is very dear to me because my grandmother had a love of cut glass. She had a beautiful collection of cut-glass bowls. Officially called American Brilliant Cut Glass, the bowls and serving dishes were created between 1876 and 1914. During my grandmother's last few years, she mentioned her cut-glass collection to me and my sister several times, hoping that we would enjoy it after she was gone. She wanted to tell us about it and explain where the pieces had originated. My sister and I had no interest in her cut glass, so we didn't have those discussions with her. We provided the classic response, "Oh, Grandma, you are not going to die," that is typical of people not willing to acknowledge death.

After she died, I received most of the cut-glass collection, and I treasure it. I wish I would have had those conversations with my grandmother so I would know how she acquired it and the stories behind each piece. It is now a part of her legacy. The glass items remind me of her and of our wonderful times together. The lesson I learned from this experience is that we should never pass up the opportunity to have honest conversations with those we love. This topic is addressed in Chapter Six.

Relections: A Middle-Class Upbringing

I grew up in a middle-class household in Evansville, Indiana. We always had plenty of food, clothing, and a nice house. My parents owned a small business, and they both worked hard. When I was a small child, my mother, father, sister, and I all piled into the car every August for the long drive to Clearwater Beach, Florida, for a vacation.

My sister and I went to public grade schools and high schools, and the colleges I attended were state universities where I received a very good education. Our lifestyle was not extravagant, but we were living the American dream.

I have happy memories of spending Saturday nights with my grandparents when I was young. When my sister and I stayed overnight with one set of grandparents, we would walk to church together on Sunday mornings. I recall that it was an incredibly long walk, but we would stop at the "five and dime" store on the way and buy grape gumballs. Since pondering this memory, I now understand why I love grape gumballs. They will always hold a special place in my heart.

Another happy memory includes my other grandmother. When we would spend Saturday night with her, we always ate buttered popcorn while watching the Lawrence Welk Show on TV. I still allow myself the pleasure of buttered popcorn. And, yes, occasionally I watch reruns of the Lawrence Welk Show.

By the time I turned 12, my parents' marriage was falling apart. Alcoholism had taken a huge toll on their marriage and their ability to cope, though I was completely unaware of their problems with alcohol at the time. My teenage years were extremely stressful, and I spent most of the time in my room in an attempt to escape the hostility between my parents. I left for college at age 17 and was very

continued...

relieved to move away. They divorced when I was 19.

When I came home for Christmas a few months after their divorce, I realized they were both alcoholics. I still wonder how I could have been so naïve as to not have recognized it before. I didn't realize that always having a case of scotch on the desk in our basement was not normal. The fact that my parents started drinking as soon as they got home from work did not seem unusual. As the evenings progressed (and their drunkenness became pronounced), the tension between them escalated, erupting into rage on many occasions. I have since learned that when children grow up, they often assume that their home environment is "normal." It never occurred to me to pay attention to how much my parents were drinking or to assume alcohol was causing the problem.

From the time I realized they were both alcoholics, I became acutely aware of the sound of ice being dropped into a glass. Whenever I would visit, I would stay at my mother's house and sleep in the bedroom in which I grew up. While lying in bed in the morning, I started hearing the ice dropping into a glass when my mother got up around 7 am. That was my first realization that she started drinking as soon as she got out of bed each morning. To this day, I cringe when I hear the sound of ice being dropped into a glass. That sound became a sad reminder of my parents' alcoholism.

Interacting with my parents during my adult years had many ups and downs. My father faced his alcoholism head-on and admitted himself to many alcohol treatment programs. I attended AA meetings with him when I was in town, and I was very supportive of him. He would do well for several months after a treatment program, and would then slip back into drinking heavily.

My mother was stuck in denial regarding her alcoholism. When I was 20, I sent my father a letter stating that I was very concerned

continued...

about my mother's health, and I hoped she would accept help and go into an alcohol treatment program. Although my parents were divorced, they remained in contact and clearly loved each other until their deaths. He showed the letter to my mother, and our relationship was strained for the remainder of her life. Although our family knew she was battling alcoholism, she was not willing to admit it, and she was threatened by anyone who mentioned it. Therefore, she never received help. She held a full-time job after the divorce and was successful at keeping her alcoholism a secret from many friends.

I held many different jobs while in high school and college. During three summers while attending college, I worked at a mental health facility in Evansville. This was good work experience for the psychology degree I was earning, and each summer I had different responsibilities. During the summer when I was 20, my responsibilities involved working with five mentally disabled teenagers and teaching them janitorial skills. The objective of the job training was to prepare them for moving out of the mental health facility and into a group home, where they would be more independent and would have janitorial contracts at local businesses to support themselves. I was given an abandoned building to use to teach them basic skills, such as cleaning windows, scrubbing toilets, and emptying trash. That was an incredible summer; I learned about teaching, character, and teenagers.

The staff I worked with at the facility consisted of several fun-loving co-workers who enjoyed socializing and drinking. With my fake ID card in hand, we went to a local bar several nights each week. I built up a tolerance for several vodka gingers (vodka with ginger ale), and then drove to my mother's home each evening. Evansville has a large German community, and almost every weekend there was an outdoor beer fest (called a bierstube) that was sponsored by the local Catholic churches. These were large outdoor community gatherings in which

continued...

enormous amounts of beer were consumed. By the end of that summer, I realized I was heading down a very dangerous path. I was
following in my parents' path with far too much drinking. I made a
deliberate decision to change my course.

The next summer, after finishing my undergraduate degree, I moved
to Albuquerque. I deliberately chose to not socialize with a drinking
crowd, and I met new friends at a local church. I worked for a year
in an accounting position for a small company that was growing rapidly, and then I decided to attend graduate school to pursue an MBA.

After completing my MBA, I accepted a marketing position in the
hospital supply industry. The firm relocated me to Phoenix for a few
months and then to a suburb north of Chicago. I stayed with that company for three years and then joined a firm that was based in downtown
Chicago associated with the food industry, where I stayed for the next
four years. I ran their U.S. marketing effort, which was great fun. I trav-
eled extensively, managed a national public relations campaign,
designed marketing materials, and managed new product launches and
packaging. I was focused on my corporate marketing career.

When I was 28 years old, both my grandmothers died in Evansville. That was a very sad year. Yet later that year I met my future
husband. After dating for two years, he proposed, and we decided
to get married and move back to Albuquerque.

In the years following the wedding and the birth of our two daughters, my mother's health declined rapidly. The alcoholism was taking
its toll, evident in her sallow and sagging skin, her weight loss, and
her caustic demeanor when she was craving a drink. She was fired
from her job, and was later arrested for driving under the influence
after tapping the car in front of her in a bank drive-through lane. Not
surprisingly, this was a secret I did not learn until after she died. This
was my mother's first offense, and the judge required that she check

continued...

in each weekday to a rehab center to take an antabuse pill. (Antabuse is a medication that causes severe intestinal reactions if a person drinks alcohol. It was used as a deterrent to drinking). She continued to drink on weekends, and I suspect she felt that she was losing control. She had put up a façade for many years, but it was now crumbling. Her life ended a few months later at age 66 after a weekend drinking binge led to a coma, followed by liver and kidney failure. She had never been a binge drinker, and I think this was a deliberate attempt to end her suffering.

After my mother died, I was determined to minimize the painful memories involving her alcoholism while maximizing the memories related to her sense of humor and her warm personality. Shortly after her death I decided to start a journal in her honor. I started it one evening, purposely holed up in a hotel room so I would not have any distractions. I wrote for several hours, and cried freely. I wrote of many memories including her death, my anger at her alcoholism, and her denial that prevented anyone from helping her. I also wrote about childhood memories that were very happy and my appreciation for the many things she taught me.

There was another reason I wanted to honor my mother by writing in a journal. After her death, I feared that I needed to hold all the memories of her very close because I knew with time they would fade. I did not want to forget special memories.

A few months after my mother died, my father was diagnosed with throat cancer. I used the same journal I was using to write down memories of my mother to document my father's experience with radiation treatments over the next several months. His health declined as he lost weight, and a fall resulted in a broken hip followed by hip replacement surgery. I was very involved with my father's care during the last 16 months of his life, and sometimes it seemed like a blur. I was trying

continued…

to run my financial planning company in Albuquerque, devote time to my husband and two young daughters, and oversee my father's care in Indiana. I made many trips to Indiana and became very close to my father. He died a few months later at age 69 from pneumonia and chronic obstructive pulmonary disease (COPD). He could have been a poster child for the negative impact of many years of alcoholism and smoking.

Although many of my memories are dominated by alcoholism, some happy memories stand out in my mind. A few days before my father died, I thanked him for teaching me that I could do anything I set my mind to. In his frail, bedridden state, he squeezed my hand, smiled and shook his head. I was grateful that I had a chance to thank him.

Because my parents were divorced, there were two separate houses to clean out after their deaths. I found love letters that my father had written to my mother from Korea when they were dating and he was serving in the Korean War. They were incredibly beautiful. I wondered what happened to erode their loving relationship. They were obviously very happy when they were dating. They were a beautiful couple, and they had a very bright future. Did alcoholism creep up on them as a result of too much drinking at too many neighborhood parties? Or did strains in their relationship lead them to drink too much alcohol? Or was there a genetic component that triggered the alcoholism? I will never know, but I know alcohol in excess is deadly.

I look back on my parents' lives with admiration and gratitude. The work ethic displayed by both my parents rubbed off on me. Dad was comfortable taking risks in his business ventures, and I admired this. Mother was strong-willed, but much more risk-averse. She was not a stay-at-home mom. I followed in her footsteps, choosing to launch a company while my daughters were both very young. Mom had a wonderful sense of humor; Dad was an extreme introvert. Dad fought

continued...

his demons (alcoholism) head-on. Mom could not. She was stuck in denial as a closet alcoholic, and it led to her early death.

Reflecting on memories that are painful can have a silver lining. It can help us understand why we hold certain values. For example, I admire someone who faces their demons because I watched my father repeatedly try to conquer his alcohol addiction. It is a way of saying "We all have flaws, but it is important that we strive to improve." My father was eccentric, and very independent. I am already independent, and as I get older I plan to work on becoming more eccentric. Recognizing that 40 percent of our happiness is within our control provides us with lots of flexibility on how we become happier. As I add more spontaneity, more adventure, and more laughter to my life, becoming a little more eccentric fits in nicely.

Think through Anne Lamott's story about her father, Katherine Rosman's story about her mother's hobby, or my story about my upbringing. Do any of these stories remind you of memories from your childhood? Oftentimes, our memories are deeply suppressed. We are so busy with our day-to-day lives, we do not have time to ponder or daydream. Give yourself permission to let memories percolate to the surface of your consciousness. Then take time to reflect on your memories and think about how they have impacted who you are today.

Keep in mind that we control roughly 40 percent of our own happiness, so although memories *impact* who we are today, they do not have to define us. Now is the time to *take charge*, and make intentional changes to increase your happiness.

Invest in Yourself

Each of us has a story about our childhood, and the experiences that shaped us into the adults we are today. What is your story?

- Set aside 30 minutes to reflect upon memories from your past. Think about your parents, grandparents, and siblings. Think about the home you grew up in, the city or town, and other families in your neighborhood. Think about holidays, summer vacations, and trips with your family. Think about your elementary school, about teachers you liked and didn't like. Were you a good student, or did you get into trouble? Think about your childhood friends. Think about sad times, such as deaths of close family members. Memories that you have not thought about for many years may come to the surface. Step back from them and just observe, without judgment.

- Write your memories in a journal. This can be to honor someone who is dear to you, or it may be simply to write down the memories so you won't forget them.

- Discuss the memories with those close to you. If you have children or grandchildren, tell them stories about your childhood, and pass along stories told by your parents and grandparents.

- If you did not complete the exercise to determine your values or the questions pertaining to money messages you learned as a child, go back and do so now. In Chapter Twelve, these will help you decide what changes you would like to make.

PART TWO

■ ■ ■ ■ ■

Happiness Strategies

I n our society money and happiness are intertwined. Sometimes the relationship between money and happiness is healthy, and sometimes it is not. Creating a lifestyle in which your money is aligned with your values will help increase your happiness.

Chapters Four and Five are called "Compound Benefits" because the strategies bridge both concepts: They influence our happiness *and* our financial security. The happiness topics covered—such as finding a sense of purpose, focusing on gratitude, and nurturing your creativity—can pay huge dividends in your personal life. Likewise, the financial topics—such as spending money on experiences rather than things, simplifying your finances, and "controlling the controllables"—can positively impact your finances in significant ways. Chapter Six leaves the compound benefits behind and focuses exclusively on happiness strategies.

As you read through Part Two, feel free to highlight the strategies you may want to try, scribble in the margins, and jot your thoughts in your journal or notebook. The number of strategies you can use to increase your happiness and become more financially secure is unlimited. Lucky for you, the choice is yours!

CHAPTER FOUR

■ ■ ■ ■ ■

Compound Benefits:
Small Changes
with Big Rewards

*In daily life we must see that it is not happiness
that makes us grateful, but gratefulness that makes us happy.*
— BROTHER DAVID STEINDL RAST

Family, Friends, and Experiences

Relationships with Family and Friends

cademia is often accused of being theoretical and abstract—providing very few practical ideas that can be applied to our real lives. Positive psychology is an exception, as it focuses on what we can do to increase our happiness and overall well-being. Ed Diener, professor of psychology at the University of Illinois, has devoted his entire career to the study of positive psychology and happiness. He summarizes much of his research this way: "Family and friends are crucial. The wider and deeper the relationships with those around you, the better."

In the United Kingdom, more than 1,000 people were asked what happiness meant to them. The question was open-ended, allowing participants to respond in their own words. The most common answers fell into six different categories in the following order: relationships, contentment, security and money, health, transcendence, and fulfillment. Relationships were mentioned by 73 percent of the respondents as having a major impact on their happiness.

Social interaction is important throughout our lives, but it is especially important for senior citizens. Oftentimes, people become more secluded as they get older. They may be less mobile if they aren't able to drive or access public transportation. They have more aches and pains, and they become less active. A spouse may have died. While trying to protect their independence by staying in their home, they unintentionally become isolated. One study reported that isolation triggers multiple health problems, including increased stress hormones in the brain, increased blood pressure, reduced inflammatory control and immunity, and sleep disturbances.

In his book *Spontaneous Happiness*, Andrew Weil states that social isolation and loneliness are strongly correlated with depression. He shares a personal story, disclosing that after living in rural and remote areas near Tucson for over 50 years, he recently decided to move into the city of Tucson. For many years he enjoyed the isolation, justifying it by telling himself that he often spoke in front of large audiences, and appeared on radio and TV programs. In recent years, he came to realize that writing is a lonely occupation and being isolated is not healthy.

Recognizing that social isolation can negatively impact our health, it is important that we routinely spend time with friends and family. The relationships my clients have with their families is often apparent in their level of happiness and well-being. As an example, I have worked with a married couple who live in northern New Mexico on a cattle ranch. They are in their 60s, and they have two grown sons who are each married with children. I have thoroughly enjoyed watching this extended family interact over many years. My clients invited one of their sons and his wife to move from Seattle to the ranch in New Mexico a few years ago. They realize they cannot keep up the hard work needed to run a working ranch for many more years, so they are mentoring their son and daughter-in-law, preparing them to take over the family ranch.

I recently learned that my clients were asked to manage the ranch many years ago by the wife's parents. This intentional "passing of the baton" down through the generations is inspiring to watch. Although very few people have a ranch or farm to pass down to future generations, the same concept works well for passing down one's values and family stories.

The other son lives near Seattle, where he and his wife have demanding careers with a large corporation. My clients fly from New Mexico to Seattle to babysit the three grandchildren when their son and his wife travel, and they relish this opportunity. After working with the parents for several years, I now have the opportunity to work with their sons and daughters-in-law. Clearly, the parents make family a very high priority. Their reward is a rich and loving family.

Although we tend to think about family members or close friends, relationships with pets can also add joy to our lives. A purring cat on our lap or a loyal dog at our feet provides companionship. Hospitals and nursing homes often arrange for volunteers to bring pets to interact with patients and residents, but people of all ages can benefit from a pet's unconditional love. Pets also provide health benefits, ranging from lowering our blood pressure (when we pet an animal) to better survivorship rates for heart attack victims, to a calming effect for Alzheimer's patients.

Unexpected interactions with strangers can also increase our happiness. While writing this book, I stayed at a nearby hotel to write for a few days, several times each year. My financial planning company keeps me busy on a full-time basis, so these little escapes allowed me to focus on writing.

On one of my writing excursions, I went to a local pizza restaurant for dinner. One of the employees appeared to have a minor mental disability, and he clearly loved to talk while cleaning tables and refilling customers' drinks. He told me about a recent vacation he had taken and about how much he enjoys his job. He said he gets wonderful benefits from the restaurant during the winter holidays when the owner gives employees cookies for their families.

This small interaction with a complete stranger made me happy. I have learned to be alert for these opportunities and to not pass them up. If I had given this young man the impression that I did not want to talk with him, I would have missed the benefit of his joyful, positive attitude.

Spend Money on Experiences Rather Than Things

Experiences have a far greater impact on our happiness than spending money on "things" and possessions. This clearly bridges the concepts of financial security and happiness. Planning a day with family or friends and including new experiences—such as eating at a nice restaurant, visiting a museum, exploring a section of town you don't frequent, or going to a park or a concert—may enrich your life.

Planning a vacation can create a significant amount of happiness because you have several weeks of anticipation leading up to the vacation. Reading tour books and learning about the area you will visit is a part of the experience. Buy a souvenir from your destination, such as a T-shirt, because it will remind you of your trip each time you wear it. My husband and I occasionally buy Christmas ornaments while we are on a vacation. When we decorate our Christmas tree each year, we have keepsakes from many of our trips that bring back warm memories.

Experiences do not need to be major vacations. They can be as simple as devoting one Saturday a month for new experiences. This requires committing to not letting anything interfere. Get up on

Reflections: Relationships Take Work

I don't know anyone who had an idyllic childhood, and aside from my parents' alcoholism, my childhood seems rather typical. If we were all limited to bland experiences, life would be boring. I am aware of my strengths and weaknesses that were formed as a result of my childhood, and I am able to deal with them honestly. That appeals to my rational way of thinking.

Having two parents who were alcoholics provided me with some useful coping mechanisms. I consider myself to be far more resilient and self-sufficient than most people. This has served me well as an entrepreneur and small business owner. I like the fact that I can dig deep within myself to find an inner strength that never lets me down. These are positive traits.

No doubt, I also have some negative personality traits that cause me problems. One characteristic that likely resulted from my childhood experiences is that I will do almost anything to avoid a confrontation. When faced with dissension in the family, I retreat. This is a common trait among children of alcoholics. As a child, I was not allowed to voice an opinion or challenge my parents; I walked on eggshells. Children with alcoholic parents often are expected to act like adults at a very young age, never rocking the boat. When my parents were fighting or the tension was high, I would retreat to my room. As a result, I am an introvert who avoids confrontation. In addition, I am a workaholic. It is common for children of alcoholics to have some sort of addiction, such as to alcohol, drugs, food, or work.

How does this impact my family now? Avoiding confrontation does not work well with teenage daughters, and it is not great for a marriage, either. Being a workaholic is also not healthy for a family. After

continued...

getting married in my early 30s, I launched my financial planning firm when my daughters were very young. I dove in and worked full time, plus most weekends and many evenings. Although there was no doubt in my mind that my family was my top priority, my actions did not support this. When my family felt neglected, our relationships suffered.

For several years, I tried to reduce the amount of time I spent at my office so I could spend more time at home. It was a losing battle; my company was growing quickly and my clients and employees demanded far more than a 40-hour workweek. In early 2007, an out-of-state company contacted me with an offer to buy my business. At first, I said it was not for sale; I considered the offer simply as a compliment. Over the next few months, however, I started feeling as though the offer had appeared for a reason—it was a way to finally have time for my family.

I agreed to sell the business in September 2007 and began telling clients of my decision in October. The sale was finalized in December. I worked as a consultant for the buyer throughout 2008 and planned to take 2009 off to honor a non-compete clause in the sales contract, write this book, and have more time with my two teenage daughters. I anticipated lazy, unstructured days during the summer, with leisurely breakfasts and lunches with my daughters. Imagine the irony when I suddenly had more time, but my daughters had grown into very independent teenagers. They didn't want to spend time with me.

I now understand that teenagers need to develop their own identity, which typically requires refuting their parents. Many friends have told me they were very disrespectful during their teenage years. They recall what seemed to be endless battles with their mothers, which later evolved into healthy, loving relationships when they were in their mid-20s.

I felt blindsided by the impolite behavior of my teenage daughters because I had never been allowed to disagree with my parents, and

continued...

I had no confrontation skills. My inability to stand up for myself during disagreements with my daughters led me to retreat even more. The whole ordeal was emotionally painful, yet I learned from it. As a personal challenge, I now force myself to practice my confrontation skills in my business whenever the opportunity arises. Each time I confront someone, I find it slightly less painful. My tendency will always be to retreat and avoid a confrontation, but I am improving. During my daughters' teenage years I found comic relief in the following quote from Nora Ephron: "When your children are teenagers, it's important to have a dog so that someone in the house is happy to see you."

Most people do not have perfect relationships with family members. Relationships take work, and they ebb and flow over the years, much like our happiness. As you assess your relationship with friends and family, give yourself permission to focus on those people in your life who are supportive of you. They want what is best for you, and they truly care about you. These are the relationships worth cultivating.

Saturday morning and decide what you would like to do. It may be enjoying a lazy morning at home, drinking coffee and reading the newspaper. It may be going for a hike in the mountains. It may involve running some errands but not your typical errands (such as grocery shopping). Perhaps you go to a new garden store to look at plants you may want for your garden. Maybe you go to a new bookstore or to a movie you have wanted to see. You may have lunch or dinner at a new restaurant or drive to a nearby town.

If you have a spouse or partner, having a spontaneous Saturday can be a great time to enjoy each other's company while stepping away from the normally hectic pace of a workweek. If you do not have a spouse or partner, call a friend and ask if he or she would like to join you for a part of the day.

Building new experiences into your routine does not even require an entire Saturday. You may decide to take a new exercise class one night after work, or go to a lecture or a recital at a nearby university, or avoid turning on the TV for one day or one week. If it is a nice summer evening, set up lawn chairs in your front yard. You may meet some neighbors walking by your home. Focusing on experiences will take you out of your normal routine, which is analogous to inviting more happiness into your life.

Invest in Yourself

- Think about how much money you spend on *things* and how much you spend on *experiences*. What is the balance between the two? If your conclusion is that you spend too much on things and not enough on experiences, commit to changing the ratio. Think about what changes you can make quickly. Going to lunch or dinner with a family member or friend, spending money on special activities (such as concerts, plays, or a trip to the zoo), or planning a weekend trip will likely make you happier than buying a new piece of clothing.

- Think honestly about your relationships with family members and friends. Do you want to change or improve any of them? If so, list a few specific actions you will take. For example, you may decide to be in touch with your family more often; send them flowers for no reason, except to let them know that you love them; write a hand-written note to a friend who lives far away; invite a friend to lunch; or call a neighbor you haven't talked to recently. Do just one thing this week and see how it feels. Try a different action next week.

- Think about how you can meet new people. Join a hiking club or an exercise class, and you can make friends while becoming healthier. Clubs for activities you enjoy—or want to learn—can introduce you to new, interesting people who share your enjoyment of knitting, cooking, gardening, travel, environmental issues, etc. Attend a community lecture, or a nearby church or synagogue. Become a volunteer and experience the added benefit of giving back.

- Reach out to others. If you are shy or consider yourself an introvert, this will take deliberate effort. Push yourself to take time to meet a new neighbor or to talk to a stranger in the line at the grocery store. It could lead to a new friendship.

- Do something this week that forces you out of your normal routine. It could be as simple as taking a new route to work, trying a different kind of ethnic food, or starting a conversation with a co-worker you don't know well. These mini-excursions open you to new experiences, friendships, and opportunities. Decide that you will try something new and adventurous each week.

Filling the Fun Bucket

Here is a question that I received in a recent workshop. It is a common problem, with an easy (and fun) solution.

Q: The money messages I learned as a child still dominate the way I interact with money. I was taught to be very frugal. In my family, money was for saving, not enjoying. I have enough money that I do not need to pinch pennies, yet spending money makes me anxious. I live with a woman who has a healthier attitude about money. She is very responsible and has saved wisely throughout her career. How can I adopt a healthier attitude about money so we can enjoy more experiences together?

A: You may think that as a financial advisor, I am constantly forced to advise people to quit spending too much. However, among my

continued...

clients, your situation is very common. Many folks raised by parents who lived through the Great Depression were taught to save for a rainy day and are fearful of spending money for pleasure.

My advice is twofold: First, take time to prepare retirement projections to see if you are on track for retirement or—if you are already retired—if you have enough money to live comfortably for the rest of your life. Assuming your retirement is secure, the next step is to carve out an entertainment budget. It can be $500 or $5,000. The amount is irrelevant. This is what I call your "fun bucket." It can be used for a weekend getaway, a special trip, concert tickets, ballroom dance lessons, and more. Give yourself permission to spend it—but only for fun experiences. As you realize that spending money on fun will not impact your long-term financial security, you will start to feel less anxious each time you take out your wallet. And having a fun bucket is a reward you have earned for being so financially responsible!

A Sense of Purpose

When researchers strive to determine the factors that make an individual happy, a "sense of purpose" is high on the list. That may mean loving your career or giving time to volunteer work that is fulfilling. It may also include your beliefs about spirituality.

Do What You Love

If you already know what you love, congratulations! Maybe you are passionate about your job or your career. Or maybe you are retired and doing volunteer work that is stimulating and fulfilling. Maybe you are athletic and have your sights on an upcoming race or a goal that requires training and focus. Or you are a stay-at-home parent who enjoys spending time with your children. Maybe you are driven to accomplish a specific goal or to leave the world a better place.

Comedian and actor Gene Wilder has written three books. When asked during an interview for *Time* magazine, "Will you act again?" he said, "I'll always leave the door open, but it's not open very wide. I like writing so much now. I write after breakfast, then have a cup of tea, give my wife a little kiss, and write some more. Then I have a tuna salad sandwich and write some more. It's very relaxing."

Maria Shriver was asked to speak at a high school graduation ceremony in 2008. While preparing her talk, she wrote a small book called *Just Who Will You Be?* In it, she shares her personal story. Her identity had been tied to her 25-year career as a TV newswoman and journalist. Her stimulating career provided glamour and excitement. When her then-husband Arnold Schwarzenegger decided to run for governor of California, her employer asked her to resign because of a potential conflict of interest. Her career came to a screeching halt. It triggered an identity crisis, which led her on a journey to determine just who she wanted to be.

She comes from a family in which public service is expected. Her mother, Eunice Kennedy Shriver, founded the Special Olympics. Her father, Sargent Shriver, founded the Peace Corps and Head Start. Maria Shriver says in her book, "I was raised in a family that equated self-worth with personal achievement. Achievement brought not just acceptance, but power, recognition, and love. I felt that overachievement was expected of me. That's the way my parents and my family had lived their lives—and they had changed the world."

Many expectations were placed on Maria Shriver due to her legacy as a part of the Kennedy family. Rather than be limited by those expectations, however, she embarked on a personal journey to decide just who she wanted to be. She realized that the true answer involved her heart, her values, and her soul. She continues, "I've also learned it's OK to change. Sometimes it's not just OK, but mandatory. You can let go of some beliefs that maybe served you well along the way, but just don't work for you anymore. We're *supposed* to grow and evolve. We have to give ourselves permission and freedom to stay open to change."

Deciding who we want to be is not a simple task. It is an ongoing process. We may need to answer the question many times throughout our lives. With a divorce pending, Maria Shriver's life is evolving into a new season, which brings new opportunities.

As we get older, we become wiser. We can make new choices and change directions. Thankfully, our lives are not static. Sometimes change is necessary to jolt us out of a rut we have fallen into or to open new doors. If you are contemplating making some changes in your life, remember the adage "embrace change."

Reflections: Living Life on Purpose

After selling my first financial planning company in December 2007 and working for the buyer throughout 2008, I had a year to contemplate my future. An essential component in my decision to sell my firm was the assumption that the junior advisor I had mentored for several years would stay with the new buyer and provide excellent service to my former clients. I anticipated a smooth transition.

Instead, the junior advisor (my replacement) resigned just a few weeks after the new buyer took over. Clearly, this was not in the plan. The continuity for my clients, which I had taken for granted, disappeared. The buyer hired a new financial advisor within a few months.

During 2009, I honored a non-compete clause as stipulated in the sales contract. It prevented me from giving financial advice to clients,

continued...

but it allowed me to do speaking engagements, work on this book, and attend financial industry conferences. The time away from working with clients allowed me to step back and reassess my priorities. I missed helping my clients achieve their personal and financial goals. Several clients contacted me to ask if I would consider returning as their financial planner.

As a financial planner, I am, obviously, strongly in favor of making plans. However, plans must be flexible. This quote by John Lennon fit my situation perfectly: "Life is what happens when you're busy making other plans." I had allowed my company to monopolize my life for too many years, and I sold it to have more time for my family. Part of that plan was for the junior advisor I had mentored to continue providing great service to my clients. When he left, my plan went awry. I realized I had an opportunity to return to financial planning—an option that I had not considered.

Yet I recognized the dangers of returning to financial planning. The biggest danger was that I would slip back into my old habit of working too many hours each week. That would likely happen unless I set strict boundaries. I was determined to make my family a top priority and to have more fun in my life.

In 2010, I returned to the financial planning industry with a commitment to limit the number of clients to one-third of my previous firm. My business is not on a growth path because I decided to focus on having a balanced life. Today, I recognize how fortunate I am to have wonderful clients as well as a lifestyle that allows time for other priorities, such as family, friends, exercise, and writing.

Flow

Psychologist Mihaly Csikszentmihalyi has spent his career researching a concept called *flow*. He defines flow as "the psychological state that accompanies highly engaging activities." The state of flow is an optimal experience where "concentration is so intense that there is no attention left over to think about anything irrelevant or to worry about problems. Self-consciousness disappears, and the sense of time becomes distorted."

The state of flow can result from a creative or artistic activity, such as painting, dancing, writing, or playing a musical instrument. It is also common in athletics. However, it can also be attained with much more mundane activities, such as those required of a factory worker or someone focusing on a project at work. It requires "presence, a problem-solving attitude, and the conviction that you are going to do the best job you can at the task at hand." An optimal experience for flow may be challenging, but you know you have the necessary skills to meet the challenge. Because you are so engaged in the activity, you lose track of time.

Csikszentmihalyi is quick to admit that he did not invent or discover the concept of flow. However, he gave it a name and made it the focus of his career. After studying the concept for many years, he states:

> What I "discovered" was that happiness is not something that happens. It is not the result of good fortune or random chance. It is not something that money can buy or power command. It does not depend on outside events, but, rather, on how we interpret them. Happiness, in fact, is a condition that must be prepared for, cultivated, and defended privately by each person.

He believes that optimal experience (flow) is something we *make* happen and that achieving a state of flow can increase our happiness. The frequency in which we experience flow is based on our intentional actions. If you discover that you enjoy playing the violin, then you should play it often. If you discover that you are in a state of flow when you write poetry, then write poetry more often.

Do you recall a recent activity or task that put you into a state of flow? It could be a project at work that you found engaging, such as preparing a presentation. It could be playing an instrument or drawing a picture. It could also be writing in your journal, gardening, or cooking a special meal. Pay attention to what puts you into a state of flow. This may give you a clue as to what you love to do, how you want to spend your free time, or new interests you would like to pursue.

It may be difficult to recall activities in which you were in a state of flow. Our rushed lives are not conducive to flow. Csikszentmihalyi believes that negative emotions, such as frustration, dissatisfaction, boredom, and anxiety may prevent the state of flow. Attaining the state of flow requires being in the present moment and focusing on the task at hand. Like many topics in this book, attaining a state of flow more frequently is within our control and it gets easier with practice.

Spirituality

Our spiritual beliefs, faith, and actions are very personal, which makes deriving conclusions and patterns very challenging for researchers. However, psychologists are striving to determine the impact of religion and spirituality on our happiness.

Religion can be defined as beliefs and actions originating from traditional organized religions, such as Protestant, Roman Catholic, Jewish, and Muslim. Most religions focus on a belief in a god or higher being. The term *spirituality* is often used in a broader context than religion. Psychologist Ken Pargament characterizes spiritualism as "the search for the sacred." Christopher Peterson, a psychology professor at the University of Michigan, says spirituality "may include religious experience but also one's compassionate experience of nature or humanity." Under this broader definition, spirituality can take many forms, including traditional religion, prayer, meditation, or a relationship with nature.

Researchers Ed Diener and Robert Biswas-Diener have found

that organized religion provides an emotional benefit through the social support that frequently comes with regularly attending a church or synagogue: "Being a member of a spiritual community provides not only a sense of identity and belonging to a group, but the knowledge that like-minded individuals will help if you fall on hard times."

Religious and spiritual beliefs provide us with many benefits. Believing in a higher being makes us feel that we are not alone in this world. Spiritual beliefs also provide a sense of purpose, and religions often encourage helping others and being charitable. The rituals that are inherent in organized religion may also elicit strong memories. You may have childhood memories of attending services with your family, beautiful church weddings, or heartfelt memorial services.

Invest in Yourself

- If you are not certain you are doing what you love, do some soul searching and personal exploration. What activities make you happy? Write down what you love. Don't edit your thoughts; just write as each thought comes to mind. Some people are passionate about certain things. Others may say they are not passionate about anything. They go to work each day only because they need to earn money to keep food on their table. Ponder the concept of doing what you love.

- Find a comfortable chair and give yourself 30 minutes of uninterrupted silence. Think about your current job or volunteer work or the ways you spend your time. Write down what you like about your job and what you do not like. Perhaps you will realize that you love your job, but you need to set some boundaries (such as working only from 8 am to 5 pm, or not working on weekends).

Or perhaps you will discover that you do *not* love your job. Consider changes that may make you happier. Explore other career paths. This doesn't require that you quit your job now. You can simply research other opportunities and start networking with people in those fields.

Let's assume you love gardening, but your current job is in the medical field. You may decide to make gardening in the evenings or on weekends a priority. You could sign up for classes to become a master gardener or volunteer to take care of the garden for a local library or church. Ask at your local garden store whether they have positions open or whether they get calls asking for referrals for gardeners.

Continuing with the same example, let's assume you don't know if you like or dislike your current job in medicine. Including more gardening in your life on evenings or weekends might mean that you feel better about your current job because you are happier with your life overall—or it might help you recognize that your current job is not fulfilling and you want to change to a job in gardening or landscaping, or take a different career path.

- Perhaps you are retired, and you want to explore volunteering. Think about the types of things you like to do: If you like to work with children, volunteer with local schools or child-care facilities. If you like to work with seniors, volunteer at a nearby assisted living facility or nursing home. If you like to work with those in need, consider helping at a food bank, shelter, or local charity.

- Go to a service at a nearby church, synagogue, or temple with an open mind. Try to avoid being judgmental, and just enjoy the experience. Watch the people around you. Observe the rituals, the environment, the music, and the message. Meet people after the service. Once you are home, think about your reaction to the service and the people you met.

The Purpose of Money

Having a sense of purpose in our personal lives directly impacts our happiness. How does money fit into our sense of purpose, and what is the purpose of money? Your money should work for you, and it should be aligned with your personal goals. You should be able to do what you love and align your money to support what you love.

First, let's reiterate: Money does not *buy* happiness. Money can certainly *impact* our happiness, and if used wisely, it can lead to greater happiness. Many people give money too much power in their lives. It is important to remember that money is just a tool, and it needs to be carefully managed.

Giving money too much power can lead to being overly materialistic. Wanting more is a pervasive problem in our society. Often, this is not intentional. Placing too much emphasis on "things" can creep up on you. Feeling like you need a bigger house, a newer car, a designer wardrobe, or another flat screen TV may not initially seem to be a problem. A friend who has fought with money problems for many years calls this the "trappings" of money. Before you know it, the bills become overwhelming. Often, an occurrence like the recession in 2008-2009 creates a crisis. Suddenly, your big house has a lower market value than the mortgage balance. Perhaps you lost your job, and the lack of income affects your ability to pay your bills. The big house payment, the car loan, the credit card bill, and all your other financial responsibilities start feeling like anchors weighing you down.

Taking control of your money—and making it work for you—requires stopping the materialistic cycle. Recognize that happiness is not dependent on the size of your house or on having the newest car in the neighborhood. In fact, the bigger house and new car may actually reduce your happiness.

Money may increase your happiness if you pay off your debt and establish an emergency fund. Saving on a regular basis, paying for your children's education, having access to quality health care, being able to afford family vacations, knowing that you can retire, and achieving financial security can all increase your happiness. These topics are all discussed in Part Three.

Other factors that have a major impact on our happiness do not pertain to money at all. These include focusing on relationships with family and friends, leading a healthy lifestyle, nurturing your creativity, having a sense of purpose, finding the humor in life, and focusing on gratitude.

Focus on Gratitude

Gratitude in Our Personal Lives

We often float through life aimlessly, with each busy day flowing into the next. It is easy to forget why we are working so hard. Yet when we express gratitude, we stop taking things for granted. By taking a moment to focus on what you are grateful for, you engage your mind and the fog clears. You once again recognize the beautiful things in the world, the wonderful people in your life, and how much you have to be thankful for. Psychologist Tal Ben-Shahar discusses the idea of cultivating happiness by focusing on gratitude with a play on words: "When we appreciate the good, the good appreciates."

When we focus on the positive aspects of our lives, those positive things increase and grow, creating an upward spiral. Intentional behavior (such as expressing gratitude, or focusing on family and friends) can significantly increase our level of happiness.

Several years ago, during financial planning meetings with my clients, I passed out an article about gratitude and gave each client a blank book. I suggested they use it as a gratitude journal during the next few months. Most of my clients didn't follow through, but one couple did. They told me that every night before bed, they tell each other at least one thing they are grateful for. They live in

Florida, and they both travel extensively for their jobs. The husband told me, "We have been doing this for over five years, and it is rare that we miss a night." Sometimes making a change in our routine seems monumental and hard. Yet this couple made a very small change, realized they were benefiting from it, and made it a habit. And it has significantly improved their relationship.

The ways to focus on gratitude are endless. One research study looked at several different forms of expressing gratitude, trying to determine the strategies that had the greatest impact and lasting effect. One strategy, which the researchers called "Three Good Things," involved writing down three things that went well at the end of every day, along with a brief comment about why each event was good. The participants were asked to do this before going to bed each night for one week. They were told the three things could be minor ("My husband picked up my favorite ice cream on the way home from work today") or significant ("My sister just gave birth to a healthy baby boy").

The researchers found that "counting one's blessings increases happiness and decreases symptoms of depression for up to six months." Although the study only required participants to do this for a week, 60 percent of the participants reported that they were still counting their blessings six months later.

Psychologist Robert Emmons, who has focused his research career on gratitude, talks about the freedom that a gratitude practice provides: "By appreciating the gifts of the moment, gratitude frees us from past regrets and future anxieties. By cultivating gratefulness, we are freed from envy over what we don't have or who we are not. It doesn't make life perfect, but with gratitude comes the realization that right now, in this moment, we have enough, we are enough."

There are many ways to express gratitude. One of them is to simply thank those around us, in a genuine and heartfelt way. Keeping a gratitude journal is another strategy. Psychologists Robert

Emmons and Michael McCullough found that people who keep gratitude journals exercise more regularly, feel healthier, and are more optimistic. Research has shown that translating thoughts into words—either spoken or written—has advantages over just thinking the thoughts.

With practice, anyone can shift their outlook from a glass half-empty to a glass half-full, simply by focusing on the many blessings we have.

Invest in Yourself

- Keep a journal. A journal can help you focus on your feelings and is an important step in releasing your emotions and unleashing your creativity. If the idea of writing in a journal is intimidating, call it a notebook. Have a free-spirited attitude as you write in your journal.

- Write down a list of 10 things for which you are grateful. When you reach 10, if you are still going strong, keep going. You will be amazed at how this simple act can profoundly change your outlook. Keep your gratitude list or journal in an accessible place and review it occasionally. Add new items to the list when you think of them.

- Make a list of three things for which you are grateful each day for a month. The three things may seem minor, such as waking up to the sound of birds chirping, or they may seem very significant, such as being grateful for your children, spouse, friends, and pets. Starting your morning with thoughts of gratitude can have a positive impact on your entire day. Conversely, ending your day with thoughts of gratitude can help you drift off to sleep in a positive frame of mind. If you don't think you can do this every day, set aside some time each Saturday or Sunday morning to devote to your gratitude practice.

- Make gratitude part of your daily routine. For example, think about what you are grateful for while having your morning cup of coffee or tea, or while brushing your teeth or taking an evening walk.

- Say a gratitude prayer before a meal or bedtime or upon waking.

- Write a gratitude letter to someone who has had a positive impact on your life. This action will provide tremendous benefits to you and the person receiving the letter. If possible, hand-deliver the letter. If that isn't possible, send it to the person and follow up with a phone call a few days later.

- Tell someone what you appreciate about them. This may feel awkward, but it gets easier with practice. You will be making someone happy, and that will also make you happy.

Gratitude and Your Finances

Gratitude exercises often focus on families, friends, health, and other personal areas of our lives. I encourage you to also be grateful for the material items in your life, such as your home, a recent vacation, or the ability to send your children to college.

We have tremendous freedom in the United States because we live in a democracy, we are safe, and we have easy access to healthy food, jobs, leisure activities, and travel. Many people throughout the world do not have these luxuries; we should not take them for granted.

Often, we worry that we do not have enough money, and we want more. I encourage you to shift your perspective (the topic *reframing* is discussed in Chapter Five) to realize that we are incredibly wealthy, both monetarily and personally. Establishing a gratitude practice (that includes your finances) will help you focus on the positive.

Invest in Yourself

- As you try some of the recommended gratitude exercises, include topics that relate to your finances. If you have a good job, plenty of food for your family, good health care, and a place to call home, give thanks.

- If your thoughts continually return to wanting more money, watch a documentary or go to the library and check out a book on an impoverished or war-torn country. Many people live in constant fear for their safety and are unsure how they will provide food for their families. This may change your perspective and help you realize how incredibly fortunate you are.

Give Back

You can give back in different ways, including volunteering your time and talents or making charitable monetary gifts. Both involve being compassionate toward others. Often, people derive a strong sense of purpose from these acts. Maya Angelou captured the spirit of giving back when she wrote:

> *The charitable say in effect, "I seem to have more than I need, and you seem to have less than you need. I would like to share my excess with you." Fine, if my excess is tangible, money or goods, and fine if not, for I learned that to be charitable with gestures and words can bring enormous joy and repair injured feelings.*

Giving Your Time

Volunteering your time to help others can enrich your life. A client named Marjorie "adopted" a family from Afghanistan that needed assistance after relocating to the United States. As a speech and language pathologist with the local public school district, Marjorie was returning a student to his classroom in 2002, when she noticed a 6-year-old boy who did not speak English.

She learned that his family had recently relocated to Albuquerque. They had escaped from Afghanistan due to the violence triggered by the Taliban. Before the Taliban takeover, the family had enjoyed a middle-income lifestyle in Afghanistan. The father had been an Olympic soccer player. When their home was bombed in Kabul, the mother and oldest daughter suffered shrapnel wounds in their backs and one of the father's brothers was killed.

Although the boy was not assigned to Marjorie for speech therapy, she started helping him learn English. After a few months, she was invited to his home for tea. There, she met the mother and father and six children. During the next few years, the father and one of the daughters were diagnosed with cancer. Marjorie became more involved with the family as they spent many long hours at the hospital. Throughout their illnesses and their deaths, Marjorie's relationship with the mother and remaining five children became stronger.

The mother was diagnosed with post-traumatic stress disorder after arriving in Albuquerque, and she did not speak English. The kids attended public schools where only English and Spanish were spoken. Over 10 years have passed, and Marjorie says (half-jokingly) that she is their "9-1-1." She has helped the kids with homework over the years. She has counseled them as they have chosen colleges and careers, from medical school to criminal justice. She has been a steadfast friend to the mother. She has helped them with many of the things we take for granted—opening a bank account, paying the utility bill, and filing their taxes.

Marjorie does not talk openly about helping this family. She is very humble. After relaying the details of this story to me, she simply said, "I am very grateful to have them in my life."

I suspect that if most of us were told we should assume responsibility for a family for many years—and be supportive through very hard times—we would run in the other direction. We would assume the responsibility would be too large for us to handle. Marjorie had no idea that helping a 6-year-old boy would lead to volunteering her time and energy over many years. Yet the experience has enriched her life.

If you decide you want to do volunteer work, you can match it to your interests and to the time you have available. Many of my clients are retired, and they describe their volunteer work to me with enthusiasm. Some of the volunteer jobs include working as a docent at a local museum; working one day a week at a homeless shelter; helping a community after a natural disaster; participating in archeological digs; teaching a gardening class; helping out at a local school, hospital, church, or nursing home; helping mentor students in science; and helping elderly neighbors pay their bills.

Jackie regularly volunteers as an assistant in a classroom at an elementary school near her home. When I talk with her, I am impressed with her enthusiasm and her commitment to helping the children. She laughs about how often kids she has worked with at the school run up to her when she is buying groceries or running errands. Clearly, she is having a positive impact on many children's lives, but she is also benefitting personally from giving back.

According to Robert Putnam, professor of public policy at Harvard, communities with high rates of volunteer activity, club and church memberships, and social entertaining all enjoyed a higher well-being than communities that were low in these characteristics.

Some of my clients give back to their family members. One retired couple, Shirley and Ben, left their home in Arizona and moved to Utah to care for their 42-year-old daughter, who had been diagnosed with brain cancer. They moved into her home, took her to all of her doctor appointments, and lovingly cared for her until her death, a little over a year later.

Giving Your Money

One of my clients, Alma, told me that she had given away $40,000 the year before, and it gave her great joy to do so. She is not wealthy by most standards, but she clearly understands the benefits of being charitable. Scientists in the field of neuroscience have studied human empathy and have shown that reward centers in the brain light up when we give to charity. There is no doubt that my client is altruistic, but she may also feel a physical reaction to giving away money. In essence, doing good feels good.

When appropriate, I discuss charitable giving with my clients. Sometimes they ask me to help them research charities before they make a monetary gift. It is often personally rewarding to get involved in local charities, where they can actually see the benefits of their financial gift. There are local, national, and international charities that do excellent work. Many people want to know that a large part of their donation goes directly to the cause, rather than to administration or marketing expenses. Most charities provide their financial statements and required IRS forms on their websites.

There are often tax benefits for giving to charity, but that is rarely the primary reason someone makes a gift. The amount of the gift is not important; even small gifts of our money or time can help us maintain a healthy attitude toward money.

I think it is unfortunate when older people die with a large amount of money. Typically, they have an estate plan that describes who will receive the money after their death. That is important. However, in my view, they missed an opportunity to give money to family members or to charities while they were alive. Giving money to children, grandchildren, and friends while still alive has multiple benefits. First, it gives the recipient an opportunity to show their gratitude for the gift. Second, it makes the giver feel good, knowing they are helping others. Third, it can help the children or grandchildren learn how to manage money wisely. Fourth, it is often needed by the recipient. Once it is determined that a person has much more money than they will need to support their lifestyle for the remainder of their life, I encourage them to start giving it away.

Another impactful way to spend money is to arrange family reunions. Typically, the grandparents or parents pay for everyone's travel expenses, and these events often coincide with celebrating a major birthday or anniversary. Several of my clients have done this, and they arrange for family members to all meet in one location for several days. With family members scattered throughout the U.S., this may be the only way the family can all get together. By providing months of advance notice, most family members can arrange vacation time to attend. A travel agent can be selected to handle all of the details, and the expenses can be very high for a large family. However, spending money on family events is always worthwhile.

In addition to funding a family gathering, I encourage clients to pay for their friends' travel expenses. It is very common that one person may be wealthier than others among a group of friends, or that one person may not visit because they do not have the money. In this case, I would encourage the wealthier person to offer to pay for the travel expenses, and to host their friend.

Invest in Yourself

- Give away some money to someone who is less fortunate. The amount is irrelevant; the gesture is what is important. For the week after you make the gift, focus on your feelings. Did the act of being generous make you happier? If it did, give money away more often. Researching charities that you may support can be enjoyable, or you may decide to give money spontaneously to people you know who need the money. Spontaneous gifts may not include a tax receipt, and that's fine too.

- Consider giving money to a family member, simply as a nice gesture with no strings attached.
- Pay for travel expenses for family members or friends to get together.

Leave a Legacy

Closely related to "giving back" and volunteer work is the concept of leaving a legacy. This may involve generous gifts to family members, friends, or charities. Or it may mean leaving a lasting impression from memories that are left behind as a result of your actions.

There are still many stigmas surrounding how people communicate about money in our society, and oftentimes my clients don't know *how* to give money to their children or grandchildren. Some clients are concerned that their gifts will cause their children or grandchildren to be less motivated to be self-sufficient or financially secure on their own. Warren Buffett, the founder of Berkshire Hathaway, exemplified this attitude when he said: "The perfect amount of money to leave children is enough money so that they would feel they could do anything, but not so much that they could do nothing."

The quote is thought-provoking, and I understand it was stated from a perspective of children feeling entitled to large monetary gifts. We have all known persons who seemed to be negatively impacted by large inheritances. However, I believe that leaving money to children or grandchildren can be very effective, as long as they are taught how to manage it and to have a healthy perspective regarding the money.

A Legacy of Family Wealth

A proverb called "Shirtsleeves to shirtsleeves in three generations," describes a common tendency in many cultures. Estate attorney James E. Hughes Jr., in his book *Family Wealth: Keeping*

It in the Family, describes the proverb from the perspective of an Irish family:

> *The first generation starts out wearing work clogs while digging in a potato field, receives no formal education, and, through very hard work, creates a fortune while maintaining a frugal lifestyle. The second generation attends a university, wears fashionable clothes, has a mansion in town and an estate in the country, and eventually enters high society. The third generation's numerous members grow up in luxury, do little or no work, spend the money, and leave the fourth generation to find itself back in the potato field, doing manual labor.*

There are programs designed to stop the rags-to-riches-to-rags cycle. Although they are focused on preserving the wealth in a family for hundreds of years, they do not focus primarily on the money. For example, the program designed by Hughes has the following premises:

- The greatest assets of a family are its individual members.

- A family's wealth consists primarily of its human capital (all the individuals who make up the family) and its intellectual capital (everything each individual family member knows), and secondarily, its financial capital (money).

- To successfully preserve its wealth, a family must form a social compact, which Hughes defines as "an agreement among a group of people that expresses their values and goals and their voluntary decision to govern themselves according to those values and goals." Each successive generation must reaffirm and readopt the social compact and participate in the governing system.

- The family must emphasize the importance of the dignity of work to an individual's sense of self-worth and assist each family member with finding work that most enhances their pursuit of happiness. All work is of equal value to the growth of the family's human capital, regardless of its financial reward.

Notice the emphasis on values, human capital, and multiple generations working together. Preserving wealth within a family takes effort and organization. The first step is to acknowledge that it is of paramount importance.

As a financial planner, I have the privilege of talking with clients about how to leave a legacy. Conversations about how to pass values and wealth to younger generations are extremely rewarding. The process can include writing a family mission statement, documenting family stories (either in writing or in a video), and organizing a family retreat.

Clients often do not know how to pass down their legacy, so having a financial advisor (or other trusted advisor) is helpful. The agenda for a family retreat may include time to discuss values, family stories, charities, and investments. Sometimes, the agenda will include showing old family movies or looking through photos of the family's history. When older family members talk about living through the Great Depression or surviving hard times, the younger members learn not only about family history, but about family values.

This is a time of tremendous sharing, which usually improves the family dynamics and communication. Most families find it difficult to discuss money, and talking about their legacy can be even more difficult. These family reunions build understanding, communication, and compassion among family members.

A Legacy of Journals

There are many ways to pass down your legacy. One of my clients has journals that were written by her mother over many years. Her mother left them for her and her sister. There are several different journals, which the two sisters trade back and forth, referring to them often. Because of her mother's legacy to her, she keeps her own journal, to pass down to her children someday.

A Legacy Letter

Another excellent way to pass down your legacy is to write a letter to your children and grandchildren. The letter can convey how important they are to you, your values, what you want to tell them about your life, and your wishes for them. If you choose, you can also include your feelings about money, especially if they will be inheriting money.

Barry Baines, M.D., expanded the idea of a legacy letter into what he terms an ethical will. This is very different from the standard legal document called a will. In his book, *Ethical Will*, Baines describes it as a "voice of the heart."

A Family Loan Fund

Some families set up a family loan fund. Oftentimes, these are interest-free loans so family members can attend college, buy a first home, or start a business. Berry Gordy Jr. founded Motown Records with money from a family loan fund. Because they are no-interest loans, they must meet requirements set by the IRS. Occasionally, family members serve as trustees, and persons wanting loans must go before the trustees. Sometimes, they are funded by contributions from all family members, who pool their money for the benefit of the entire family.

A Legacy of Your Life

A few years ago, I attended the memorial service of one of my favorite clients, Jeff. One of the greatest gifts I receive from my financial planning clients is the privilege of getting to know them well and learning from their stories, values, and wisdom. Although there is tremendous sadness when one of my clients dies, I often gain inspiration from their life.

Jeff's doctor recommended that he have triple bypass heart surgery. He was told that his heart was strong enough to handle the surgery, although the doctors had serious concerns about whether his lungs would tolerate it. Jeff consulted with numerous doctors and decided to proceed with the surgery.

Unfortunately, his lungs did not cooperate; after the surgery, the doctors could not transition him off the ventilator. Weeks passed and his health continued to decline. Nina—his wife, ally and spokesperson—was always at his side. She knew Jeff would only want to live if he had a high quality of life. Her unconditional love and devotion was an inspiration in itself.

Exactly two months after the surgery, Nina arrived at the rehabilitation center one morning, and Jeff said to her, "It's time." She knew immediately what he meant. He had made the decision that the ventilator should be turned off. The doctors and nurses tried to persuade him to change his mind, suggesting he wait until his children could visit him again. His children—who all lived in other states—had visited him recently. Jeff had made up his mind and did not waver. The doctors had Jeff put his thumbprint on the authorization form to turn off the ventilator so Nina did not have to make this painful choice. He was given some medication to relax him, and the ventilator was turned off. Within a short while he died, with only Nina at his bedside.

Jeff had been a teacher his entire career. By all accounts, he had been an incredible teacher, leaving a legacy of students who had loved and admired him. During the weeks leading up to the surgery, he wrote his own memorial service, which took place at a Unitarian church. The woman who led the service spoke warm words about Jeff. His best friend spoke about some of the values that were important to Jeff and recited Jeff's favorite readings. The songs during the service had been selected by Jeff, and several of his children spoke during the service.

Near the end of the service, attendees were given an opportunity to speak. One of his prior students read a letter she received from Jeff after she graduated. The letter conveyed Jeff's devotion to teaching, as well as his encouraging words on the values she should take forward throughout her life.

The memorial service was an incredible tribute to Jeff's life. I am grateful that I knew Jeff, and I continue my professional relationship and friendship with his wife. Jeff left a powerful legacy that touched his students, his friends, and his family.

Invest in Yourself

- Write your own memorial service. This idea may seem a bit daunting, but it also may intrigue you. Use ideas you have seen in other memorial services.

- Start a journal for your children or grandchildren. Simply buy a blank journal and write your first entry. Write each week, each month, or whenever an event occurs that you want to document. You could also write on special occasions, such as birthdays and holidays.

- Write a legacy letter to your children or grandchildren.

- Set up a family loan fund.

- Start the process of preserving your wealth for future generations. Refer to the book *Family Wealth: Keeping It in the Family* by James E. Hughes Jr. Another service that provides similar guidance is the Heritage Institute, at www.theheritageinstitute.com. The Heritage Institute trains "Certified Wealth Consultants" to work with families throughout the process.

Control the Controllables

The concept of "Control the Controllables" covers aspects in our personal and financial lives. From a personal standpoint, it often involves contentment, satisfaction, and acceptance.

Contentment

Researchers conducting the British poll on happiness were not surprised that 73 percent of the more than 1,000 people surveyed answered that relationships with friends and family had the greatest impact on their happiness. However, the next highest response was contentment, which 56 percent of the respondents equated with happiness. This was much higher than the researchers had expected.

Responses from the happiness opinion poll regarding contentment included: "Happiness is about personal tranquility." "Being at peace with the way things are going." "Happiness is when you are OK inside about where you are and who you are."

What does it mean to have peace of mind? The researchers concluded that contentment is a mixture of several things, but one commonality is that the person is not fighting with himself or herself. This implies that we are content when the different parts within us make friends with each other. This is an intriguing idea, because it suggests that your perception (and acceptance) of yourself can lead to greater happiness.

In addition to conducting an opinion poll on happiness, the BBC presented a six-part TV series about happiness. One segment looked at how age impacts happiness. It reported that men and women tend to be happier after they reach age 50, following the lowest point of satisfaction during their 40s. One explanation is that we grow to accept the world as it is and we have a healthier perspective on our lives. Another explanation may be that the physiological aging process reinforces being more accepting. Neuroscientists believe that the prefrontal cortex portion of our brain calms down the negative emotions coming from the amygdala, and that this dynamic is more pronounced as we age. This same dynamic may impact our memories as we age, encouraging us to have more positive memories.

We are most likely to feel content and satisfied when we know we are honoring our priorities and our values. Contentment, satisfaction, and acceptance are all closely related. Can we accept the fact that we may never be as thin, as beautiful, as charming, or as popular as we would like? Wouldn't accepting ourselves as we are be a healthier approach? If we were more accepting of ourselves, we would likely be more content, more satisfied, and happier.

If you don't like something in your life, consider whether it is within your control to change it. If it is within your control—such as a job that is not fulfilling—then change it. If it is not—such as a body shape that will never meet your definition of perfect—then accept it.

Accepting our bodies is difficult for some because the media has chosen a very thin young woman as a typical role model for females. The role model for men is a muscular, tall male with lots of hair. Recognizing that very few women and men look like those images—and that life would be very boring if we did—is a much healthier attitude.

The Serenity Prayer exemplifies the importance of not trying to control everything in our lives and to be more accepting. After my father died, I found a small card in his wallet. One side of the card contained information from Alcoholics Anonymous, and the other side contained the Serenity Prayer. Although it is very short, it is extremely powerful:

> *God grant me the serenity to accept*
> *the things I cannot change,*
> *Courage to change the things I can,*
> *and the wisdom to know the difference.*

The concept of acceptance is not simple. It requires that we acknowledge—and accept—that there are many things we cannot control. Attaining personal tranquility (which can result from contentment, satisfaction, and acceptance) has a positive impact on happiness.

Take Control of Your Finances

The Serenity Prayer also applies to our finances, because many factors that impact our financial security are outside our control. As individuals, we could not control or prevent the September 11 terrorist attacks in 2001. We could not control the turmoil in the stock market between 2000 and 2002, or the recession in 2008 and early 2009.

Fortunately, we *can* control many factors that affect our finances, and they have a much greater impact on our long-term financial security than those we cannot control. Financial advisor Bert Whitehead developed this concept, and he termed the items within our control *endogenous* and the items outside of our control *exogenous.*

Review the endogenous and exogenous items listed on the next page, and recognize that the items on the left (which you control) impact your finances much more than the items on the right.

Whitehead states in his book *Why Smart People Do Stupid Things with Money*:

> *You have a great deal of control over the volatility that your portfolio will experience when the markets go up and down. You can even make money in years when everybody else is losing their shirts. This is not by timing the market, but by making sure that your assets are properly allocated in relation to your stage in life and the amount of risk that is appropriate in your particular situation.*

We cannot control stock market fluctuations, but we can control the asset allocation and diversification within our investment accounts. We can also control our attitude about money. One of my clients contacted me in 2010 and suggested I watch a YouTube video of someone claiming that our economy was about to collapse. It was a very "doom-and-gloom," alarmist message. I watched a few minutes of it and then told my client that I have no control over

Control the Controllables

Items We CAN Control (Endogenous)	Items We CANNOT Control (Exogenous)
Our Savings Rate	Stock Market Fluctuations
Our Spending	Greed and Corruption
Our Investments (Asset Allocation, Diversification)	Tax Rates
	Interest Rates
Whether We Live a Healthy Lifestyle	Inflation Rates
	Unemployment Rates
Whether We Live Within Our Means	The Federal Deficit
Having an Emergency Fund	Wars
Our Education	Natural Disasters
Our Career	Global Suffering
Marriage, Divorce, Children	Political Infighting
Whether We Support Charities or Do Volunteer Work	Recessions
	Economic Downturns
Managing our Money (and Not Neglecting It)	The Behavior of Others (in Terms of Flaunting or Worshipping Money)
Whether We are a Role Model to Our Children	

the U.S. economy. I can only be responsible with my own finances and encourage my clients to be responsible with theirs so we are not at the mercy of the economy or the stock market. I told him I do not want to live my life in a state of fear, and I do not want to be influenced by people who choose to have a negative view of life.

Invest in Yourself

- Think about something in your life that you are not satisfied with. Write it in your journal. Next, think about whether changing it is within your control. If it is, write down some ways you may decide to change it. For example, if you are not satisfied with your job, write down some other jobs that may be more satisfying. Lay out a plan for exploring other jobs and for possibly making a job change when the time is right.

- Make a list of the things you can control regarding your finances. Chapters Seven through Eleven will provide more details on financial topics, but start to think of the areas in which you would like to focus.

CHAPTER
FIVE

■ ■ ■ ■ ■

Compound Benefits:
Lifestyle Shifts

Go confidently in the direction of your dreams!
Live the life you've imagined.
As you simplify your life,
the laws of the universe will be simpler.
—HENRY DAVID THOREAU

A Healthy Lifestyle

eading a healthy lifestyle is a key component of happiness. Being healthy includes many different variables, such as eating healthy food, getting regular exercise, maintaining a healthy weight, getting enough sleep, controlling your stress levels, being kind to yourself, and adding more laughter to your life.

It is commonly said that all of the money in the world will not help a person if they don't have their health. Most of us have seen this firsthand. Some of my financial planning clients are in their 70s and 80s. When their health starts to fail, they become frightened, regardless of the amount of money they have.

We sometimes neglect our health because of our busy schedules. By the time we have put in a long day at the office and devoted time to our families, we are exhausted. Yet there is clear evidence that our health is very closely related to our happiness. Our health deserves our attention.

Healthy Eating

Many excellent books are available on nutrition and healthy eating. Whether you want to lose weight or simply improve your eating habits, below are some key points.

- Eat a variety of healthy foods. Diets that severely restrict your food choices typically do not work.
- Eat plenty of fresh fruits and vegetables.
- Drink lots of water.
- Avoid processed foods, such as those high in sugar, white flour, additives, and salt.
- Prepare fresh food at home, rather than eating out frequently.
- Eat small portions if you are eating at a restaurant. Consider taking home half the meal for tomorrow's lunch.

If you decide to eat healthier food, be patient. Give your body four weeks to feel the difference when you have implemented a healthy change. Be content with small changes initially. For example, if you start eating more fruits and vegetables, you may realize you feel better. Next, you may replace soda with water, followed by exchanging your daily dessert for a weekly dessert. Small changes are easier to maintain, resulting in long-term benefits.

Invest in Yourself

- Go to a farmers' market in your area. In addition to buying fruits and vegetables, buy some flowers or some homemade jams or jellies. Select the most appealing fresh produce, then try some new recipes. Make a salad or stir-fry the vegetables. Eat the fruit by itself, or use it over cereal, oatmeal, yogurt, or ice cream.

- Pay attention to when you eat. Are you physically hungry, or are you eating due to boredom, habit, or stress? If you find that you are not physically hungry, take a walk instead. Even a 10-minute walk can make you feel better—physically and mentally.

Exercise

Consistent exercise is one of the easiest ways to improve your health *and* increase your happiness. Research studies show that regular exercise can lower blood pressure, improve cholesterol levels, and help prevent heart disease and Type 2 diabetes. Although researchers disagree on how much exercise is needed to reap significant benefits, 30 minutes, five days a week is often advised. Unfortunately, this often leads to an "all or nothing" attitude. If you don't feel that you can get 30 minutes of exercise, you don't get any. Experts warn against falling into this trap. A 2010 study found that just 10 minutes of exercise produced measurable reductions in anxiety and depression.

Exercise does not have to be strenuous to be healthy. Although a slow stroll through the park may not be enough, a brisk walk is one of the healthiest forms of exercise. Getting oxygen and fresh air into our bodies is good for our lungs. Getting our bodies moving helps our heart, muscles, and joints.

An eight-year study by the National Cancer Institute, which included 250,000 Americans, concluded that participants who watched television for seven hours or more each day had a much higher risk of premature death than participants who watched less. Even exercising seven hours per week didn't cancel the devastating effect of sitting in front of a television screen for seven hours a day. Television viewing is often used as a measure of a sedentary activity. Sitting at a desk or in front a computer for long hours may have similar effects.

Another study by the Baker IDI Heart and Diabetes Institute in Melbourne, Australia, demonstrated that being sedentary for seven hours per day can negatively impact blood sugar and insulin levels. These studies indicate that we need to build frequent activity into our daily routines, along with regular exercise.

Exercise provides far more than just physical benefits; it also improves mental health and well-being, reduces depression and anxiety, and enhances cognitive functioning. Exercise has been called a natural antidepressant. The serotonin and endorphins that are released within our bodies during exercise are natural mood enhancers.

The extensive benefits of exercise are clear: Exercise improves our physical health (heart, lungs, joints, cholesterol levels) and provides benefits to our mental health. It also has financial benefits, because healthy people often require far less medical care as they age.

In Chapter Twelve, you will be encouraged to select two happiness strategies and two financial security strategies. These will be the small changes you choose to make. If you do not have a consistent exercise routine, I encourage you to select increasing your exercise as one of your two happiness strategies. It provides many (compound) benefits to your happiness and your health. You may also want to add eating healthier foods to your exercise goal. As we get older, maintaining good health must be a high priority.

Making changes is not easy. What may seem like a small change may feel insurmountable as you slip back into your old, comfortable habits. Chapter Twelve provides many tips for making changes. For now, simply ponder the changes you would like to make.

Invest in Yourself

- Exercise doesn't have to be strenuous to be beneficial. Experts advise us to choose forms of exercise that we like so we will exercise more often. From walking to jogging, biking to swimming, and yoga to dancing, the options are endless. Most communities have a variety of exercise classes available to the public, often at no charge. If you are not aware of any classes in your community, call your local chamber of commerce or city government, or search on the website for your city.

- Stretching is good for our bodies, but is often forgotten. You can simply sit on the floor and do some stretching and flexibility exercises while watching the nightly news, or first thing in the morning to start the day off in a healthy way. Yoga is also helpful for stretching and flexibility.

- Create a social group that promotes a healthy lifestyle. Encourage a friend to meet you for a walk or a hike in the mountains. Or, call a friend and arrange to meet at a health club, for a tennis match, or for a bike ride.

- Setting a goal will help motivate you to keep your exercise on track. For example, maybe you want to walk or run a 5K race (approximately three miles), 10K race (a little over six miles), or a half marathon (approximately 13 miles). Maybe you decide to take a bike or walking tour as part of a vacation. Often, group training programs are offered to help you train for biking, walking, or running events. In addition to the health benefits, these are a great way to meet new friends and expand your horizons.

- If you would like to improve your health by getting more exercise, write down an exercise goal for the next week. For example: I will walk on Monday, Wednesday, and Friday, from 5 to 6 pm before I make dinner. When you get home from work, immediately change into your exercise clothes and head out the door. Don't sit down and turn on the television. If you decide to exercise in the morning, lay out everything you need the night before.

- Making a healthy change to your exercise or eating routine requires much more than simply knowing what you need to do. Often, you need to implement some changes that will hold yourself accountable. If you are trying to lose weight, take a few minutes each evening to write down what you have eaten that day. Knowing that you must write it down helps keep you accountable so that you choose an apple at 3 pm rather than a candy bar. There are plenty of online websites and apps to help you track your food and exercise, too. The camaraderie of having a support group can be very motivating as you make changes. Another strategy for weight loss is to plan your food for the next day. Knowing what you will have for breakfast, lunch, and dinner makes you more likely to make wise choices.

- Likewise, if you set a goal of exercising three times next week, write down the goal, and then log your exercise at the end of each day. The act of writing it down is a much bigger step than just planning to do it. By writing your goals down, you are making it a much higher priority and are more likely to be successful at achieving them.

Laugh More

What can strengthen your immune system, reduce your stress, and shift your perspective so you see situations in a more positive way? Laughing can do all of this and more! Laughter reduces the levels of cortisol, epinephrine, and dopamine, commonly known as stress hormones. Laughter triggers the release of endorphins, the "feel-good" hormones that increase a sense of well-being.

Most of us are far too serious. We work too hard and play too little. Making intentional changes that lead to more laughter can have a significant impact on your happiness. Spend more time with friends who are silly and playful, and give yourself permission to laugh. Rent funny movies. Start looking for funny situations or events in your everyday life. Learn to laugh at yourself.

I am fortunate to be a part of a special group of women. Our paths crossed in the early 1980s when we all worked in management positions for a hospital supply firm located north of Chicago. We started getting together for dinner each month and named ourselves the "Broad's Bunch." Now, more than 30 years later, we are still close friends. We get together at least once a year somewhere in the United States. The group is very diverse, with ages ranging from mid-50s to over 80. Whenever we get together, there is lots of laughter. Often, my jaws hurt for several days from laughing so much. Some of the members are natural comedians, while others (like me) just go along for the ride. In between get-togethers, the humorous emails fly fast and furiously between us throughout the year.

Below is an email excerpt from one of the women in the Broad's Bunch. She is a Southern belle, a business owner, and a very funny woman. It is common for residents in Highpoint, North Carolina, to rent out a portion of their home for a week when the annual furniture market occurs. She has done this for many years, because she has a full apartment in the basement that she moves into. The friend she refers to (Sheila) was staying with her temporarily when she wrote this email. Ted is her son, who is serving in the military.

Dear Donna,

Sheila and I moved to the basement yesterday. My market people will be coming today so we spent the weekend cleaning the house. As it turned out, Ted was home for the weekend and he was a huge help also. I've been trapping raccoons for the last two weeks. They started trashing my garage about three weeks ago looking for food. They have been scavenging cat food but are now looking for more. So, I bought an animal trap, placed it in front of the cat door and in the last two weeks have caught ten raccoons. I bring them to work with me and let them loose in the edge of the woods. I've been spraying their butts with red paint so I can tell if I get any repeat offenders. So far, the red butts have not returned or at least I haven't trapped them. Who knew I'd be a raccoon trapper at age 56?

Now, when I read this I can just picture her looking in her garage each morning, and going through all of the trouble of moving the trap into her car so she can release the raccoons in the woods. I also picture her getting her can of red spray paint ready so when she opens the cage she can spray them quickly as they scamper off. No doubt, they are not happy raccoons! I suspect the animal rights activists may complain that this is cruel, but I would counter that trapping them and letting them loose is humane. (Note: I recommend that you not try this at home. Raccoons have sharp teeth and nails, and they may even have rabies. Simply enjoy the humor).

Invest in Yourself

- What has happened to you recently that makes you laugh? Start a list of funny experiences. This will help you remember them; then when you need a good laugh, refer to your list.

- Write a stand-up comedy routine using some of your funny experiences. Recognizing that no one needs to see you practicing your stand-up routine allows you to be very silly.

- Think about what would be fun to you. Most of us are lacking in fun and playtime. Go to a funny movie, go to the beach, get together with friends to laugh, or read a funny book. Plan something special during the next week that would add some fun to your life.

Enjoy Nature

Include outdoor activities in your exercise program. Health clubs or home exercise equipment are great when the weather is bad, but when you get outside, there are benefits beyond the exercise. Getting into nature lets you enjoy the sunshine, clouds, rain, wildlife, flowers, and trees. Enjoying nature can reduce your stress levels and improve your overall well-being.

I routinely walk and run in an undeveloped area of Albuquerque. It has numerous trails, a variety of wildlife, and plenty of natural vegetation. It is truly wonderful, and I am grateful that it is available. Dogs are allowed as long as they are on a leash. Many other people walk and run there, and I have met some great people over the years.

One man, Joseph, was a "regular." He was a tall, lanky man, who was always eager to say hello. He had a strong Christian faith that was apparent from his comments as we would pass. I would say something like, "Isn't it a glorious day?" and he would respond, "Yes, I thank God that he created this day and this world so we can enjoy nature." One day he told me that he prayed as he walked. I saw him several times each week for several years, and he was always incredibly cheerful. I looked forward to seeing him because he had such a bright spirit about him.

One day we were ending our walk at the same time, and we started talking. I learned that he had been battling brain cancer for several years. He had already had multiple surgeries, and walking was his way of trying to sustain his physical and mental health as he battled the cancer. He typically walked twice each day. He told me he had a website that told his story, and that he gave motivational speeches about staying positive through his battle with cancer. I did not ask for the website address and I never knew his last name.

I saw him less frequently over the following months, and the next time I saw him, I noticed he was wearing a baseball cap and his hair had fallen out. Then I stopped seeing him. I continued looking for him, hoping to see him and hear his cheerful greeting. One day I saw a woman walking who also knew Joseph. I stopped and asked her if she had seen him. She said he had lost his battle with cancer.

I tried to determine why Joseph had left such an impact on me. How do we know when someone is going to leave a lasting impact? How can we know if we will leave a lasting impact on someone else? I decided it was his positive attitude and his zeal for life that impressed me. I did not know him personally, although I regret that I was not able to say goodbye. As I get older, I am more aware of people who are "out of the norm." Maybe they don't care about fitting in; maybe their self-confidence permits them to be authentic. For whatever reason, being eccentric is more appealing to me, along with tolerance of other people who may not be clones of the status quo.

Be Kind to Yourself

Being kind to yourself is sometimes called self-care or self-compassion. Many of us are constantly working on behalf of others. We may work all day and then go home to prepare dinner, help our children with homework, clean the house, or do the laundry. Our weekends are often full of errands and chores. Some people also care for senior relatives or grandchildren. Our responsibilities and hectic lifestyles often make us feel depleted. Being kind to yourself may require experimenting to discover what nourishes you physically and emotionally.

You may think that making time for yourself is selfish and that you should always put the needs of others ahead of your own. But you *must* take care of yourself to do a good job taking care of others. Kate Larsen, author of *Progress Not Perfection,* states: "When putting off self-care becomes a habit, you drain or diminish the very energy you need to serve others. Giving yourself permission to take care of yourself is not an indulgence; it's a necessity."

Self-care consists of activities that nurture and sustain us. They may involve pleasure or relaxation, such as a hot bath, a massage, a nap, or lying down to read a book on a weekend. Self-care may also mean getting out into nature or buying flowers for yourself. It may mean spending several hours by yourself on a weekend or taking a long walk with a friend. Eating nutritious food, getting adequate exercise, and getting enough sleep are all forms of self-care.

Below is a list of potential self-care activities.

Self-Care Activities

- Buy yourself a journal (and write in it!)
- Take a hot bath with bubbles or scented oils
- Take a walk in nature
- Go to a movie and buy popcorn
- Go out to breakfast
- Put on some lively music and dance
- Catch fireflies on a summer evening and then let them go
- Go for a hike and enjoy the wild flowers
- Bake your favorite dessert
- Make a food from your childhood (a warm and fuzzy memory)
- Take a nap in the afternoon
- Buy yourself flowers
- Watch the sunset
- Dance in the rain
- Stomp in puddles
- Rent a funny movie and have a good laugh
- Rent a sad movie and have a good cry
- Paint one wall in your house a color that you love (it cannot be white)
- Buy an audio tape on meditation and listen to it while lying on your bed
- Call an old friend you haven't talked with in years
- Go to a park, a museum, or the zoo
- Treat yourself to a banana split or other decadent dessert
- Treat yourself to a lazy Sunday

continued...

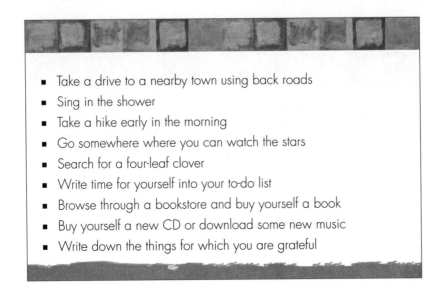

- Take a drive to a nearby town using back roads
- Sing in the shower
- Take a hike early in the morning
- Go somewhere where you can watch the stars
- Search for a four-leaf clover
- Write time for yourself into your to-do list
- Browse through a bookstore and buy yourself a book
- Buy yourself a new CD or download some new music
- Write down the things for which you are grateful

Invest in Yourself

- Take 15 minutes to list in your journal acts of kindness that you could do for yourself. They can be as practical or as eccentric and far-flung as you choose. Plan to give yourself at least one treat per week to add more joy to your life. You deserve it.

- Consider how much money you spend on yourself. This may include buying flowers for yourself, getting a massage, hiring a personal trainer, or hiring a physical therapist for treatment for a sore back. Consider taking a vacation that includes physical exercise, such as a walking or biking vacation or a visit to a health spa that includes exercise or meditation. Spending money that benefits your health is a wise investment.

Sleep

Many Americans are sleep deprived. Our bodies require an adequate amount of sleep to function well. Sleep is critical for a healthy metabolism and plays a large role in keeping our immune system working properly. Our body repairs itself during sleep. Yet recent studies have shown that a rigid expectation of sleeping eight hours straight during the night may not be realistic. Countries such as China, Spain, and Mexico often include a mid-day nap. Researchers have determined that even a very short nap (as short as 24 minutes) can increase cognitive performance.

Researchers have also found that many people naturally tend toward a split schedule for nighttime sleeping. They concluded that people often sleep a few hours, are awake for a few hours, and then fall back to sleep. Fighting to sleep eight hours in a stretch causes many people to take sleeping pills unnecessarily. Once the research subjects stopped fighting the fact they were awake, they adjusted to looking forward to their time awake as a period of reflection, deep thinking, or looking ahead. Most of us do not work in industries that encourage a mid-day nap. However, when you get the opportunity, indulge in a nap.

Invest in Yourself

- If you know you are not getting enough sleep, try going to bed one hour earlier each night. If this seems impossible, try sleeping an extra 30 minutes on weekend days. If possible, take a short nap on weekends.

- Make your bedroom a relaxing place. Eliminate electronic gadgets. Get rid of clutter.

- Wind down before bedtime by reading, taking a hot bath, doing some gentle stretching, or meditating. (Do not check your emails or do work just before bedtime.) When you turn out the lights, think about the things for which you are grateful. It puts you in a relaxed, peaceful state of mind for sleep.

- If you wake up during the night, do not be concerned. Use the time to reflect on the things you are grateful for, to pray to a higher being, think about what you will do to add more happiness to your life, enjoy the silence, or let your mind wander. Do not use electronic gadgets, watch TV, get up to eat a snack, or start doing the laundry.

- Recognize that physical exercise can lead to more restful sleep—another benefit of exercise.

A Healthy Attitude About Finances

A healthy attitude about money fits nicely with a healthy lifestyle. The two topics below—Don't Reach for the Stars and The Rule of 72—support the idea of having a long-term investment plan and using discipline to follow it.

Don't Reach for the Stars

Deciding to *not* reach for the stars takes discipline. We all want to participate in a winning investment, and human nature seems to push us to "win big." However, trying to win big (which usually means taking a large risk) can easily result in losing big. Having a clear plan and the discipline to stick with it is the best strategy.

What are the stars? Buying stock in Microsoft on December 31, 1986, at the closing price of 17 cents per share and selling it on December 31, 1999, at the closing price of $58.38 per share would have been a shining star. An investment of $10,000 would have grown to over $3.4 million! This explains why Bill Gates is so wealthy.

Many of the technology companies looked like shining stars in the late 1990s, but only until March 10, 2000. After that date the "dotcom crash" began, and by October 9, 2002, the Nasdaq Composite (technology sector) had declined 78 percent. Investments in technology companies became *falling* stars.

What about Enron? I recall a client asking me in 2000 why I was not recommending that she buy Enron stock. The company imploded in late 2001, and its investors lost everything. The problem with reaching for the stars is that it's almost impossible to know what will become a star. As a financial advisor, I receive numerous phone calls from investment firms and large banks touting the next "latest and greatest" investment, hoping I will recommend it to my clients. Many years ago I established a three-year rule that allows me to avoid these sales pitches.

Here are the terms of my three-year rule: The investment must prove itself (with good performance) over three years, and I must have access to three years of reliable, transparent data I can analyze. After analyzing the data, I determine if the investment is one I would recommend to my clients. Very few of these "latest and greatest" investments make it through this process. This three-year rule protected my clients from many of the scams of recent years. It became evident in less than three years that many of the investments that were being touted in 2007 and 2008 were not wise investments.

You can have a similar rule for any investment you may decide to purchase. For example, if your neighbor, Joe, brags about his latest stock tip that sounds appealing to you, set some boundaries. Typically, a hot stock tip does not fit into a long-term plan. Most stock tips are high risk, and your goal should be to protect and grow your finances. Recognize that folks like Joe often brag about their big winners but fail to mention that they have also had many big losers. If you were to ask Joe to show you his performance data for all the stocks he purchased over the past five years, I suspect he would tell you he doesn't have performance data. (This makes it much easier for him to recall the one winner and forget the five losers!)

Let's assume, however, that you are intrigued by the stock tip. Do your homework. Research the company carefully. (Investment research firm Morningstar provides data at no charge for many stocks and mutual funds at www.morningstar.com.) Next, determine if the stock fits into your investment portfolio. It needs to complement your other holdings and provide diversification. If you decide that Joe's investment tip fits into your long-term plan, and assuming it has at least three years of history that you have researched, put it on your watch list for at least three months. After the waiting period, you may decide to include it in an investment account. At that point it becomes an investment you have researched, rather than a hot tip. Or you may find that it has lost its luster and you are no longer interested.

The Rule of 72

There is a "Rule of 72" that is a very practical investment tool. It states that if you have an average annual return in your investments of 7.2 percent a year, you will double your money in 10 years. Or, if you have an average annual return of 10 percent per year, you will double your money every 7.2 years.

We all want the highest return possible in our investment portfolios each year. Knowing that a return of 7.2 percent will cause your money to double in 10 years is very encouraging. Let's assume you currently have $100,000 invested and you are 40 years old. If you average an annual return of 7.2 percent, your money will become $200,000 in 10 years, and $400,000 in 20 years. If you are saving and investing consistently through your 401(k) at work or in an investment account, your net worth will grow even more quickly.

Of course, it is impossible to experience a return of exactly 7.2 percent each year. The goal is to *average* 7.2 percent or more. In a year such as 2008 (when the stock market plummeted), your return may be far less than 7.2 percent. In other years, your return may be far higher. In Chapter Ten we will review historical stock market data that show that 7.2 percent was attainable for a balanced portfolio over the long term.

Simplify Your Life

Simplifying your life may include many different factors. It may be decluttering your house or office or getting rid of some responsibilities that are causing you stress. It may require that you stop being a perfectionist. It might mean saying "no" when people ask you to do something you don't want or need to do, or taking tasks off your to-do list.

In terms of your finances, simplification may include reducing the number of investment accounts you have and consolidating them to make managing your finances easier going forward. It may include setting up most of your bills so they can be paid online. It may also include setting up a system so you don't have piles of mail (bills, receipts, insurance statements) that seem overwhelming.

When you simplify your life, it frees up time to do other things that you enjoy. Having more time is a valuable benefit. You may devote the extra time to your family, exercise, hobbies, or even exploring a new career.

Another significant benefit of simplifying your life is a reduction in stress. Because we are so busy, our lives often feel out of control. Sometimes we feel like we are just working to keep "all of the balls in the air." And finally, simplifying our lives helps bring peace of mind.

Get Rid of "Stuff"

Speaking of "stuff," in a hilarious skit (you can find it on YouTube), comedian George Carlin reminds us that our homes are places to hold our stuff while we go out to get more stuff. "More stuff doesn't make people happier," says Bill McKibben in his book *The Wealth of Communities and the Durable Future*. McKibben, a Harvard-trained economist, states: "The idea that more is better, which has been orthodoxy for the past 50 years, no longer matches reality." He believes that our quest for a bigger home, more electronic equipment, and more possessions may lead to people being more cut off from friends and family.

There are ways to live better with less. McKibben suggests that we choose to buy a few high-quality items instead of lots of cheap, trendy, largely disposable items. Our "throw-away" society is often apparent in our children's behavior. When a new technology gadget becomes available, teenagers often think they should throw away the old one and buy a new one. This wasteful philosophy has been encouraged by the computer industry. A computer technician for my financial planning firm told me our computer equipment is obsolete after three years. With my middle-income background, I am constantly working to stretch equipment as long as possible— I'm especially proud that my Hoover vacuum cleaner lasted 27 years and my KitchenAid mixer for 25 years. I was told recently that most major appliances are now made to last only seven years, rather than the 20-plus years we could expect just a few years ago. I am hopeful this trend will change, as people realize the long-term benefits of making high-quality, durable items.

Clear Out the Clutter

If you clear away much of the clutter in your home or office, you will likely discover that the benefits are much greater than you would expect. Pilar Gerasimo, editor in chief of *Experience Life* magazine, says: "There's a corrosive quality to clutter. As it accumulates, slowly but surely, it eats away at my peace of mind, my confidence, my sense of order, my pleasure in my physical environment. On bad days, clutter pecks away at my whole outlook on life."

Clutter looks bad and causes us stress. For most of us, our homes and offices are overstuffed. Clearing out the clutter can seem overwhelming, because it is everywhere. Where do we begin? As one of my employees said, "How do you eat an elephant? One bite at a time." Breaking the task into a series of decluttering sessions makes it more manageable. You can also hire professional organizational experts who can help you get your office or home in order. They are not emotionally attached to your stuff, so they will encourage you to let go of more items than you may do on your own.

In her book *Organizing from the Inside Out*, Julie Morgenstern says clutter often results from something "not having a home." If you have a huge mail pile, create files or baskets for each category: "To Read," "To File," "Bills to Pay," etc. When the "To Read" collection gets too large, go through it and toss quickly, knowing there are no bills to pay or documents to file.

When cleaning out a closet or drawers, sort items into three piles: "Donate," "Throw Away," and "Keep." If you donate clothing and other items to charity, you can feel good that someone else will be able to use it. You can also often take a tax deduction for the donation.

There are many different ways to declutter. Some people like to set aside a specific period each day for the task. This works well for a kitchen, mail pile, or office. Using a 60-minute kitchen timer can help you stay on task.

Others prefer to set aside a couple of hours on a weekend day. This works well for cleaning out one part of your house each weekend. Follow this strategy, and your house could be decluttered within a few months. Take everything out of the closet, shelves, or drawers, and then sort through what you want to put back. This forces you to deal with the entire closet, shelves, or drawers rather than just part of it.

Regardless of which strategy you choose, you must set boundaries. If you are going to clean out a closet, then you must focus only on the closet; you cannot decide in the middle of the project to start cleaning out bedroom drawers. Morgenstern calls this "zigzag organizing." You want to see progress. Focusing on one area at a time will lead to that area being organized, which will motivate you to move on to the next section.

Decluttering requires perseverance, but the rewards are liberating. Visualize a clean closet (no more than 80 percent full), a clean house, a clean office, and no mail piles. Some people have speculated that clearing out the clutter frees up space for new and wonderful changes in your life.

Invest in Yourself

- Commit to decluttering your home or office. Decide ahead of time what you will do to reward yourself for a job well done— maybe treating yourself to a movie, giving yourself a free evening to read a book, taking a hot bath, or going for a massage. Set a timer if necessary. Don't allow yourself to be distracted.

- Consider enlisting a friend to help you declutter a closet full of old clothes. Friends can be brutal, encouraging you to let go of those items that don't fit or are never going to come back into style.

Learn to Say "No"

Wanting to please other people is deeply ingrained in many of us. There is nothing wrong with making others happy, but we need to set boundaries. When someone asks you to do something you do not want to do, remember you can say "no." The problem lies when you do not want to disappoint the person asking for your help. In *The Art of Extreme Self-Care*, Cheryl Richardson offers some tips on how to say "no." The next time you are asked to do something you do not want to do, consider saying:

- I've recently made a decision to limit the commitments I make, so I am not able to do this.

- I feel bad about letting you down, but I need to.

- To take better care of myself and spend more time at home, I need to decline your offer, although I'm honored that you asked.

It is important to be honest, but you do not need to waver. If you have committed to saving your evenings for exercise, say that. If you want more free time for your family (or for yourself), say so. You can thank the person for asking, but state clearly that you are going to have to decline their request.

Tame Your To-Do List

Our to-do lists are an indication of just how obsessed we are with getting things done each day. I am a list maker, and my to-do list is essential for running my business. I have a computer software program solely for tracking all the tasks I need to do for each of my clients and a separate to-do list on the computer for everything else. As useful as it is, there is no doubt that a never-ending to-do list can stifle our creativity and negatively impact our lives.

If you can successfully avoid your to-do list for a day, try to do it one day each month or on weekends. Do not look at emails or do anything work-related on your days off. Warning: Trying to avoid your emails and to-do list may make you aware that you are focused too much on work and you need to move your personal life (family, friends, exercise, relaxation) to a higher position on your priority list. This may not be realistic during the workweek, but it is possible on weekends. Unplugging from work occasionally can give you time to clear your mind, and you will feel refreshed and more energetic when you return.

Another way to deal with the to-do list is to put yourself on it. Consider scheduling an hour to read a book, take a walk, write in your journal, or focus on your gratitude list. Putting yourself on the to-do list reinforces the idea that taking care of yourself is a high priority.

Invest in Yourself

Go through your to-do list and eliminate any unnecessary items. Would the world end if 75 percent of those tasks didn't get done this week? If deleting items is difficult or stressful, just move the nonessential items into a to-do-later list, which will make your to-do list—the things that need to get done quickly—much shorter and more manageable. Over time, you may realize that many of the items on the to-do-later list don't really need to be done at all.

Make sure your to-do list includes at least one task each day that helps you move forward on your top priorities. For example, if one of your priorities is to:

- improve your health, include a 30-minute walk (or any other form of exercise).

- improve your eating habits, include planning the next day's meals or buying fruits and vegetables.

- meet new friends or try new activities, your to-do list may include looking in the local newspaper for events to attend in the upcoming weekend.

- be kind to yourself, carve out time for treating yourself to something you enjoy.

Simplify Your Financial Life

In addition to simplifying your personal life, your home, and your office, you can also simplify your finances. This makes it easier to manage your finances going forward (discussed in Part Three). Simplifying your finances can also reduce your stress levels and make you happier.

Are your investment accounts scattered? Do you have accounts at three different banks and four different brokerage firms? Or do you have three different 401(k) accounts from previous employers? People who are good savers often respond to offers to open accounts at different banks and brokerage firms. With accounts at different places, it is much harder to manage your finances.

If you have multiple accounts with a variety of banks and brokerage firms, consolidate them. Retirement plans, such as 401(k)s from former employers and traditional IRAs, can often be merged into one account. Decide which brokerage firm or financial advisor you want to use. Typically, brokerage firms will help you complete account applications and transfer forms, and financial advisors will handle all the paperwork for you.

If you are comfortable with a computer, pay your monthly bills online. If this seems difficult, ask the customer service agent at your bank to show you how.

If clutter is a problem with receipts, bills, and monthly investment statements, establish a filing system in your home. Remember that clutter often results from items not having a home, so creating file folders for each category will help you keep your financial papers organized.

Many of my clients have chosen to not receive paper statements or documents through the mail. They prefer to receive everything via email. This can work well, but it requires that you set up folders on your computer for bank statements, investment statements, tax documents, etc. I prefer statements on paper, but I ask the investment firm to bundle the monthly statements into one envelope each month. I put everything in that envelope into a file labeled "Investment Statements." When the next month's statements arrive, I put them in the front of the file. If I need to refer back to the statement, I know they are filed by month.

Trade confirmations are mailed separately and are filed in a separate file folder. My husband and I also keep a file for the current year's tax information, and anything we receive that pertains to taxes—such as charitable receipts or tax documents from banks or brokerage firms—goes into that folder. When we are ready to prepare our tax information for our accountant, everything is in one file.

If you keep your files for many years, you may feel as if you're drowning in paper. My rule is to keep your tax returns forever (the actual tax returns, not all the supporting documents). Put them in a storage bin labeled "Old tax returns." I recommend that my clients keep the supporting documents for the returns (W-2s, 1099 statements, charitable receipts, etc.)

for six years. The IRS has six years to initiate an audit from the due date of your return if they claim that you failed to report over 20 percent of your income. For more minor issues, the IRS has three years to initiate an audit.

If you are afraid to destroy anything because you think you might need it someday, put those files in a banker's box or a bin labeled "Archives" with the years listed (such as 2005-2010). These boxes can go in the garage or even under the bed. If you don't open the boxes during the next five years, you should feel more comfortable about shredding the contents. (Anything with your name, Social Security number, investment or bank account numbers, or other personal information, should be shredded.)

There are many other ways to simplify your financial life such as by reducing your spending. For example, you may significantly reduce your budget by not buying new clothing, and that money can be redirected into savings and investments. Instead of buying a new car, decide to stretch it another four years.

What is the reward for simplifying your lifestyle and finances, and reducing your expenses? One reward is that you may be able to retire at a younger age. You will also be able to manage your finances more easily because they are in good order. Another is that you may immediately start feeling happier.

Nurture Your Creativity

In recent years, neuroscientists have conducted fascinating research on creativity. Once thought to be a trait we inherit, creativity is now recognized as a skill we can nurture and develop. When researchers look for the physiological location for creativity, they study the surface of the right hemisphere of the brain.

This is the basis for the belief that people who favor the right side of their brain tend to be more creative, artistic, and spontaneous. Artists, poets, dancers, actors, writers, and performers favor the right side of the brain. Similarly, people who favor the left side of the brain tend to be more comfortable within the realm of logic and analytical thinking. Engineers, scientists, and accountants favor the left side of their brain. However, the "right brain and left brain" notion is only a guideline because scientists have found that many different parts of the brain interact for various actions.

Researchers can study the brain using MRIs, and they can see the brain "light up" in specific areas. Neuroscientist Joseph LeDoux states: "We can trace a stimulus from the eye to the neocortex and follow that stimulus through pathways that give rise to our perceptions. We know a great deal about how memories are formed as information is routed from neuron to neuron and, ultimately, stored in patterns of synaptic connectivity."

However, LeDoux considers the right-brain, left-brain concept to be an oversimplification. "Just because an area is slightly more active on the right side of the brain in a given task does not mean it is a right brain task. Sure, the task may engage the activated area a little more on the right side, but not the whole right side, and it probably also engages the same or other areas on the left side, just not quite as much."

In her book *The Artist's Way*, Julia Cameron offers suggestions for unblocking the creativity within ourselves. Even if you have no desire to be a writer, singer, illustrator, or entertainer, this book can help you unleash your creativity. Cameron recommends writing three pages every day, first thing in the morning. You can write in complete sentences or just write in a stream-of-consciousness style. The idea is to get your thoughts out of your head and onto the paper.

The choreographer Twyla Tharp believes that creativity is a result of good work habits. In her view, there are no natural geniuses. Good work habits require discipline, rituals, and lots of practice. During her 50-year career, she choreographed more than 130 ballets as well as numerous movies and Broadway musicals. In her book *The Creative Habit*, Tharp describes how she starts every day in New York

City: waking at 5:30 am, putting on her workout clothes, walking outside and hailing a taxi, and going to the gym for two hours. She says the ritual is not the stretch training and weight training she puts her body through each morning at the gym. The ritual is getting up, getting dressed, and getting into a cab. She believes it is vital to establish some rituals—automatic but decisive patterns of behavior—at the beginning of the creative process. She says, "It's Pavlovian: Follow the routine and you get a creative payoff."

She recommends finding a working environment where you can be creative, and she describes a writer who writes on his outdoor patio and a chef who is most creative in his garden. For you, it may be your kitchen table or a little table near a window. She recommends sticking with it as you develop your creative habit. She describes obstacles to the creative process, including newspapers, magazines, TV, music, and emails. She even considers numbers to be a distraction. Her goal is to give the left side of her brain (which includes numbers and logic) a rest, while allowing the right side of the brain (creativity) to become more prominent.

Tharp discusses the importance of honing one's skill through practice, which leads to confidence and self-reliance. She then addresses passion: "Without passion, all the skill in the world won't lift you above craft. Without skill, all the passion in the world will leave you eager but floundering. Combining the two is the essence of the creative life."

Like Tharp, author Walter Mosley believes creativity doesn't come naturally—it requires discipline. Most well known for his crime fiction novels, Mosley also wrote a nonfiction book titled *This Year You Write Your Novel*. In the book he explains his use of discipline and rituals. While he is writing a novel he writes for three hours each day, seven days a week, 52 weeks a year. If he takes a vacation, Mosley writes for three hours each morning. He believes in the power of rituals, and his three hours of writing is an unbreakable ritual for him.

Tharp and Mosley both employ discipline and rituals in their creative process. Nurturing creativity is not only for artists and writers. It's for businesspeople, teachers, engineers, truck drivers, restaurant employees, parents, and children. Nurturing our creativity enhances our life. It moves us away from the linear thinking that is often dominant in our work and our schools, and into an entirely new way of looking at the world. Researchers are studying strategies that may help us be more creative. Consider the following:

- Surround yourself with certain colors. For example, blue is often associated with relaxation, using your imagination, and creating new ideas.

- Watch a short video of stand-up comedy.

- Experience other cultures through travel, which can lead to open-mindedness. If traveling is not an option, simply learn about other cultures.

- Think like a beginner. The famous cellist Yo Yo Ma said, "One needs to constantly remind oneself to play with the abandon of the child who is learning to play the cello. Because why is that kid playing? He is playing for pleasure."

- Think outside the box. Don't allow yourself to get into a rut. Try new things. Meet new people. Enjoy the diversity among us.

- Remember that practice is an essential component of creativity. If you want to become a better tennis player, practice. If you want to become a better musician, writer, or artist, practice.

I am blessed to live among immensely creative and talented people in New Mexico. Many artists make this state their home, and I have been fortunate to have several artists, filmmakers, and writers as clients. I have heard them talk about how difficult it is to move from the right side of the brain to the left side, and back again. I have seen them go into a creative mode and not want to re-emerge. The simplest thing (paying the bills, making a phone call, watching the evening news) can distract them and disrupt their creative energy. I used to think this was a bizarre phenomenon until I experienced it myself while writing this book.

I learned that I cannot write for one or two hours a day and then move back into my financial planning responsibilities. I am most creative when I can slip away for several days and go into a writing mode. I also learned that I am most productive if I can work outdoors with minimal distractions. I enjoy having the birds and the bugs nearby (butterflies and lizards are great), but I avoid music in the background or people talking nearby. Fortunately, living in New Mexico provides many days of perfect weather for my outdoor writing.

Invest in Yourself

- Plan adventures that allow you to embrace and immerse yourself in creativity. Go to art galleries, museums, movies, lectures, plays, musical performances, and dances. Exercise in a new way, such as taking a yoga or dance class. Get creative as you plan your adventures.

- Decide what activities might nurture your creativity, then write down the steps you need to take. If you want to learn how to paint, sign up for a painting class. If you want to write a poem, book, or song, follow Julia Cameron's advice and write three pages each morning. Read Twyla Tharp's book for ideas and inspiration on designing a creative habit. Give yourself a gift of nurturing your creativity.

- Select an area where you can be creative. Design it to be conducive to creativity. Perhaps you need to declutter an area in your home, create a small space with an overstuffed comfy chair, or a space by a window with plenty of natural light. Consider a location in nature where you can go nurture your creativity.

Learn to Reframe

Reframing in Our Personal Lives

We perceive situations based on our beliefs, our values, our personal experiences, our perspective, and many other variables. This frame of reference then leads to our opinions and actions. We often assume that our personal frame of reference is the only accurate way of perceiving a situation, but others may see the situation differently. We can teach ourselves to look at the world with a different perspective or to *reframe* the situation. Think of reframing as looking through a different picture frame.

The concept of reframing is not new. Founded by Aaron T. Beck in the 1960s, cognitive behavioral therapy uses reframing. Cognitive reappraisal therapy (a form of cognitive behavioral therapy) teaches people to reframe adversity (change their perception), resulting in the individual recognizing a situation is not as extreme as originally believed. Neuroscientist Richard Davidson believes cognitive reappraisal therapy may be useful in increasing resilience. Davidson states: "This type of cognitive training directly engages the prefrontal cortex, resulting in increased prefrontal inhibition of the amygdala, the pattern that exemplifies resilience."

If we can learn to reframe, then can we also learn to be more optimistic? Martin Seligman did much of his early research (in the 1970s) on learned helplessness before turning his attention to topics such as well-being and optimism. In his 2011 book *Flourish*, Seligman talks about people who tend to be optimistic: "We found that people who believe that the causes of setbacks in their lives are temporary, changeable, and local do not become helpless." They think, "It's going away quickly, I can do something about it, and it's just this one situation." Seligman concludes that we can learn how to be more optimistic. "Once you get into the habit of disputing negative beliefs... your daily life will run much better, and you will feel much happier."

Reframing is helpful in many ways. If you perceive that you have too many problems and are overwhelmed, your behavior (and level of happiness) will be different than if you consider each problem as a situation waiting to be solved. Reframing can be described as "turning obstacles into opportunities."

Many life events can benefit from reframing. Psychologists have shown that losing a job often has a severe impact on happiness, and many people lost their jobs due to the economic recession that began in 2008. Reframing can be used to change the perspective, realizing that the job loss could create an opportunity to pursue a different career and find a better job. The unplanned time off can be used to enjoy your family, or focus on improving your health or your education.

A friend once told me that she considers exercise to be a privilege, because she is so thankful that her body is healthy enough to do it. If you look at exercise as a privilege rather than as a chore, you are likely to make greater progress toward your physical fitness goals. Changing your attitude about exercise is an example of reframing.

Reframing allows us to intentionally look at a situation with a new perspective. This can increase our tolerance of other viewpoints by realizing that persons with drastically different views on politics, environmental issues, and social issues simply have a different perspective. We could even decide that the diversity of opinions, cultures, and beliefs is a positive feature of our society. For example, if you hear someone complaining about political viewpoints, you can focus on the fact that we are very fortunate to live in a democratic country where we can voice opposing viewpoints. If you hear someone complaining about prices in a grocery store, you can choose to focus on how fortunate you are to have enough money for food for your family.

Researchers are finding that we have far more control than previously believed over our thoughts. If you are feeling stressed, take a slow, deep breath, and change your thought pattern. One strategy is to think about something you are grateful for. This reframes your thoughts and puts you in a healthier and happier state of mind. Eating healthy food or taking a walk can make you feel better, both physically and mentally. Similarly, intentionally changing your thought patterns can have a positive impact on your attitude. This gets easier with practice, and I encourage you to try it.

Reframing and Your Finances

Reframing also applies to your attitude about money. If you know that you have a serious problem with trying to keep up with the Joneses, change your perspective. Rather than lusting over the new car in your neighbor's driveway, think about the positive lessons you are teaching your children about living within your means. Realize that managing your finances in this manner will help you attain financial security, which is far more rewarding. Remind yourself that life is about choices, and you are making wise choices for your family's future. Discuss these issues with your family, and recognize that reframing is a useful tool for achieving financial security.

Reframing can also apply to your investing experiences. If you lost a significant amount of money in the last recession, reframe your thinking and be thankful for the money you have now. You probably have much more now than you had when you were on a tight budget in college. Take steps to reduce your investment risk going forward so you are less vulnerable when the stock market takes another nosedive. A downturn is inevitable; only the timing is uncertain.

Reframing also applies to the question, How much is enough? English writer G.K. Chesterton was reframing when he wrote: "There are two ways to get enough. One is to accumulate more and more. The other is to desire less."

Reframing may apply to how many "things" (possessions) you want and whether you decide to place more value on family and friends, experiences, laughter, creativity, generosity, and time. Reframing means stepping back and saying, "Let's look at this issue another way." When practiced effectively, it can lead to powerful changes in your level of happiness and financial security.

CHAPTER SIX

■ ■ ■ ■ ■

Happiness: Pure and Simple

Money itself doesn't make you happy.
What can make you happy is what you do with it.
— PSYCHOLOGIST DANIEL GILBERT

Be a Work in Progress

ccepting that you are a work in progress is saying, "I am still changing. I am not finished. I am still exploring. I am an active participant. I am not just floating aimlessly through life."

Change is often very difficult. We are set in our ways, and we return to what feels comfortable. Consider our eating and exercising habits. If we are accustomed to not planning healthy meals or not getting adequate exercise, then changing those habits into healthier ones takes very intentional actions. Likewise, starting a gratitude practice or deciding to include more fun in your life can be difficult.

Many of us were taught at a young age that failure is unacceptable. This mindset is detrimental because we learn by failing. Not being allowed to fail interferes with our ability to try new things and causes us to be overly cautious. A healthier attitude is to change this mindset and consider failure as a learning opportunity. Thomas Edison emphasized the importance of allowing for failure when he said: "I failed my way to success."

Seek Solitude

Carving out some downtime and solitude in your routine is healing and refreshing. Many Americans are running a rat race. Often, we feel like we are on a treadmill running faster and faster, but going nowhere. A client recently described her life as a performer on the old *Ed Sullivan* show who spins plates on the top of poles. She said she is working as hard as she can to keep the plates spinning, but people keep throwing her more plates.

Solitude requires "alone time," but this can take many forms. The solution may be simply turning off the noise. Rather than playing the radio on your drive to work, turn it off. Or get up earlier than the rest of your family to enjoy a few minutes of quiet before you start your busy day. Find a quiet room in a library, a museum, or a church, and savor the silence. Take a hike in nature to escape the noise of the city. Your body and your mind will appreciate the silence.

Solitude can also be a retreat. Being alone provides an opportunity to really listen to your body and your mind. In her classic book *Gift of the Sea*, Anne Morrow Lindbergh describes living in a small house by herself on the ocean. Writers and artists often prefer to work in complete silence, and solitude is often associated with creativity and innovation. Picasso said, "Without great solitude, no serious work is possible."

Invest in Yourself

- Think through your day, and decide when you can carve out 15 minutes of quiet time. For many people, it is early in the morning.

Set aside 15 minutes each day when you can sit quietly and let your mind relax. Don't think about your to-do list or the problems in your life. If your mind is racing with thoughts, just practice letting the thoughts drift off. With practice, this becomes easier.

- Carve out two hours on a weekend to have no plans. You may decide you want to read a book, take a nap, or write in a journal. The idea is to leave this time unscheduled so you can decide how to fill it, with the only rules being that you cannot work during this time and you need to be alone. It cannot be used to clean the house or pay the bills. It is time devoted to solitude.

- Start planning an "ultimate day off." This will be a day when you completely unplug from your normal routine. Checking emails, taking work-related phone calls, and running errands are not allowed. Is there a part of your town or city that you have not explored? A museum or state park you have never visited? A trail you have been wanting to hike? A restaurant you have been wanting to try? As mentioned in Chapter Four, spending money on experiences is far richer than spending money on things. Decide if you would like to share your ultimate day off with a family member or a friend. If not, make it an entire day just for you. The key is to get out of your normal routine and treat yourself to a day of new experiences.

- After experiencing an ultimate day off, start planning a retreat for several days. Your retreat can be as simple as visiting a nearby city or region you want to explore. Or it could be staying in a small inn and taking some books with you that you have been wanting to read. Take a journal with you so you can write down your thoughts and experiences. Treat yourself to a slower pace. Go to bed when you are tired and wake up without an alarm clock. While you are clearing your mind, it may provide you with a new perspective on your life and changes you would like to make.

Enjoy the Moment

"Enjoy the moment" is easy to understand but difficult to implement. We are driven to always be looking ahead, and it is hard to slow down to savor the moment.

One of the barriers to living in the moment is our tendency to multitask. Researchers have found that we are really not multitasking, because our brains don't allow it. Instead, we are shifting our focus very quickly from one thing to the next. Studies have shown that our productivity goes down as much as 40 percent when multitasking. Peter Bregman of the *Harvard Business Review*, decided to avoid multitasking for one week. He experienced enormous benefits, especially while interacting with his children. At work, he reported that his stress levels declined dramatically and he was extremely productive in tackling challenging projects.

Learning to enjoy the moment takes practice, just like many of the happiness strategies in this book. When you are doing something you enjoy, try training your brain to focus on the current moment. For example, if you are gardening, focus on the sunshine, the birds, the bugs, the feel of the dirt, the beauty of the flowers, or the new growth on the vegetables. Do not think about all the many other things you need to do. When your mind wanders to other topics, simply stop your thought pattern and bring your focus back to gardening. With practice, focusing on the moment will get easier.

Gardening is just one example. If you are at a movie, relish the movie (or the buttered popcorn). If you are at a picnic with your family, be grateful for your children or grandchildren as you watch them play. Act silly and play on a swing set at a playground. Walk your dog and feel the sunshine on your face. Go outside during a rainstorm and feel the rain on your skin.

Invest in Yourself

- If you have young children, devote at least one hour each evening to them, without multitasking. This means you cannot open the mail, cook dinner, or watch TV during that hour. Give them 100 percent of your attention. If you typically multitask, this may be very difficult. Approach it as a challenge, recognizing that this special hour may become a part of your child's memory about growing up.

- If you do not have children, but you have a spouse or partner, spend an hour focusing on each other, without distractions. Take a walk together or have an uninterrupted conversation. If you live alone, give yourself an hour of quiet time.

- Be open to unexpected experiences as you enjoy the moment. You may be rewarded by seeing wonderful—and previously unnoticed—things around you. You may notice a bird that sings outside your window each morning or take delight in someone being kind to a stranger. As you experience these moments, take time to reflect on how they enrich your life.

Cultivate Positive Traits

Sometimes we rely on experts too much. When it comes to reviewing your life and looking at what is out of balance, *you* are the expert. Only you know if you are working too many hours and not getting enough exercise. Only you know if you are short-changing yourself on fun or relaxation.

The great news is that we have the control, and we can cultivate positive traits. Recall from Chapter One that research has shown our behavior is a result of our *nature* (the DNA we inherited), our *nurture* (our environment), and our *choices*. Also recall that roughly 40 percent of our happiness is based on the choices we make. The fact that we have control over our choices is the exciting message of this book. It allows us to significantly increase our happiness and our financial security.

Keep in mind that many positive traits can be cultivated through your choices and your behaviors. The following traits (and many more) can be cultivated: creativity, a sense of purpose, meaningful relationships, patience, resiliency, self-discipline, an optimistic attitude, gratitude, a sense of accomplishment, and personal satisfaction. We have an incredible opportunity to shape our lives into the people we choose to be.

Have Rich Conversations with Family and Friends

Think about the people who have enriched your life. Initiate heartfelt discussions with your parents, grandparents, or older friends while they are still alive. I did not do this often enough, and I regret it.

I regret that I never talked with my dad about the Korean War, where he was stationed, or about dating my mother during the war. I wish I had talked with my Uncle Allen about his year as a prisoner of war in Germany during World War II. My mother and grandmother told me they baked cookies and mailed them to him every week at the prison camp where he was held. After he was released, they learned that none of the cookies ever reached him. Presumably, the German guards enjoyed lots of cookies.

Don't pass up the opportunities for these discussions. What is the worst thing that can happen if you ask a relative or friend about their life? They can say, "I don't want to talk about it." You can then say to yourself, "So what, at least I tried." More likely, they will appreciate that you asked.

Practice the Art of Meditation

Meditation is a 2,500-year-old ancient tradition most often associated with Buddhism. Richard Davidson, a neuroscientist and psychologist based at the University of Wisconsin at Madison, has researched the benefits of meditation for most of his career. As a graduate student at Harvard, he practiced meditation in his personal life and was intrigued by the idea that it may have a positive and lasting impact on the brain. Since then, he has conducted numerous research experiments on people who meditate, some including Buddhist monks. He was curious whether a meditation practice could cultivate positive qualities of mind as well as compassion and loving kindness.

Richardson designed a study in 1999 that would examine whether very limited exposure to meditation changed the brain. He mapped the brains of employees at a bio-tech company in Wisconsin, after roughly half the employees completed an eight-week meditation course (one session per week for 2½ hours). It was led by Jon Kabat-Zinn, PhD, who is the founding director of the Stress Reduction Clinic at the University of Massachusetts Medical School. Dr. Kabat-Zinn developed a type of meditation known as *mindfulness-based stress reduction* (MBSR).

After only four months, Davidson found that the employees who had been meditating noticed a boost in mood and a decrease in anxiety, while their immune systems became measurably stronger. He concluded that MBSR (often called mindfulness meditation) caused the level of activation in the left pre-frontal cortex to triple as compared to the activation levels before the meditation classes. The higher levels of activation in the left prefrontal cortex have been shown to lead to a higher level of resilience and having a more positive outlook. While referring to the benefits of MBSR, he stated: "being able to cope with stress means you are more able to bounce back from a setback, and it can cause you to see the world through more optimistic eyes." This relates to neuroplasticity (discussed in Chapter Two) and the neuronal pathways within our brains.

Mindfulness meditation (as developed by Jon Kabat-Zinn) is now being taught throughout the United States and Europe. It is easy to learn and is focused on nonjudgmental awareness. In addition to the benefits that Davidson identified, MBSR is being used to help patients deal with chronic pain, heart disease, high blood pressure, anxiety, depression, sleep issues, and weight issues.

MBSR has been shown to reduce the levels of stress hormones and inflammation in the blood. The key to meditation is practice. It can initially take as little as 15 minutes a day, increasing to 30 minutes or more. Although meditation has an aura that makes it intimidating to many people, it is quite simple. References regarding MBSR meditation are listed in the Resources section at the back of the book and on *www.joyoffinancialsecurity.com*.

Invest in Yourself

- Research books, articles, or audio tapes on meditation. There are guided meditations available by Jon Kabat-Zinn, Andrew Weil, Sharon Salzburg, and Pema Chodon. Or look for a local class on MBSR. These classes are often offered in many communities by hospitals or colleges.

Focus on Breathing

This topic is closely related to meditation. In fact, it is very common while practicing meditation to focus your attention on breathing. If starting a meditation practice seems daunting to you, simply focusing only on your breath may be much less intimidating.

Andrew Weil, M.D., is a leader and pioneer in the field of integrative medicine, which encompasses body, mind, and spirit. He is a proponent of what he refers to as *breath work*. He explains that focusing on your breath automatically directs your focus away from emotionally upsetting thoughts. What tends to clutter our minds? Often, it is our ever-overflowing to-do list or problems that seem insurmountable. The stress can feel overwhelming. Dr. Weil has recommended the following to his patients and medical students for many years:

- Put your attention on the breath whenever possible.

- Whenever you can, make your breath deeper, slower, quieter, and more regular.

- Let your belly expand outward when you inhale.

- To deepen breathing, practice exhaling more air at the end of each breath.

When we are anxious, angry, or upset, our breathing typically becomes rapid, shallow, and irregular. You can calm your body and your mind by focusing on your breath. Deep breathing is a tool you can practice many times a day. You can do it while waiting at a red light in traffic, when you feel stressed at work, or at the end of a long day.

Live in a State of Completion

This topic is similar to decluttering, which was discussed in Chapter Five. Having unfinished projects can be very stressful, just like a cluttered environment. There are two components to living in a state of completion. First, commit that you are going to complete new tasks and projects that you begin. This applies to projects that you start from this point forward. If you finish a project and put it away before moving to another task, you will experience a sense of accomplishment that feels great. This applies to opening the mail, paying the bills, filing documents, putting away the groceries, or making your bed each morning.

Second, if you have unfinished projects from the past, decide when and how you can complete them. This takes time and planning. You can gradually complete the old projects, such as unfinished filing or cleaning out the closet you started two months ago. Or, you may decide a project is no longer a priority and does not deserve to be completed. Reassessing your priorities is always encouraged.

Invest in Yourself

- Commit to completing new tasks and projects going forward.

- Make a list of the projects (from the past) that are unfinished. This may be a long list, so don't get discouraged. Decide which projects you want to complete, and which you want to tackle first. Set aside some time each week to clean up old projects. Within a few weeks, you will start to see significant improvement. If you decide to discard an old project, throw it away, give it away, or put it out of sight.

Reinvigorate a Relationship

Many of the topics in this book pertain to activities for you to do alone. Topics such as seeking solitude, improving your self-care, and starting a gratitude practice are focused on increasing your personal happiness. Yet improving relationships with people we love can also significantly increase our happiness.

Rabbi Naomi Levy wrote a book called *To Begin Again: The Journey Toward Comfort, Strength, and Faith in Difficult Times.* In her book she describes a couple from her congregation. She had performed their wedding ceremony and had been impressed that they seemed to have it all—money, success, looks, and love. Then one day they came to see her, and they were worried about their relationship. They both worked long hours at high-pressure jobs and looked seriously stressed. They told her they rarely had any time to enjoy being together.

She persuaded them to try observing a Sabbath day, just to see how it felt. Starting that Friday at sunset, she convinced them to leave their workweek behind and allow their spirits to be revived. The next week they came back to see her and reported that they hadn't experienced such peacefulness since their honeymoon. They seemed like different people—calm, patient, and affectionate with each other. Levy states that true rest doesn't just affect us when we are resting. It spills over into our weeks, our years, our lives. Even the most harried workdays become tolerable when you know a day of holy peace is coming soon. The days after the day of rest become better, too, because they shimmer with the afterglow of a revived spirit.

Invest in Yourself

- Devote extra attention to your spouse or partner. Often, it seems that we neglect each other because our lives are too busy. Talk with your spouse or partner and plan some special time together. Maybe you want to start a date night tradition. Many couples do this, and they look forward to the evening together each week. Consider planning to save one day each weekend for each other. Perhaps you plan a weekend away or a vacation for just the two of you. Remember that our relationships are keenly important to our happiness, and experiences are far more valuable than things.

Other Happiness Triggers

The number of potential happiness triggers is unlimited. Here are few you may want to try:

- Put special pictures, sayings, inspirational quotes, photos, and cards throughout your home and office where you will see them. If you have set a goal, put a reminder where you will see it often. A note that says, "I'm getting healthier" or "Reframe" or "I am grateful" can be a reminder of the changes you are trying to make.

- Hang photos of your children, grandchildren, spouse, or pet where you will see them often. Put a piece of artwork from your child or grandchild on the refrigerator (even if it is 20 years old). Put your child's baby shoes on your desk.

- Use colors to brighten your mood. The color yellow is associated with joy and energy. Blue is considered to be relaxing and to induce creativity.

- Listen to music. It doesn't matter if you choose classical, country, rock and roll, jazz, or rap. Listening to music can increase your endorphins (your "feel-good" hormones).

- Turn off the TV. There are numerous studies that show the negative impact of watching TV. This may be an easy solution for you to find more time for reading, exercising, writing in your gratitude journal, or whatever makes you happy.

- Buy yourself a little something once a week, to reinforce the idea of self-care. A fancy bar of soap, some special after-shave, a scented candle, or flowers can brighten your day.

- Buy a friend or family member a little something as a surprise. It will make you both feel great.

- Give someone a sincere compliment. Look directly into their eyes as you congratulate them on a job well done or on something you admire about them. This will make them feel great, and you will also reap happiness rewards. Begin complimenting others more often. It becomes easier with practice.

- Spend time with your dog or cat. This has been shown to increase oxytocin, a calming hormone.

- Evoke happy memories. Whenever I think of my 4-year-old daughter (many years ago) trying to stay awake on Christmas Eve while looking out her bedroom window for Santa Claus, I am grateful for my family.

- Treat yourself to at least one small pleasure each day. It may be savoring a cup of coffee on your patio early in the morning, enjoying a piece of chocolate, or lying down for 10 minutes before dinner.

- Appreciate nature. Author Francine Prose fell in love with a crabapple tree in her yard. It has been there over 30 years, and she looks forward to each spring when it blooms. There may be plants in your garden that are special, or you can enjoy the wildflowers you observe while hiking.

- Odds and ends: a trip to the beach; a hike in the mountains; hugging a family member or friend; ice cream; giggling; gardening; enjoying your grandchildren; breakfast at a restaurant; a massage; a movie; a great newspaper; trying something new; calling a friend; grilling outdoors; s'mores; a good book; seeing a ladybug, a hummingbird, or a butterfly; baking your favorite dessert; writing in your journal; taking a nap; going to a farmer's market; treating yourself to a day off.

Invest in Yourself

- Make your own list of happiness triggers, and then treat yourself to two (or more) of them this week.

PART
THREE

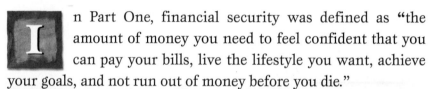

Financial Strategies

n Part One, financial security was defined as "the amount of money you need to feel confident that you can pay your bills, live the lifestyle you want, achieve your goals, and not run out of money before you die."

Attaining financial security is not a simple process. It is multi-faceted. Chapters Seven, Eight, and Nine cover many financial planning topics, such as how to track your net worth, increase your savings, and minimize your taxes. You will also learn how to protect yourself from unscrupulous tactics that are pervasive in the financial industry. Chapter Ten covers investment topics, including how to select the appropriate asset allocation and how to design your portfolio. Chapter Eleven addresses retirement issues, such as how to prepare psychologically and financially for retirement, and how to calculate how much money you will need in your retirement "nest egg." The latest research regarding how much you can withdraw during retirement (termed *sustainable withdrawal rates*) is also covered.

Note: The financial information provided in Part Three is general and is not intended as specific advice to any reader. Each person's financial situation is different, and the financial strategies must be customized for each individual person. If you have any questions regarding the applicability of topics in the book to your individual situation, you are encouraged to consult with the professional advisors of your choice.

Throughout the book I discuss the services I provide my clients. These comments are included to demonstrate the services that a full-service financial planner *may* provide. Financial planners (and financial advisors) vary significantly in the services they offer and the way they interact with their clients.

CHAPTER
SEVEN

■ ■ ■ ■ ■

The Essentials of Financial Security

Money is better than poverty,
if only for financial reasons.

— WOODY ALLEN

Beyond the Investments

When you hear the phrase "manage your finances," you may immediately think of your investment accounts. Investment strategies are addressed in Chapter Ten, but for now I encourage you to think more globally. Financial security encompasses far more than just investments. Managing your finances means getting your financial life "in good order." Organizing your finances allows you to see progress as your net worth increases and you become more financially secure.

There are many factors that impact your finances. Consider the following questions:

- Have you established your financial and personal goals?

- Do you know how much you are saving each year? Does the savings occur automatically?

- What are your plans for retirement? At what age do you plan to retire?

- Do you have retirement projections showing several different scenarios? Do you update the projections annually?

- What financial decisions have you made regarding paying for your children's or grandchildren's private schools or college expenses?

- Are you currently supporting adult relatives financially, or do you anticipate needing to in the future? (This could be parents, adult children, or siblings.)

- Are you anticipating receiving any inheritances?

- Do you "gamble" with your investments by keeping them very aggressive? Do you have a tendency to act on stock tips and other speculative investments?

- Are your investments diversified? Do they match your tolerance for risk?

- Do you know how your investments are performing?

- Do you know what investment fees you are paying?

- Are you carrying credit card debt that is not paid in full each month? This is a clear sign of living beyond your means.

- Do you have the lowest mortgage interest rate available? Are the mortgage terms consistent with your goals (for when the mortgage will be paid off or when you may be planning on moving or downsizing).

- Are you using wise tax planning strategies to maximize your income and assets on an after-tax basis?

- Do you drive cars that are more expensive than you can afford?

- Do you have adequate insurance to cover major risks?

- Are your estate planning documents current, and do they convey your wishes?

- Do you have an estate planning binder that would help your family or executor settle your estate if you were to die suddenly?

- Do you discuss your finances with your spouse, partner, or other household members?

If you have not completed many of the topics listed above, do not worry. Getting your finances in good order is a process—one that does not need to be done all at once. Take it a step at a time. Start by reading through the chapters in Part Three. Then in Part Four, you will be encouraged to select a few strategies that will set you on a path to improving your finances.

Manage Your Human Capital

In financial planning, we focus on *financial* capital, which is basically *money*. This includes your investments, how much you save, how much you spend, the growth within your investment accounts, withdrawals during retirement, and many other factors.

Another important concept is called *human* capital. Human capital is your ability to earn income over your lifetime. This is an enormous asset, and it is much more within your control than your stocks, bonds, or real estate investments. Human capital encompasses your education, the career you select, job changes during your lifetime, and your earned income. It also includes part-time work during retirement, which may result from needing extra income or from choosing to work for enjoyment. Financial advisor Paula Hogan describes human capital as "what you do with your skills and talents and how society chooses to pay you for your endeavors."

Human capital is a major determinant of an individual's lifetime standard of living. Rather than focusing only on investment accounts (and the money that has been saved and invested), the focus shifts to the income stream resulting from our careers. A steady income stream allows for consistent savings over the years, which can lead to a larger investment portfolio and financial security.

Human capital emphasizes the importance of deciding the type of education you want to pursue, how much education you want to obtain, and what career path you choose. A college degree is considered the clearest path to the American middle class, and it can significantly increase a person's earning power. Not too many years ago, a college degree was a ticket to a good job. Unfortunately, this is no longer a guarantee. Careful thought needs to be applied to matching your skills and talents (what you love to do) with a career path that can pay you what you want to earn. Nurturing and managing your human capital is essential throughout your career.

Note, however, that managing your human capital is not the same as saying, "Maximize your income." Consider a person who loves teaching grade school children. Most likely, being a teacher is not going to provide a high income. Yet a person who loves teaching can design his or her lifestyle around the income that a teaching career provides. Furthermore, teaching positions often provide a defined benefit pension after retirement. If a teacher works for the same employer for many years, the pension can be very rich indeed.

One of my long-term clients retired from a teaching career several years ago. During her working years, she routinely contributed the maximum allowed to her employer's retirement plan. When she retired, her monthly take-home pay was higher than her teacher's salary. How was she able to do this? There were two contributing factors: 1) She had been an employee for the same school district for many years, and her pension was substantial; and 2) once she retired, she was no longer contributing to her retirement plan, which had been reducing her take-home pay.

Managing your human capital entails thinking through what you love to do and then obtaining the necessary education to pursue that career path. It may also include researching the career paths and potential employers that may provide you with a retirement pension and excellent employee benefits (health insurance, disability insurance, vacation days, etc.). Your research may include investigating opportunities for advancement, an enjoyable work environment, and jobs close to home (with short commutes). Networking with others in your chosen field is essential.

The concept of managing your human capital applies to teenagers and college students who are just embarking on their careers. However, most college-age kids do not know where their passion lies. That comes with trial and error, experience, and wisdom. The concept also applies when someone is contemplating a career change or preparing for retirement.

There are plenty of examples of professionals who were highly paid investment bankers, corporate executives, doctors, and lawyers who chose to leave the stress and high income behind. Maybe they moved to the country, to a simpler (and less expensive) lifestyle. Maybe they pursued their dream of changing careers and became farmers, raised goats, and made cheese, or devoted their talents to a charitable venture for which they were passionate. In some cases, they had saved plenty of money when they were in their highly paid profession. In other cases, they drastically simplified their lifestyle and reduced their expenses to match their new lifestyle. Clearly, these people were interested in more than just maximizing their income.

The key in managing your human capital is to determine what you love to do and to design your life around doing it. If you can find a way to be paid for doing what you love—and to create a consistent income stream throughout your working years—then you can consistently save for the future and attain financial security.

Track Your Net Worth

Many people neglect their finances, and this can threaten their financial security. A net worth statement is a valuable tool for managing your finances. It summarizes your overall net worth by listing your *assets* (what you *own*) minus your *liabilities* (what you *owe*). A Net Worth Statement Worksheet is provided in Figure 7.1 for you to complete. You will also find an easy-to-use, downloadable version at *www.joyoffinancialsecurity.com*. I recommend updating your net worth statement annually and keeping the prior net worth statements so you can monitor your progress over the years.

A common problem is that people let their finances get scattered. If investors are good at saving, they often open accounts with multiple brokerage firms or mutual fund firms over the years. People may also have three or four different 401(k) accounts from past jobs. Or they may have several IRAs and bank accounts. This makes it very difficult to manage their finances. One of the first things I do for a new client is to consolidate their investment accounts into a small number of accounts. For example, all the old (inactive) 401(k)s can usually be consolidated into one IRA, and all of the taxable accounts can be consolidated into one account. Getting your investments organized is the first step in gaining control of your finances.

To begin completing your net worth statement, gather recent statements for your investment accounts and bank accounts, and start listing them under "Assets." Include all stocks, bonds, and money market accounts. Include any CDs, retirement accounts (such as traditional IRAs, Roth IRAs, traditional 401[k]s or 403[b]s, Roth 401[k]s or 403[b]s) and annuities. (Only include annuities that have not yet been annuitized. This means you are not receiving payments from the annuity). Do not forget savings bonds that may be stored in a safety deposit box or in a Treasury Direct account. Use estimates for the value of your home and other real estate. If a life insurance policy has a cash value—and you expect to cash it in early—include it on the net worth statement. If you do not plan to cash it in early, it should not be listed. Do not include the death benefit for life insurance policies.

If you will receive a pension during retirement, but you are not yet receiving any payments from it, do not list it on the net worth statement. Some people think the present value of the future pension benefits should be listed as an asset. I disagree. The pension benefits will become an income stream (much like your Social Security benefits) when you start receiving payments. It will be included in the retirement projections, but does not belong on the net worth statement.

If you own valuable personal items, you may wonder whether they should be included in the "Assets" section of the net worth statement. I generally recommend that clients not list the value of their cars as an asset, because they are not going to sell them, and cars often have little value. However, there is an exception. If you have a car loan that will be listed as a liability on the net worth statement, then you should list the estimated value of the car as an asset. Electronic equipment (such as computers or stereos) should not be listed as an asset because it loses value quickly. If you have expensive art, jewelry, or antiques that you do *not* intend to sell, do not list them as assets. Alternatively, if you have items such as an extensive art collection and you *do* plan to sell the items, then the art collection should be listed as an asset.

Once all your assets are listed, calculate the total for the "Assets" column.

Next, start listing your liabilities. Include your current mortgage balance, as well as the current balance for education loans, car loans, or a home equity line of credit. Include credit card debt if it is not paid off each month. Once you have listed all your liabilities (debts), calculate the total for the "Liabilities" column.

The net worth statement does not need to be exact. It serves as a snapshot of your total net worth at this point in time. I recommend you update it each year to track the changes.

Once you have listed all your assets and liabilities, you are ready to complete the form. Your net worth is simply your total assets minus your total liabilities (debts). The goal is to increase your net

FIGURE 7.1 NET WORTH STATEMENT WORKSHEET

Net Worth Statement   Date _____

Assets: What You Own		Liabilities: What You Owe	
Cash and Cash Equivalents	Value	Home mortgage balance	
Checking accounts		Second mortgage balance	
Savings accounts		Home equity line of credit	
Money market funds		Credit card balances (only if not	
Certificates of deposit (CDs)		paid off in full each month)	
Savings bonds		Education loan balance	
Other		Business loan balance	
Other		Notes payable	
Investment Assets (Taxable)	Value	Other	
Account		Other	
Account			
Account			
Retirement Assets	Value		
Traditional IRAs			
Roth IRAs			
Traditional 401ks, 403bs			
Roth 401ks, 403bs			
Annuities (not yet annuitized)			
Other			
Other			
Real Estate	Value		
Home			
Second home			
Rental property			
Commercial property			
Other			
Other			
Other	Value		
Cash Value of Life Ins. (only			
if you plan to cash in soon)			
Business assets			
Other			
Other			
Total Assets	$	Total Liabilities	$

Total Assets	$
Subtract **Total Liabilities**	– $
Equals **Net Worth**	= $

worth over time. The increase from year-to-year will not be linear. In other words, you cannot assume the net worth will increase by 10 percent or 20 percent per year. In some years, it may increase 40 percent; in other years, only 15 percent. It may decrease 20 percent if the stock market performs poorly or if you need to withdraw money from your investment accounts. Tracking your net worth is extremely important, because it keeps your focus on the big picture.

Congratulations! If you prepare a net worth statement you have taken a huge step forward in improving your financial security.

Monitor Your Saving and Spending

Monitor Your Saving

Do you think people with high incomes are wealthier than people with average incomes? This is a myth that needs to be dispelled. Many people with high incomes do not have a high net worth.

The key is not how much you earn but how much you save. *The amount you save is the primary factor in becoming financially secure.* Many people with high incomes live a "high-consumption lifestyle" in which they spend everything they earn. Often, they spend *more* than they earn, which lands them in debt. This is a common example of living beyond your means. People like this tend to be very status-driven as they strive to keep up with the Joneses. Clearly, you do not want to follow this destructive—but very common—path.

In the classic financial book *The Millionaire Next Door*, Thomas Stanley researched the common traits of millionaires during the 1990s. He discovered that, on average, they saved and invested 20 percent of their income.

How much of your income do you save? Do you know? Most people do not. The average savings rate in the United States is less than 5 percent, and many people do not save at all. I recommend that my clients save at least 15 percent of their gross income, and preferably 20 percent or more. Many of my clients save over 25 percent of their income. A high savings rate is the very best way to ensure that you will not run out of money during retirement. I sincerely hope that this book provides you with many ideas that result in positive changes in your life. However, if the only thing you do is to increase your savings rate, you will have taken an enormous financial step forward.

"Your Current Savings Rate" worksheet in Figure 7.2 can be used to calculate your current savings rate and track your income. Look at your year-end tax documents or investment statements to see how much you contributed to your retirement plans last year. Do not include the amount your employer contributed—only include your contributions. If you saved money in a bank account or a taxable account, fill in that amount. However, only include the money that was truly saved for the long term. If you spent the money later, it should not be counted as savings. Follow the steps provided in the instructions below to calculate your savings rate.

If you didn't save anything last year, strive to save at least 10 percent this year. If you saved 10 percent, strive to increase it to 15 or 20 percent this year. Increasing your savings usually comes from two sources: Either you increase your income (possibly by taking on a second part-time job), or you decrease your expenses.

Pay Yourself First

Establishing a savings plan so it occurs automatically—and before you pay your other bills each month—is called "pay yourself first." It is a valuable tool as you strive to become more financially secure. Setting up a "pay yourself first" system so that the amount you want to save each month is automatically swept into a savings or an investment account will quickly increase your savings percentage. Instead of *hoping* there will be money left over at the end of the month for savings (and knowing that there rarely is), you will be proactively taking control of your financial future.

FIGURE 7.2   YOUR CURRENT SAVINGS RATE

Date:_____

Savings (Type of Account)   Amount Saved

_____ $ _____

_____ $ _____

_____ $ _____

_____ $ _____

_____ $ _____

            Total Savings (A) $ _____

Gross (Before Tax) Income (Source)   Amount

_____ $ _____

_____ $ _____

_____ $ _____

_____ $ _____

_____ $ _____

            Total Income (B) $ _____

(A÷B) X 100 = C Savings Rate (C)   _____%

Instructions for Completing
"Your Current Savings Rate"

1. List each account where you saved money last year and the amount saved in each. Calculate the total savings.

2. List each source of income from last year (such as your wages, your spouse's wages, Social Security, a pension, or an annuity). Show the amount of gross income from each source, (before any taxes were withheld, or before retirement plan contributions were subtracted). You can access this information from your last paycheck of the year, or from the first page of your IRS federal tax return. If you are self-employed, use your income from Schedule C or from a corporate tax return. If you are retired and are receiving Social Security benefits, list your annual gross Social Security income (before deductions). If you receive a pension, list the gross annual amount (before any withholdings). If you receive payments from an annuity (that has already been annuitized), list the gross amount you receive each year (before any taxes are withheld). Calculate the total income.

3. Take the total savings (A) and divide it by the total income (B). This is your savings rate. For example:

   If you contributed $6,000 to your 401(k) and you earned $50,000 (gross), then you saved 12% ($6,000 ÷ $50,000).

   If you saved a total of $15,000 (in any combination of retirement accounts, taxable investment accounts, or savings accounts) and your income is $100,000, then you saved 15% ($15,000 ÷ $100,000).

   If you saved $30,000 and your income is $150,000, then your savings rate is 20% ($30,000 ÷ $150,000).

Financial advisor Kenneth Robinson, in his book *Don't Make a Budget*, states: "The key to saving is not to figure out where you can cut back so you can add up your potential savings. Rather, it is to *make a decision about how much you are going to save.* Then the decision about where to cut back will take care of itself."

The "pay yourself first" strategy will also help you reduce your expenses. During the first few months, you may have less money at the end of the month, but you will tighten your budget and realize that you no longer want to spend money on unnecessary items. Within a few more months, you will no longer notice because you will have adjusted to spending the lower amount.

Tax refunds and bonuses are another savings opportunity. Often, people look at tax refunds and bonuses as "free money," and the money is spent quickly. Instead, recognize that this money provides a golden opportunity to increase your savings, and therefore, your financial security. I recommend that my clients save and invest at least 50 percent of any tax refund or bonus. (The remaining 50 percent can be spent on a nice weekend away, home improvement, or a new washer and dryer.)

There are also periods that lend themselves to drastically increasing your savings. Paying off a mortgage or a car loan frees up that monthly payment to all go into savings. When kids move out of the house, the grocery bill may decrease significantly. Be diligent in looking for these opportunities. These are sometimes referred to as "burst" savings because they are like a burst of energy to your investment accounts and your financial security.

Salary increases also provide an excellent opportunity to direct the additional income to savings. If your employer provides an annual raise, direct the amount of the increase to savings. You will still be receiving the same take-home pay so you will not notice a change, but your savings will benefit.

Discussing your savings with your children can plant a powerful seed for how they handle money throughout their lives. Teach your children and grandchildren that they should save at least 15 percent and preferably 20 percent—beginning with their first summer job. If they can continue saving at least 15 percent throughout their career, they will be on the path to financial security.

Monitor Your Spending

Most people do not like adhering to a budget, which is why the term *spending plan* is often used. However, I typically do not recommend that my clients keep a spending plan. Let me explain.

A spending plan is very useful if you do not know where you are spending your money. If you take $200 out of an ATM machine each Monday, and by Thursday it is gone, then tracking your spending for a few weeks can be very helpful. If you know that you spend too much money on clothes, eating out, travel, or birthday and holiday gifts for family members, then track your spending for a few months to pinpoint the problem. Often, overspending is limited to one or two areas, and becoming aware of the problem is the first step in correcting it.

So why do I often *not* recommend that my clients keep a spending plan? There are two reasons. First, most of my clients are already financially secure, and they tend to be very responsible with their money. They have saved and invested wisely over many years, and as a result, they have significant assets. They tend not to overspend, so exceeding a spending plan is rarely a concern.

However, the second reason is more important. I do not ask them to keep a spending plan because I am monitoring their saving and spending for them. This is not done at a detailed level, but I do it at least once each year. Together with my client, I review the amount they are saving and the amount they are withdrawing from their investment accounts. This is not an exact analysis, but it will identify a problem if one exists.

My working clients (not yet retired) typically contribute the maximum allowed each year to their employer retirement plans. In addition, most of them save through automatic monthly deposits in their taxable investment account. These contributions and deposits are all added together to arrive at a total amount saved for the year. That figure is then divided by their gross (before-tax) income to arrive at a saving percentage. For my younger clients who are still working, the savings percentage is very important.

The process is slightly different for my retired clients. They are usually taking monthly withdrawals from their investment accounts. If they are over age 70½, they are withdrawing Required Minimum Distributions (RMDs) from their IRAs. It is easy to determine how much they are withdrawing on an annual basis. I divide their total withdrawals by the current balance in all their investment accounts combined, and that gives me a withdrawal percentage. A sustainable withdrawal percentage is discussed in Chapter Eleven.

You may already see the obvious shortcut to this strategy. If you are not yet retired, the most important factor is your savings rate. If you know you are saving at least 20 percent, and you are not withdrawing from your investment accounts, then this indicates that you are living within your means and you are using your income (*after* the 20 percent savings) to pay your monthly bills. In this case, it is not important that you closely monitor how you spend your money.

The above shortcut (monitoring the savings and withdrawals each year) requires monitoring all debt. For example, having a fixed-rate mortgage is fine. This is tracked in the retirement projections and the net worth statement that we update each year. Carrying credit card debt that is not paid off each month, increasing the balance on a home equity line of credit loan, or taking on car loans may indicate that a person is living beyond their means. This is not OK, and further discussions are needed. For instance, if a person is saving 20 percent of their income, but they are carrying credit card debt from month to month, then we will discuss paying off the credit card debt quickly, making sure the credit card bill is paid in full each month going forward, and then getting back on track with their savings.

Most Americans do not have the savings and investments that my clients have, and they are striving to become financially secure. For many people, the idea of saving 15 or 20 percent seems unreasonable, even impossible. So let's look at strategies that may help you increase your savings to the 15 or 20 percent level.

A Need or a Want?

Financial planner Carl Richards astutely asks, "What if financial happiness is not about getting more but about wanting less?" Following this rationale, we can categorize our expenses and purchases as either a "need" or a "want." Buying groceries for the week is a need, but going to a movie or out to dinner is a want. Paying the mortgage and the utility bill are both definitely a need. A want may be the deluxe cable TV package or the clothes you buy each month.

Becoming aware that much of your money is probably being spent on wants rather than needs is an important first step. Go through your past three months of credit card bills or bank statements and circle all of the expenses that would be considered a want. If you typically eat out four times a week, reduce it to twice a week. If there are lots of clothing purchases, commit to reducing those purchases. The idea is not to put yourself into a deprivation mode. The goal is to identify where you can reduce expenses, thereby freeing up money that can be saved.

Discuss the topic of needs versus wants with your family. Share with them that you want to increase your savings rate, which will benefit the entire family.

There are numerous ways to reduce your expenses. One piece of advice that was trendy in recent years was to eliminate the expensive cup of coffee you purchase on your way to work in the morning. Another strategy may be to take your lunch to work three days each week. You may decide to quit buying sodas when you eat out and ask for tap water instead. Or you may decide to use coupons for groceries and restaurants.

Another strategy for saving money is the "envelope" system. It seems old-fashioned, but it really works. When I was staying home

One Thing Leads to Another

It has probably become obvious that many of the strategies discussed in this book are intertwined. Simplifying your life (Chapter Five) encourages you to have less "stuff," which will reduce your spending on wants. Focusing on family, friends, and experiences (Chapter Four) reduces the temptation to be materialistic or to try to keep up with the Joneses. Taking steps to a healthier lifestyle will indirectly help you keep a healthy perspective on money.

with my daughters while they were very young, I began taking classes to earn my Certified Financial Planner™ certification. The courses were only offered as correspondence courses, and I wanted to go to the library to study a few times each week. That required hiring a babysitter. My husband was the sole breadwinner at that time, and our cash flow was limited. So I started an envelope system. At the beginning of each month, I put a fixed amount of cash into three different envelopes: one labeled "babysitter," one labeled "eating out and entertainment," and one labeled "groceries."

My priority was to make sure I had enough money each week for a babysitter, because getting out of the house to study was important to me. The first thing I discovered was that when I paid cash for groceries, I spent significantly less than if I bought groceries with a check or a credit card. This dynamic has been verified numerous times in research studies. A Dun & Bradstreet study found that people spend 12 to 18 percent more when using credit cards than when using cash. McDonald's restaurants found that the average transaction increased from $4.50 to $7 when customers used plastic instead of cash. Presumably, using a debit card is similar to a credit card. George Lowenstein, a professor of economics and psychology at Carnegie Mellon University said: "People experience what my research collaborators and I call a 'pain of paying' when they pay for purchases, and this pain is more intense with cash than with cards. Paying with cards is more carefree."

Using a credit card pushes the consequences to 30 days away, so it is much easier to overspend. Seeing the $50 leave your billfold when you buy groceries is immediate and real. Therefore, one easy way to reduce your spending is to use cash rather than credit cards.

With the envelope system, I also discovered that I was willing to be very frugal with groceries and with eating out and entertainment to ensure that my babysitting envelope had enough money to allow me to study two or three times each week. The envelope system helps you focus on your priorities, and using cash makes you aware of exactly how much money you are spending. It is not a surprise that credit card debt is an enormous problem for Americans.

An envelope system also works very well for saving for a vacation, and you can involve the entire family. Having the kids contribute a small amount of their allowance or birthday money to the vacation envelope is a great way to teach children the value of saving. This idea can be expanded by building a colorful paper link chain. Each time $20 is saved in the vacation envelope, a link is added to a paper chain. This can be hung from a door so everyone can see it each day, and the family will enjoy watching the chain get longer as the savings increases.

Saving money for Christmas or holiday gifts is also easier using the envelope system. This idea led to the old "Christmas Club" savings accounts that banks provided in the 1960s. My grandmother helped me open a Christmas Club account at a local bank (a money message I remember from my childhood). I would deposit $1 per week for January through November. This would total $48. The bank contributed $2, and I received $50 in early December for buying Christmas gifts for my family. At that time, $50 was an enormous amount of money, and saving $1 each week made it easy. Deciding to spend less on clothes in the coming year, eat at home more, and be more frugal when buying groceries can all add up to a significant savings.

Take a Giant Leap Forward

Identifying big-ticket items for potential savings will have a much greater impact on reducing your expenses and increasing your savings than eliminating an expensive cup of coffee each day. For example, do you live in a house that is more than you need? Often, it is not the monthly mortgage payment that is a problem. It is the never-ending expenses for maintenance, property taxes, and homeowner's insurance that become problematic. Downsizing to a smaller house or apartment may seem like an overwhelming task. However, it can lead to drastic reductions in your annual budget and much less stress. It can also free up time so you can explore new hobbies, spend more time with friends, or exercise more. A simpler lifestyle has wide-reaching benefits.

Do you need to replace your car during the next few years? Could you stretch your car's life to 10, 12, or 15 years? Do you need to take an expensive vacation this year, or would weekend or day trips nearby be just as fun? Short trips require less time to plan, and they are often less stressful. You could decide to take a major vacation every other year instead of every year. These big-ticket items can have a major impact on your savings. Instead of taking a $5,000 vacation this year, spend $1,000 on small trips and save the remaining $4,000. Multiple weekend trips also give you more to anticipate than one big vacation, which can increase your happiness.

Once you have identified some areas where you can reduce your expenses, set up an automatic saving system to "scoop" that money into your savings or investment account at the beginning of each month. Within a few months, you will not notice that you have reduced your spending, and you can celebrate that you have increased your savings rate.

If you would like to track your spending using a spending plan form, one is provided at *www.joyoffinancialsecurity.com*.

Insurance: Cover Your Assets

Having adequate insurance is very important, but the type and amount should be customized to fit your situation. The general rule with insurance is that you want coverage for losses that would be catastrophic. If your home were to burn down, that would be catastrophic, and you should cover that risk with insurance. Likewise, you need adequate auto insurance to cover the risk of an accident that results in severe injuries or property damage. A high deductible (at least $500 or $1,000) is generally recommended, because you do not want to file a claim when a rock cracks your car windshield. The high deductible means you are "self-insuring" for small losses.

Most people need homeowner's insurance, auto insurance, and a separate umbrella liability policy that covers at least one or two times their net worth. Often, a rider on your homeowner's policy is wise to provide specific coverage for jewelry, artwork, computers, and other valuable items. Whether you need flood insurance or earthquake insurance is a personal decision and is impacted by where you live. When selecting an insurance agent for your property and casualty insurance, you should interview two or three agents and request the same quotes from each of them. This will allow you to compare the quotes and help you determine which agent and insurance firm you prefer. National firms without a local presence have become very popular, but I prefer working with a local agent. I also prefer to have all my "property and casualty" policies (the types of insurance listed above) with one agent.

Parents with young children should have a significant amount of term life insurance. This is an area where a local agent is not necessary, and it is easy to compare quotes on the internet. I recommend buying a term policy that is *fixed* for 20 years or longer if possible (this means the policy will last for 20 years and the premiums will not change during that time). You can usually reduce the coverage if you decide you have too much life insurance, and you can always cancel the policy if you decide you no longer need it. It is important that you select an insurance company with a high rating.

I prefer that clients have long-term care insurance, but in many cases, they cannot qualify for it for health reasons or they cannot afford it. The premiums have increased substantially in recent years, so it is quite expensive. If someone is extremely wealthy, then long-term care insurance may not be needed. The variables that need to be reviewed are unique to each person, and buying (or not buying) long-term care insurance needs to be a personal decision.

I recommend that my clients who are in high-paying professions buy a personal disability policy. These often have better terms (for paying out benefits in the case of a disability) than the group policies offered by most large companies, and the policies are "portable" (meaning you can take them with them with you if you leave a company, or even if you decide to retire early).

Insurance is an extremely important purchase, and I recommend that you devote time and energy to finding an insurance agent who will work closely with you.

Good Debt vs. Bad Debt

This is a concept that may seem counter-intuitive. Some may say all debt is bad debt, but I disagree. Let's start with good debt.

Good debt is associated with something that has a very long benefit period. If you have a fixed-rate mortgage on your house, that is good debt. You can enjoy your home, and you can typically take a tax deduction for the mortgage interest payments if you itemize when you file your taxes. I do not recommend paying cash for a house (and not having a mortgage), because keeping your money invested and using the bank's money for leverage is wise.

The Meaning of Leverage

Leverage involves buying assets with borrowed money. For homeowners, it includes taking out a mortgage on your home rather than paying cash for the full amount. This generally works very well, as long as you can make the monthly payments and the home does not lose value. For companies, using leverage may involve using a small amount of their own money to make an investment of much larger value. Companies use derivatives (such as swaps, futures/forwards, and options) in their use of leverage. If the underlying instrument doesn't perform as expected, leverage magnifies the risk.

This was apparent with Lehman Brothers, which was reportedly leveraged 35-to-1 leading up to the 2008 financial crisis. In other words, Lehman Brothers was in debt for 35 times the amount of its capital. Other financial firms were reportedly leveraged at roughly 33-to-1. A *New York Times* article reported that "under 33-to-1 leverage, a mere 3 percent decline in asset values wipes out a company." The collateralized debt obligations (bundles of high-risk mortgages, also called CDOs) owned by Lehman Brothers declined quickly in value as home owners started defaulting on their loans and as it became obvious that the mortgages in the CDOs were very poor quality. The CDOs declined more than 3 percent, and Lehman Brothers was suddenly insolvent due to their excessive leverage and the declining value of the underlying assets. This led to their bankruptcy on September 15, 2008. Several other large banks and brokerage firms were dangerously close to a similar fate.

It is not necessary to understand the nuances of leverage, as long as you understand this: in small doses, leverage can work well. It can lead to higher profits when the underlying assets rise in value. In large doses, and when the underlying assets fall in value, it can be catastrophic.

My comments below regarding using leverage wisely are based on living within your means. This includes buying a home (if you choose) that is affordable for your current financial situation.

Let's discuss how leverage can be used wisely. Banks and mortgage companies lend money for buying houses. You can typically take out a 15- or 30-year mortgage, although 10- and 20-year mortgages are also available. The most popular is still the 30-year, fixed-rate mortgage, although my preference is typically a 15-year loan.

I do not recommend variable-rate loans (often called *floating* loans or ARMs (adjustable rate mortgages). Typically, I recommend you put between 20 to 30 percent of the value of the house down so the mortgage will be for 70 to 80 percent of the value of the house.

There are tremendous benefits to taking out a mortgage rather than paying cash for a house. Consider the following example.

Assume you buy a $300,000 house and your deposit is 20 percent ($60,000). Your mortgage balance is $240,000. Let's assume your house increases in value from $300,000 to $400,000 over five years—the house has appreciated 33 percent ($100,000 ÷ $300,000).

However, the amount of your investment (your down payment) was only $60,000. Your $60,000 investment has now increased in value to $160,000. Why? Your mortgage balance is still $240,000 (or slightly less), and the increase in value is applied to what you actually invested in the house (your down payment). For the sake of simplicity, I am ignoring the monthly payments you have been making for the past five years. Obviously, the monthly payments have been reducing your mortgage balance slightly, although during the first few years of a loan the majority of your payment is going to pay the interest. The mortgage interest is tax deductible if you itemize on your tax return and your income is not so high that you lose some of the itemized deductions. The increase in your investment (which is also called the "equity" in your home) is 166 percent (from $60,000 to $160,000).

Let's look at the alternative. You buy the same $300,000 house, but you pay $300,000 in cash and you do not take out a mortgage. The house increases in value over five years to $400,000. Your investment (the $300,000 you paid) has increased by $100,000, which is a 33 percent return over the same five years.

In the above example, using the bank's money as leverage resulted in a return on investment of 166 percent (for taking out a mortgage for 80 percent of the purchase price) versus 33 percent for paying cash for the house. Using the bank's money as leverage definitely has financial benefits. Another factor in having a mortgage is that if the loan is written with a "no prepayment penalty," you can pay off the mortgage at any time by using investment assets.

It is important to recognize, however, that leverage will increase the risk if housing prices decline drastically. If the $300,000 house you purchased falls in value to $200,000, you have lost your $60,000 down payment and your $240,000 mortgage is "underwater" (real estate lingo for "below value") by $40,000.

When homebuyers contemplate whether to pay cash for a house or take out a mortgage, some complain that they don't want to pay the interest rate on the mortgage. In their view, paying cash is a better option because it avoids the interest on the monthly mortgage payment. I would argue that if you can earn more (on average, on an annual basis) by keeping your money invested than the stated interest rate minus the tax deduction for the interest, then you would be better off keeping your money invested. Again, let's use an example. Assume a couple buys a house, and they take out a 15-year mortgage at 4 percent. Assume they both work, and they are in the 28 percent marginal tax bracket for federal taxes and the 5 percent bracket for state taxes. Their combined (federal and state) marginal tax rate is 33 percent. If they itemize on their tax return, they can likely deduct the interest on the mortgage payments. To calculate the "net," or after-tax mortgage interest rate, you would take the 4 percent mortgage rate and multiply it by 0.67

(that is, 1 – 33 percent). This causes the 4 percent rate to decline (after taxes) to 2.68 percent. Now, the question is whether the couple can earn more than 2.68 percent after tax (on average, on an annual basis) by keeping their money invested. For my clients, the answer is almost always yes.

Another benefit of having a fixed mortgage is that your mortgage payment does not increase and it is not impacted by inflation. A fixed-rate mortgage is considered to be a hedge against inflation. If inflation increases above 10 percent as it did several years between 1974 and 1981, having a low fixed-rate mortgage becomes a valuable asset.

What else is considered to be good debt? A student loan can be good debt. Generally, getting a college education will increase your wage-earning ability for the rest of your working years, so the college education has a very long benefit period. Of course, you want the interest rate to be as low as possible, and you don't want to build up too much debt. Depending on income limitations, the interest paid on student loans may be tax-deductible. Getting financial aid, scholarships, or working a part-time job during college can all help minimize the amount of loans required.

What is bad debt? Credit card debt (that is not paid in full each month) is bad debt. You may have used your credit card to pay for a nice dinner, clothing, or a new electronic gadget. None of those items have a long benefit period. A common problem is buying Christmas or holiday gifts on a credit card. In January, the credit card bill arrives, and the experience of the holidays and gift-giving is just a memory. Yet it may take several months to pay off the purchases from December.

A car loan is typically considered to be bad debt. This is because you should only spend as much on a car as you can afford to pay in cash; therefore, taking out a loan is usually not recommended. There are some exceptions, such as the deals in recent years when car loans are available with a low interest rate of 1 or 2 percent. In this case, make sure the car loan payments fit easily into your monthly budget. However, the rule still stands that you should only spend as much on a car as you can afford to pay in cash. If you do not have much cash, then a used car is a good choice, as well as keeping your car for as long as possible before replacing it. Another argument against taking out a car loan is that a new car loses approximately 25 percent of its value as soon as you drive it off the car lot. Unlike a home or a college education that provide long-term benefits (that often appreciate over time), a car does not hold its value well.

Should You Own or Rent a House?

I will never forget a question that a man asked me when he and his wife were interviewing me as their potential financial advisor many years ago. He asked, "Are you going to *make* us buy a house?" Both spouses had very successful academic careers on the East Coast, and they had just recently retired in Albuquerque. I was stunned by the question for several reasons. First, I never *make* my clients do anything. I provide recommendations, but the decisions are all theirs. In addition, I would never recommend that someone buy a house if they preferred not to. I answered that I certainly would not make them buy a house and that they should only consider buying a house if it fits in their lifestyle and if they *want* to buy a house. From a financial standpoint, it is certainly not necessary that anyone own a house.

This couple became a client in 2003, and the wife is still a client today. (Sadly, the husband died a few years ago.) They chose to rent an apartment rather than buy a house, and that was a very wise decision for them. They did not want the responsibilities that come with owning a home. There are many other reasons to not buy a home. If you are not planning on living in a home for over five years, then I recommend you rent. Often, renting a house is a good choice, and landlords are eager to find a good tenant who will stay for several years.

As a former writer at the *Wall Street Journal*, Jonathan Clements analyzed the expenses involved in owning the home he purchased in 1992 for $165,000. He estimated the value in 2005 to be $500,000, which would be roughly a 200 percent gain. On first glance, this appears to be a very successful investment. However, he calculated he spent $130,000 for upgrades and $147,000 on property taxes and mortgage interest (after subtracting the tax deductions he received). He did not include any routine maintenance, and he noted that if he were to sell the house, he would owe real estate commissions on the $500,000. All in all, he concluded that his house appreciated very little over the 13 years. However, there were two benefits that he pointed out. One is that he has thoroughly enjoyed living in the home, and the second is that if someone is making mortgage payments (as opposed to paying rent), the mortgage payments eventually end.

Family Issues

Discuss Finances with Your Spouse or Partner

It is essential that spouses (or partners) discuss their finances. Secrets do not work when it comes to money. For most of my clients, both spouses or partners attend every meeting together. However, sometimes one spouse is more involved in managing the finances for the family than the other.

I have had several clients over the years who have hired me to manage their finances because the husband was comfortable managing the finances and the wife was not. In these cases, the husband wanted the wife to have someone she could trust if anything happened to him. I also have some clients where the wife manages the money and the husband is not involved. It varies for each family. However, if one spouse is in charge of the finances for the family, I often request that both spouses attend at least one meeting a year together. During that meeting, we discuss financial goals and retirement projections.

If you and your spouse do not routinely discuss financial issues, plan a time when you will discuss them. Oftentimes, having dinner together (without the kids) provides a good opportunity to focus on financial matters and listen to each other's viewpoint. The collaboration is important when making decisions pertaining to money. Plan to discuss financial matters at least once a month, and more often if necessary. Discuss any major purchases or changes that will impact your finances. Discuss setting up an automatic savings plan and establishing goals to improve your finances.

Teach Your Kids by Example

All parents hope their children will grow up to become responsible adults. What is a responsible adult? No doubt there are an unlimited number of definitions, but a few may include being a productive member of society, a giving person, a creative person, and a happy person. How do we assist our children in developing the desired traits? There are many ways we teach our children. The best way is to set a good example for your kids. They will follow your actions much more than your words.

Earlier in Chapter Seven we discussed saving at least 15 percent of your income and preferably 20 percent. This same advice pertains to kids, and they have the added benefit that they are starting early. This simple rule should be followed starting with a child's allowance and should continue through teenage jobs, adulthood, and even retirement. This will ensure that a person will never run out of money. If your kids see that you have a savings program (through your employer's retirement plan, through an automatic investing plan, for their college savings plan, or just by talking about how much money you save each month or each year), they will see that you are responsible with your money.

Teach your children money skills at a very young age. Children as young as age six can understand the concepts that money buys things, saving now allows me to buy bigger things later, and money does not grow on trees. Some parents use a jar system for their children's allowance. For example, if you give your child an allowance of $5 a week, you could require that the child put $2 into a jar labeled "Spending," $2 into a jar labeled "Savings," and $1 into a jar labeled "Charity." The child can use the money in the spending jar on things that provide immediate gratification (candy, toys, etc.). The savings jar is kept for big-ticket items, such as a bicycle, upcoming school trips, or extra-special clothing or sneakers the parent doesn't feel are necessary. The money in the charity jar is given to any charity the child chooses.

The method selected for determining the amount of an allowance and the rules for how it can be spent are issues the parents must determine. Children are excited about receiving an allowance, and when started at a young age, they will accept the rules (for saving, charity, etc.). Parents will be teaching their children the value of saving as well as the value of helping people who are less fortunate. This also encourages rich family discussions about having a healthy attitude about money.

Another strategy that can be used with the jar system involves the parent "matching" whatever is in the savings jar. With this approach, the savings jar is kept for major expenses in the future, such as college or paying for a high school trip. When the amount in the savings jar reaches $25, the parent matches the $25 and deposits $50 into a savings or investment account for the child. The matching feature is similar to traditional 401(k) plans (or 403(b), Roth 401(k), or Roth 403(b) plans) where the employer matches a portion of the employee contribution. This strategy provides a further incentive for the child to save for long-term goals, because the child will quickly realize that the money he or she saves will be matched by the parent. It also provides an opportunity to introduce the concepts of interest, growth, and compounding when an investment or savings account is used.

Children are extremely vulnerable to bad spending habits when they leave for college. At that point, banks and credit card companies make it enticingly easy for students to run up a large credit card balance and suddenly be in debt. It is important to let your child make mistakes at a young age, thereby preventing more expensive mistakes later. If a 14-year-old child uses his money to buy a $150 pair of name-brand sneakers and then realizes the $50 pair would have saved him $100, this is a valuable lesson. It is far less expensive than a college freshman who runs up credit card debt of $8,000!

Teach your children that money is a tool. Money can buy nice things, such as a home, a lifestyle, a college education, a vacation, or an early retirement. It certainly does not buy happiness, and it should be managed wisely. This is a valuable lesson to teach your child or teenager. Include your children in discussions about money. If you, as a parent, want to improve your family's financial security (by saving more, paying off the credit card balances, etc.), include the children in these discussions. This is a classic example of practicing what you preach, and everyone will benefit!

Estate Planning

Current Legal Documents

It is important that you have current legal documents that convey your wishes. Some financial advisors recommend that everyone have a revocable living trust, but I disagree. A simple will may be sufficient, and there is no reason to make your legal documents more complicated than necessary.

There are several variables that may lead you to decide that you need a revocable living trust. These include owning real estate in more than one state, having children from a prior marriage, having a large estate, or wanting to stipulate that your assets be distributed to your beneficiaries over many years rather than all at once upon your death. I recommend hiring an estate attorney who will discuss your wishes with you and give you advice regarding different legal strategies.

At the very least, you need a will, a Power of Attorney document for finances, and a Power of Attorney for health care. The will is the document where you state who will receive your assets upon your death. You will be required to name an executor to distribute your assets according to your wishes as stated in the will. If you have young children, it is important that you name someone in your will to serve as a guardian for them until they become adults.

A will typically goes through a probate process, which is a legal proceeding designed to take inventory, provide appraisals of your property, pay outstanding debts, and then distribute your assets. Some states are known for very lengthy and expensive probate processes. If you live in one of those states, then having a revocable living trust (which avoids probate), may be wise. New Mexico (where I live) is known for an efficient, inexpensive probate process, which is why a revocable living trust is often not needed.

If you have a revocable living trust prepared, it is typically recommended that you re-title your assets into the name of the trust. You should insist that your attorney help you with this for any real estate, and a financial advisor can help by providing the necessary forms to re-title your investment accounts. IRAs and retirement plans do not go into a trust, so they do not need to be re-titled.

You need to review your beneficiaries on retirement plans, annuities, and life insurance products. The beneficiaries you have named on these products will supercede your will. In other words, the beneficiaries will be honored, even if they conflict with the wishes conveyed in your will. You must understand that the beneficiaries you have named will inherit the asset, so it is essential that your beneficiaries are in alignment with your will. For example, it is common that someone goes to a tremendous effort to have a will prepared that shows who they want to inherit their assets.

But they do not realize that their large IRA account or their work retirement plan will *not* be distributed according to the will.

When hiring an estate attorney, I recommend you interview two or three, just as you would if you were selecting a financial advisor. You want to select an attorney who will be available to you whenever you need legal guidance. Estate planning laws vary by state, and everyone's situation is unique. For example, in some states it may be recommended that real estate not be placed in a trust, in some instances IRAs and 401(k)s may be left to a trust (rather than naming a person as a beneficiary), and there are ways to avoid the probate process without having a revocable living trust.

Decisions about selecting a guardian for young children or an individual or corporate executor or trustee are very important decisions. Decisions regarding naming a person as a Power of Attorney to manage your finances are also very important, especially in terms of whether the person has the authority to act on your behalf immediately, or upon your incapacity. For all of these reasons, I do not recommend that people prepare their own legal documents. Instead, I recommend that you seek the advice of a competent estate attorney.

An Estate Planning Binder

It is very important to have your papers in order so that members of your family or an executor can more easily sort through everything in case of your disability or death. At *www.joyoffinancialsecurity.com*, you will find a template that I created for my clients to keep all your pertinent financial information in one place.

The document encourages you to fill in the following information:

- Your advisors: (financial advisor, accountant, attorney, and insurance agent, as well as your employer (regarding pensions and benefits)

- Your investment and bank accounts, including where they are located

- A list of money that flows into and out of your checking account each month (such as a Social Security or pension check), bills that are paid automatically from your credit card, or bills that are set up online for automatic bill pay

- Doctors and current medications

- The locations where you store important documents. This includes titles to your home, car, and other real estate; the location of jewelry or valuables; and documents, such as life insurance policies and tax returns. If you have a safety deposit box, who has a key? If you have a home safe, who has the combination or key?

- Passwords to access your computer and commonly-used websites so a family member may access information if you become disabled or in the event of an unexpected death. If you are concerned about creating a paper copy of your passwords, you can encrypt the list or tell family members how to access them on your computer. It is common to keep family photos and contacts on a computer or social media sites, and these are items that family members will want to be able to access.

The document can be placed in a three-ring binder labeled "Estate Planning." Next, insert a current net worth statement, a set of your legal documents, and a recent statement for each investment and bank account. Include information about life insurance policies, disability policies, and homeowner's, auto, and umbrella insurance policies. If you have made funeral plans, those documents should be included, too. If you have written an obituary or you have wishes regarding a memorial service or funeral, include them in your binder.

A Letter of Instruction

Often, at the back of a will, an estate attorney will include a blank template that is titled "Letter of Instruction." Most people never fill it out, and they are probably unaware of the document. Or maybe they are avoiding the task because it involves thinking about death. A letter of instruction conveys your wishes for who should receive your personal items. It is especially important for family heirlooms, jewelry, artwork, or furniture that is not specified in your will.

Many years ago, the University of Minnesota created a program called "Grandma's Yellow Pie Plate." It discussed that the item that your children or grandchildren would treasure most after you die is probably not expensive. It may not be the set of china or crystal glassware that you have always loved. It may be a yellow pie plate that holds warm memories for your children or grandchildren. It may be a skillet used for frying chicken or a cookie jar that held homemade cookies.

There are several ways to help your children or grandchildren receive the personal items that they value most. One way is to invite your children or grandchildren into your home and ask them what they would like to have after you're gone. Another way is to have them come into your home (one at a time) while you are away, and ask them to create a list of the items they would like to receive, ranked in order.

Once your children, grandchildren, or friends have created their lists, compare them and the way items are ranked. It is possible that three children may have all selected the same item, but perhaps it was listed first on the list by only one child. You can assign the items based on the rankings. Once you have decided who will receive your personal items, you can create the letter.

Keeping a sense of humor during this process will keep it from becoming depressing and difficult. We all know we are going to die one day, so addressing it honestly is a healthy approach. Sharing with your family that you want them to receive personal items they enjoy is a generous gesture, and it encourages rich family experiences.

Add your completed letter of instruction to your estate planning binder.

Invest in Yourself

- Go through the list at the beginning of this chapter and mark the items you would like to work on.

- Think about the concept of human capital. Have you chosen a career path you enjoy and that pays you what you want to earn? If you would like to change careers, do you need more education? Who could you contact for guidance in your chosen field?

- Have you calculated your net worth? If you have not, go back to Figure 7.1 and create a net worth statement. This is an incredibly important step in taking control of your finances.

- How much are you saving as a percentage of your income? If you do not know, go back to Figure 7.2 and calculate your savings percentage. Think about ways you increase your savings percentage.

- Are there certain areas where you overspend? Can you reduce your spending in those areas so you can increase your savings percentage?

- Do you have adequate insurance to cover unexpected risks? Do you need to make an appointment with one or more insurance agents to make certain you have sufficient insurance?

- Do you have any bad debt, such as credit card bills, that are not paid off in full each month? Are you living within your means?

- Do you discuss your finances with your family? Create a healthy attitude toward money within your household. If necessary, set up a time to discuss financial topics with your spouse or partner.

- Do you have current estate planning documents? If not, meet with an estate attorney to have documents drafted that match your wishes.

CHAPTER
EIGHT

■ ■ ■ ■ ■

Tax Strategies

Dear IRS,
I am writing to you to cancel my subscription.
Please remove my name from your mailing list.
— SNOOPY (CHARLES M. SCHULZ)

 on't let the tax tail wag the investment dog" is a quirky saying that has been a bastion for financial advisors for many years. It means to not let tax issues override smart investment decisions. However, with recent tax changes, smart tax planning is essential for smart investing.

Wise Tax Planning

Effective January 1, 2013, numerous tax changes went into effect that impact high-income earners. These included higher marginal tax rates, higher tax rates for capital gains and qualified dividends, new taxes for high-income earners, and a phase-out of personal exemptions and deductions. Most people anticipate more tax increases in the future.

Let's review tax rates over the past 70 years. In 1944, the top federal tax rate was over 90 percent. It remained at approximately 90 percent until 1963. It was reduced to 70 percent in 1965, where it remained until the early 1980s. Since that time it has declined significantly, with the top marginal tax rate capped at 35 percent between 2003 and 2012. Effective January 1, 2013, the top marginal federal tax rate rose to 39.6 percent.

Compared with the past 70 years, 39.6 percent seems like a reasonable tax rate. However, there are many other forms of taxes, and they can add up to a high number. For example, most states have state income taxes. The states that do not charge a state income tax tend to charge higher property taxes or gross receipts (sales) taxes to compensate. Some cities also have a separate income tax. Working people pay a Social Security tax and a Medicare tax. As consumers, we pay gross receipts taxes (or sales taxes) when we buy items, and we pay property taxes for the real estate we own. There are often additional taxes, such as when we buy a car, renew a driver's license, purchase alcohol or cigarettes, or pay for travel-related expenses, such as airlines, hotels, and rental cars.

In many cases, taxes cannot be avoided. I tell my clients we will work to maximize the after-tax money. For instance, if we sell a mutual fund that has increased in value in a taxable account, we know we must pay a capital gains tax on the gain. We accept that fact and work to grow the after-tax proceeds.

However, in many instances, wise tax planning can *save* a significant amount in taxes, leaving more money for your family and your financial security. Federal District Court Judge Learned Hand stated the following in 1934:

Anyone may arrange his affairs so that his taxes shall be as low as possible; he is not bound to choose that pattern which best pays the treasury. There is not even a patriotic duty to increase one's taxes. Over and over again the Courts have said that there is nothing sinister in so arranging affairs as to keep taxes as low as possible. Everyone does it, rich and poor alike and all do right, for nobody owes any public duty to pay more than the law demands.

Clearly, minimizing your taxes is a wise strategy.

Three Tax "Buckets"

The key with tax planning is to be proactive. The purpose of having three different tax buckets is to minimize taxes now or in the future, and to provide flexibility when taking withdrawals. This strategy is also called *tax diversification*. Figure 8.1 shows a diagram of the three tax buckets.

FIGURE 8.1 THREE TAX BUCKETS

Tax Deferred	Taxable	Tax Free
IRAs, 401(k)s, 403(b)s	Investment Accounts Bank Accounts	Roth IRAs Roth 401(k)s
Bucket #1	**Bucket #2**	**Bucket #3**

Bucket #1

This bucket is for tax-deferred assets, such as retirement accounts like traditional IRAs, 401(k)s, or 403(b)s. Typically, the money you invest in a traditional retirement account is deducted from your income in the year of the contribution. Taxes are not due until the money is withdrawn, and whatever amount is withdrawn is considered to be taxable income for that tax year. IRAs have been available since 1974, and these accounts have become the most common way to save for retirement.

Saving and investing *only* in bucket #1 was a wise strategy in the past for those who expected their tax rate to decline during retirement. Bucket #1 takes advantage of the tax deferral benefits of traditional retirement plans, so the tax rate during retirement is critical to this strategy working well. For many years, folks were encouraged to invest in a tax-deferred account (such as a 401[k] or a traditional IRA) rather than in a taxable account.

It is common for investors nearing retirement to have a large traditional IRA, but very little money in a taxable account. This could be termed "IRA rich, but cash poor." However, many people no longer expect their tax rate to decline significantly during retirement, which is why having multiple tax buckets has become important.

Bucket #2

This bucket is for taxable accounts. Many people do not realize that saving and investing in a taxable account is always wise. The gains on this money are not tax-deferred, but investors with taxable accounts have benefitted for many years from the 15 percent preferential tax rate on capital gains and qualified dividends. This was raised to 20 percent effective January 1, 2013, but only for individuals and couples with high incomes. Most investors will still pay the 15 percent tax rate for capital gains and qualified dividends. (Persons in the 15 percent or lower marginal tax bracket do not pay capital gains taxes). Even if you must pay 20 percent, it is still a preferential tax rate when compared with higher marginal income tax brackets.

Bank accounts are taxable accounts, but I always encourage people to have a taxable investment account as well. I recommend building an emergency fund (in a taxable investment account or bank account) that will cover up to six months of living expenses. Once this emergency fund is established, any extra money (such as savings at the beginning of each month, a tax refund, or a bonus) should be deposited into your taxable investment account.

Bucket #3

This bucket contains tax-free accounts, such as a Roth IRA, Roth 401(k), or Roth 403(b). This is the newest bucket because Roth IRAs only became available to investors in 1998, with Roth 401(k)s and Roth 403(b)s becoming available during the past few years. Money invested in these accounts is not deducted from income in the year of the contribution, so there are no tax benefits on the front end. However, the tremendous benefit of a Roth IRA is that the contributions and the gains will not be taxed going forward. For this reason, a Roth IRA trumps a traditional IRA in my view.

For several years after Roth IRAs were introduced, some investors were concerned that the tax-free provision of the Roth would be eliminated and gains on Roth IRAs would become taxable in the future. This concern seems to have been put to rest during the past 15 years. More information about the benefits of Roth IRAs is provided later in this chapter.

Benefits of Having Multiple Tax Buckets

The three tax buckets provide you with choices regarding where to withdraw money during retirement, while also providing significant tax benefits and savings:

- It is common for those nearing retirement to have large IRAs but very small taxable accounts and no Roth IRA. One reason having all your investments in an IRA is *not* recommended is because taking IRA withdrawals during retirement (to pay your annual living expenses) can place you in a higher tax bracket than if you took the withdrawals from a taxable account. It can also cause Social Security benefits to be taxed at a higher rate and Medicare premiums to increase.

    Let's assume you estimate you will need $60,000 per year for living expenses during retirement, and your Social Security benefits total $20,000 per year. If all of your money is in an IRA, you may need to withdraw as much as $55,000 each year in order to have $40,000 remaining after taxes for your living expenses. (This is because withdrawals from an IRA are taxed as income). Conversely, let's assume you have a large taxable account or a large Roth IRA, and you are not yet age 70½. You could withdraw the $40,000 you need for cash flow from your taxable account or your Roth IRA. This would result in much lower taxes because the money withdrawn from a taxable account or a Roth IRA is not taxed as income. This could also result in your Social Security benefits being taxed at 15 percent rather than 50 or 85 percent. Even if you withdraw a portion of the $40,000 from your IRA and a portion from your taxable account or Roth IRA, you would still owe less in taxes because only the IRA withdrawal is categorized as taxable income.

- In addition to reducing taxes by withdrawing from tax buckets #2 and #3, three tax buckets can also allow you to delay starting Social Security benefits, thereby letting the benefit accrue until a later date. Let's assume you retire at age 62 and your full retirement age (for Social Security benefits) is age 66. Full retirement age varies according to your birth date, but currently ranges from 65 to 67. If you have a significant taxable account (bucket #2), you can withdraw from that bucket between years 62 and 66 for living expenses and delay drawing Social Security benefits until age 66 or later. Delaying Social Security benefits until age 66 will result in the monthly benefit increasing by approximately 33 percent (as compared to the amount you would receive at age 62). By following this strategy, you may be in a very low income tax bracket between ages 62 and 66, which provides an opportunity to convert a portion of the traditional IRA to the Roth IRA each year.

- Converting a significant amount of a traditional IRA to a Roth IRA can reduce required withdrawals from the traditional IRA at age 70½. Roth IRAs do not have required distributions, so if the withdrawals are not needed for living expenses, then the money can remain invested in the Roth IRA, growing tax-free for many years.

More Tax Strategies

Having your money in three different tax buckets is a valuable tax strategy. Keeping your investments tax-efficient can save a significant amount of money. However, the strategies need to be customized to match each person's situation. Below is a list of some common tax strategies. I recommend you work with your tax advisor or financial advisor to determine which strategies will work best for you.

- Keep the assets within your investment accounts tax-efficient. With the tax changes beginning January 1, 2013, most investors will continue paying a preferential 15 percent federal tax rate on capital gains and qualified dividends. For this reason, holding stocks or equity mutual funds that provide qualified dividends in a taxable account is wise. Select equity investments for a taxable account that tend to be tax-efficient. Most index funds are tax-efficient. Some actively managed funds are also tax-efficient, but avoid equity mutual funds with a high turnover ratio. (Turnover relates to how often the fund manager buys and sells stocks within the mutual fund. An annual turnover ratio can range from zero to several hundred percent.)

- Try to avoid placing equity mutual funds that have a very high *unrealized* capital gain in a taxable account. This happens when a fund has had strong performance in recent years, but the fund managers have not sold their big winners and have not yet triggered the capital gains. This can happen with any fund, but is most prevalent in actively managed funds. Morningstar provides the unrealized capital gain exposure for mutual funds on their website at www.morningstar.com under the "tax" tab. When possible, these equity mutual funds should be placed in an IRA or a Roth IRA. (Because IRAs are tax-deferred and Roth IRAs are tax-free, capital gains taxes are irrelevant.)

- If you are in a high tax bracket, you may want to consider using municipal bonds (muni bonds) for the fixed-income portion of your portfolio in a taxable investment account. This could be accomplished with individual muni bonds or muni bond mutual funds. The muni bond interest will not be subject to federal taxes. When deciding what type of bonds to use in your taxable investment accounts, you should always compare the *after-tax* bond yield. In some cases a taxable bond may have a higher after-tax yield than a muni bond.

- Some advisors recommend using a strategy called *asset location*, which requires putting investments in certain asset classes in taxable accounts and investments in other asset classes in IRAs. In recent years they have typically advised putting the equity investments in taxable accounts and the fixed-income investments in IRAs. The rationale is that the equity mutual funds will distribute dividends and capital gains, which are taxed at 15 percent for most investors, and the bonds (in the IRA) will distribute interest. The interest would be taxed as regular income if it were present in a taxable account, but it is not taxed in an IRA. (Capital gains, dividends, and interest are not taxed in an IRA on an annual basis. Taxes are triggered when a distribution is taken from the IRA, and then the entire distribution is categorized as taxable income.)

    Financial planner Michael Kitces has studied asset location strategies, and he has shown that following the typical advice (noted above) may *not* maximize after-tax returns. Many variables come into play, including tax efficiency, return assumptions, and complications resulting from other asset classes. In March 2013 he recommended that it may *not* be wise to place most bonds in tax-deferred accounts.

There is another flaw in using an asset location strategy, and it involves the emotional reactions we all have as investors. If the stock market has a sudden decline as it did in late 2008 and early 2009, investors will be traumatized to see their taxable account (which would contain mostly equities if this strategy were followed) drop by roughly 50 percent. Telling them that their IRA did not nosedive (because it is in bonds) would not provide much consolation. Other tax planning strategies provide significant benefits without exposing investors to undue stress.

- Avoid excessive trading in your account. When selling an asset in a taxable account, be cognizant of the cost basis and the capital gain or loss that will be triggered by the sale. Manage your gains and losses (your winners and losers) by capturing a loss in an asset that has declined in value and using that loss to offset gains from selling other assets. This is called *tax-loss harvesting*. When selling an asset with a gain, hold the asset for at least one year so it will be categorized as a *long-term* capital gain, making it eligible for the preferential capital gains tax rate. Also, minimize transaction fees from trading.

- Consider making charitable contributions using appreciated securities rather than cash. This eliminates the capital gain taxes on the asset that is donated to charity.

- When rebalancing or taking withdrawals from a taxable account, be aware of the tax consequences of selling different assets.

With the tax changes effective January 1, 2013, attempting to keep your adjusted gross income from going above certain thresholds is wise. The tax changes have a compound effect on high income earners. In accounting parlance, the taxes are "stacked," meaning one tax increase can trigger another. For example, the new taxes for high income earners can push you over an adjusted gross income threshold so you start losing exemptions and deductions. That will cause your taxable income to increase, and force you into a higher tax bracket. If you know you are vulnerable to exceeding the thresholds that trigger higher taxes, you may want to work with your tax advisor or financial planner to strive to minimize your taxes.

Let's go back to the saying "Don't let the tax tail wag the investment dog." Paul Sullivan wrote an article for the *New York Times* about *unwise* investment decisions to avoid or defer taxes. One common example is not selling individual stocks simply to avoid paying the capital gains tax. If the stock represents a concentrated position in your portfolio (concentrated is typically defined as over 10 percent but may be only 5 percent), then a portion should be sold to reduce the risk that the share price may plummet. Not selling the stock simply to avoid paying the capital gains tax can be a very unwise decision. Sullivan's article also talks about deferred compensation plans, which are often made available to corporate executives. Unlike money contributed to a 401(k) plan—which is protected if a company goes bankrupt—deferred compensation plans do not have the same protection. The money in deferred compensation plans becomes subject to creditors, meaning the individual investor may not receive the money or may only receive a portion of it. Other examples of tax avoidance or tax deferral investments that may be unwise include investments in green energy, limited partnerships, section 1031 real estate exchanges, and even annuities. The bottom line: *Sometimes it is better to pay your taxes and focus on maximizing the after-tax money.*

The Extraordinary Roth IRA

The Roth IRA is one of the greatest gifts Congress has given investors over the past 20 years, and it has multiple features and benefits. I strongly encourage you to take advantage of this very versatile investment tool.

The concept of the Roth IRA was proposed by Senator William Roth in 1997 and became available to investors beginning in 1998. The Roth IRA was originally intended as a retirement savings tool, in which the contributions and growth of the assets within a Roth IRA are *tax-free* when withdrawn, rather than *tax-deferred* as in a traditional IRA. The primary purpose continues to be for retirement, but many other benefits have become apparent during the past 15 years. The Roth IRA is a magnificent estate planning tool because beneficiaries receive the assets income-tax free, and it works great as a first investment account for teenagers and young adults.

Building a Roth IRA Tax Bucket

There are three primary ways to build a Roth tax bucket:

1. Contribute to a Roth 401(k) or Roth 403(b) through your employer.

2. Convert a traditional IRA to a Roth IRA or a traditional 401(k) or 403(b) to a Roth 401(k) or Roth 403(b). (This requires paying taxes on the amount converted in the year of the conversion.)

3. Open a Roth IRA account and make annual contributions.

Unfortunately, there are income limitations that prevent some investors from contributing directly to a Roth IRA. The income limitations for 2013 start at $178,000 for a married couple and $112,000 for a single person. (These income limitations apply to modified adjusted gross income. See the IRS website at www.irs.gov for a definition of modified AGI). These income limitations change slightly from year-to-year, and current figures can be accessed from the IRS website. Fortunately, contributing to a Roth 401(k) or Roth 403(b) through your employer does not have income limitations, and converting a traditional IRA to a Roth IRA or a traditional 401(k) or 403(b) to a Roth 401(k) or Roth 403(b) does not have income limitations.

Are There Exceptions?

Yes! There are always exceptions. Tax strategies and Roth IRA strategies must be customized to each person, so there are plenty of exceptions. For example, although I look for all opportunities to convert a client's traditional IRA to a Roth IRA (without triggering unjustified taxes), some financial advisors prefer to not do Roth conversions. Their rationale is that they hope the person will be in a lower tax bracket when they retire, and they may convert to the Roth IRA at that time. I disagree, and prefer to take advantage of the future tax-free benefits of the Roth IRA as soon as possible.

There are also exceptions regarding the "backdoor Roth IRA." Some financial advisors recommend it for all of their high-income clients, and other advisors do not recommend it at all. Yes, there are exceptions.

Beginning in 2010, anyone can convert any amount from a traditional IRA to a Roth IRA. Prior to 2010, persons with over $100,000 in income were prevented from doing a Roth conversion.

If you are not already contributing to a Roth IRA (and your income does not exceed the income limitations shown above), I strongly recommend you open an account and start contributing. You can contribute the maximum amount allowed to a 401(k), 403(b), Roth 401(k), or Roth 403(b) through your employer and also fund a Roth IRA. The maximum contribution amounts allowed for Roth IRAs in 2013 is $5,500 for a person under age 50 and $6,500 for persons age 50 and over. Refer to the IRS website for current figures in future years.

There is a fourth way to build a Roth IRA tax bucket, but it only works in limited circumstances. If your income is too high to contribute directly to a Roth IRA, you may still be able to fund a Roth IRA via a "backdoor Roth IRA." This strategy works best for investors who do not have a large traditional IRA. Often, a person who is not retired will have accumulated a large 401(k) account, but they will not have a traditional IRA.

The backdoor Roth IRA involves contributing to a traditional IRA on an *after-tax* basis (there is no tax benefit in the year of the contribution), and then converting that amount to a Roth IRA. (I prefer doing the conversion to the Roth IRA in the same year as the contribution, but this is not required). Because the IRA contribution was on an after-tax basis, the amount of the contribution is considered as basis and is not taxable when converted to the Roth IRA. This strategy is not discussed in detail in this book, but you can find articles explaining the process by searching online for "backdoor Roth IRA." I use this strategy for my high-income clients who often have large 401(k) accounts but do not have large traditional IRAs.

Contributing to an Employer's Roth 401(k) vs. a Traditional 401(k)

Many employers have introduced Roth 401(k) plans and Roth 403(b) plans in recent years as a choice within their employee retirement plan. The tax consequences are very different from contributions made into traditional 401(k) plans and 403(b) plans.

If you contribute to a traditional 401(k) plan, your contribution will be pre-tax, which means that the contribution is *not* included in your taxable income for that year. Conversely, if you contribute to a Roth 401(k) plan, the contribution is after-tax, and it is included in your taxable income in the year you make the contribution. In the short term that appears to be a negative feature. However, the money contributed to the Roth 401(k) plan (and the earnings over future years) will not be taxed when you withdraw it. The long-term benefits of a Roth 401(k) outweigh the benefits of a traditional 401(k). Most of my working clients who are in a 28 percent or higher federal tax bracket are directing at least 50 percent of their 401(k) contributions into the Roth 401(k). (The remaining 50 percent is still going into the traditional 401(k) to provide an annual tax benefit.) If you are in a marginal tax bracket lower than 28 percent, then I recommend directing your *entire* contribution to the Roth 401(k) due to the attractive long-term benefits.

Regardless of whether your contributions are being directed to the traditional 401(k) or the Roth 401(k), many employers will match a portion of your contribution. This is extremely valuable, and at the very least, you should contribute the amount that your employer will match. Ideally, you should contribute the maximum allowed.

When to Convert a Traditional IRA to a Roth IRA

The best conversion strategy is to look for a window of opportunity when your tax bracket will be low and do a Roth conversion in that year. You can convert any amount each year, so converting gradually over many years can work well. Converting to a Roth IRA gradually may allow you to stay in a low tax bracket. Conversely, if you expect tax rates to go up significantly in future years, you may want to convert a significant amount before tax rates increase.

Young investors reap the maximum benefits of a Roth conversion because they have so many years for the Roth IRA to grow tax-free. Another strategy would be to convert money gradually from your IRA to the Roth IRA between ages 60 and 70. The taxable account could be used to pay the taxes each year. This strategy works well for investors who are eager to move money from the traditional IRA into the Roth IRA. Traditional IRAs require distributions after age 70½ (these are called Required Minimum Distributions, or RMDs). Roth IRAs do not require RMDs at age 70½. Therefore, any money moved to the Roth IRA prior to age 70½ is not included in the calculation for the RMD, thereby making the RMD lower than if the Roth conversion had not occurred.

Another opportunity for a Roth conversion is between retirement and when you start drawing Social Security benefits. This works well if Social Security benefits are delayed until your full retirement age or later.

Each person's situation is different, and there are many variables to consider. The strategy needs to be customized to match your specific situation. Having money in different buckets with different tax treatments provides you with more choices. The key is to manage your tax rate and to convert from a traditional IRA to a Roth IRA whenever it provides future benefits that exceed the taxes you would be required to pay in the year of conversion. It is best to consult with your financial planner or tax advisor on your specific situation.

The beauty of the Roth IRA (or Roth 401[k]) is that it is tax-free going forward. The longer it is left in the account to grow and compound tax-free, the more powerful the tax-free provision becomes.

Reasons Not to Convert to a Roth

- If you anticipate your tax rate going down, you may choose not to do a Roth conversion.

- If your tax rate is currently very low (and you expect it to stay very low), then a Roth conversion is unnecessary.

- If you do not have the money in a taxable account to pay the taxes due to the Roth conversion, you should avoid a conversion. Paying the income taxes from additional IRA withdrawals significantly reduces the benefit of a Roth conversion.

- If you intend to spend all your assets or you do not have any children as beneficiaries, then the estate planning benefits of the Roth IRA are eliminated.

The Versatile Roth IRA

Roth IRAs are very versatile, offering numerous benefits. This section provides information on the primary and secondary benefits.

Primary Benefit: Retirement

Roth IRAs are retirement accounts, so the money is typically not withdrawn until at least age 59½. Often, an investor will plan to tap into a Roth IRA as a last resort, because allowing the tax-free money to compound over many years is a major benefit.

When a person contributes to a Roth IRA, there is not an immediate tax benefit. You cannot take a tax deduction in the year you make the contribution. You must have *earned income* to contribute to a Roth IRA, and earned income typically includes wages, salaries, and tips. Rental income, disability income, pension income, Social Security benefits, dividends, and interest are *not* considered earned income.

If one spouse is working and has earned income and the other spouse does not work, *both* spouses can still contribute to their Roth IRAs.

When dealing with Roth IRAs, it is important to discuss the contributions separately from the earnings because they are handled very differently from a tax standpoint. Let's first review the contributions. Because there is not an immediate tax benefit when you contribute to the Roth IRA, the contributions can be withdrawn tax-free at any time. For example, if you contribute $5,000 each year for 10 years to a Roth IRA, your contributions will total $50,000. If the account has grown 8 percent per year, the total account at the end of 10 years will be over $78,000. You can withdraw the $50,000 (your total contributions) at any time and leave the $28,000 of earnings in the account until you turn age 59½. The ability to withdraw the *contributions* at any time makes the Roth IRA more flexible than a traditional IRA, which requires you to leave contributions *and* earnings in the account until age 59½ to avoid a penalty.

In terms of *earnings*, keep in mind that the Roth IRA is meant for long-term savings and investing. That means you are required to keep the earnings inside the Roth IRA for at least five years. The five years begins on the first day of the first year for which contributions are made, and only one five-year holding period is required, regardless of future contributions. For example, if a person opened a Roth IRA and contributed $5,000 on November 1, 2010, the five-year holding period would have started on January 1, 2010 and concluded on January 1, 2015. The earnings within the Roth IRA can be withdrawn tax-free as long as the five-year holding period is met, *along with one of the following*:

- The taxpayer's age is at least 59½
- The distribution is due to death or disability
- The distribution is made to a qualified first-time homebuyer

If you withdraw the earnings after meeting the above rules, the withdrawal is deemed to be a *qualified* distribution of earnings. If you take a *nonqualified* withdrawal, the earnings are taxed and you will incur a 10 percent early withdrawal penalty if you are under age 59½. The moral to this story is that the contributions are always accessible to you (for any reason, with no penalties), but the earnings should be left in the account for at least five years *and* until age 59½.

Another enormous benefit of the Roth IRA is that withdrawals are not required to begin at age 70½ like a traditional IRA requires. Because withdrawals are not required, the money can stay in the account growing and compounding tax-free for many years. Many retirees find they do not need money from their traditional IRA at age 70½. They may have plenty of money from other sources (such as Social Security, a pension, or a taxable investment account) to cover their living expenses. Yet the traditional IRA requires that distributions begin when a person turns 70½. At that point, the RMD triggers income taxes on the amount withdrawn each year. As a general rule, the RMD is slightly less than 4 percent times the value of the IRA at the end of the prior year. As a person gets older, the 4 percent increases slightly each year. (See www.irs.gov for details.)

The fact that the Roth IRA does not require distributions at age

70½ is an enormous benefit. For retirees who don't need withdrawals for their living expenses, they can leave the money in the Roth IRA to continue growing tax-free and potentially leave it to their heirs to continue growing tax-free for many more years.

Secondary Benefit: Estate Planning

From an estate-planning standpoint, a Roth IRA is a valuable account to leave to children, grandchildren, or other beneficiaries. The beneficiary will not be required to pay income taxes on the distributions from an inherited Roth IRA as they would on distributions from an inherited traditional IRA, although they must take annual withdrawals based on their age and IRS rules. In this respect, leaving a Roth IRA to a beneficiary is more favorable than leaving a traditional IRA.

However, if a person is planning on leaving a part of their estate to a qualified charitable organization, then a traditional IRA is typically the best asset to leave, because the charitable organization is not required to pay income taxes. If a person has a traditional IRA as well as a Roth IRA, it would be best to leave the traditional IRA to a charitable organization and leave the Roth IRA to a child, grandchild, or any other person.

Additional Secondary Benefit:
Teenage Savings Account

Roth IRAs are fabulous for teenagers with jobs, such as babysitting, mowing lawns, etc. The income must be categorized as "earned income." Earning an allowance does not count. However, if a parent paid a child (any age) to clean out the garage or wash the windows, this would be acceptable. A child can contribute the amount of their earned income, up to the $5,500 maximum Roth contribution for 2013, if their earned income is $5,500 or higher. Although it may not be required, I recommend that the income be substantiated by filing a federal tax return for the child or teenager. If the child does not receive a W-2 form or a 1099 form from an employer, then it is very important to keep clear records showing the dates the child worked, the hours, and the amount paid. Also, if the child does not receive a W-2 form from an employer, Social Security taxes *may* need to be deducted when calculating the amount of the Roth contribution.

Because the Roth IRA is such a valuable savings and investing tool, and because it is even more valuable when started by a child or teenager (due to the many years the investments will have to grow and compound on a tax-free basis), I often recommend that parents or grandparents fund a Roth IRA for their child or grandchild. For example, if a teenager earns $1,200 per year, he will not want to invest the entire $1,200. Let's assume he saves 20 percent of it for school trips or upcoming college expenses (starting a lifelong habit of saving 20 percent as mentioned in Chapter Seven, "Family Issues"). The parent or grandparent can gift $1,200 to the child (the amount the child earned), and the $1,200 can be contributed to a Roth IRA. It is not necessary that the actual money the child earned be contributed to a Roth IRA. The key is that the amount earned (up to $5,500 per year for 2013) is the maximum amount the child can contribute to the Roth IRA. Therefore, contributing gifted money to the Roth IRA (that matches but does not exceed the child's earnings) is acceptable—and wise.

Note: The information provided on Roth IRAs is based on current tax laws. The Roth IRA is extremely attractive because of its tax-free growth provisions, its flexibility in withdrawing contributions at any time without penalty, and its lack of required distributions at age 70½. There are many minute details involved in Roth IRAs, and the rules may change. For example, there is currently a proposal in Congress that would force beneficiaries to withdraw money in an inherited Roth IRA (or traditional IRA) within five years. This would eliminate one benefit of the Roth IRA (and traditional IRA), which is the "stretch" provision which allows beneficiaries to withdraw the money over many years. However, the other benefits would remain. It is unknown whether such a proposal may pass, or whether prior Roth IRA owners would be "grandfathered" under the old rules.

Invest in Yourself

- Are you funding all three tax buckets (tax-deferred, taxable, and tax-free accounts)? If not, refer to the net worth statement you created in Chapter Seven, and determine how much you have in each tax bucket. Decide how you can start funding all three buckets.

- Are your taxable investment accounts tax-efficient? (See "More Tax Strategies" earlier in this chapter.)

- Are you taking advantage of the extraordinary Roth IRA? Have you considered converting a traditional IRA to a Roth IRA for the potential long-term tax savings?

- Are you helping your child or grandchild fund a Roth IRA (as long as they have earned income that is properly documented)?

CHAPTER
NINE

■ ■ ■ ■ ■

Protect Yourself

Corruption in the banking industry, the investment industry, and corporate America is widespread. The basic values of integrity and honesty are often lacking. Do you remember the old-fashioned nursery rhyme "There Was a Crooked Man"? Below is an updated version:

> *There was a crooked CEO.*
> *He went a crooked mile.*
> *He found a crooked billion.*
> *It fit his crooked style.*
> *He bought a crooked yacht,*
> *which took a crooked sail.*
> *And now he's wearing stripes*
> *in a crooked little jail.*
> — REVEREND DEWEY JOHNSON

This was written in 2002, shortly after the implosion of Enron and the scandals at Worldcom, Tyco, and other U.S. corporations. The U.S. economy was resilient, and it recovered within a few years. Then in 2008, another round of corruption erupted, along with another financial crisis.

Some people would say that too many of the people implicated in the financial debacles are still roaming freely and more of them should be in a "crooked little jail." But the best advice for investors is to steer clear of any unsavory situations in the first place. As the adage goes...

Buyer Beware

Too Many Straws on the Camel's Back

Throughout 2007, members of the Federal Reserve were quietly voicing concern over the U.S. housing market, specifically the fact that the mortgage industry was encouraging folks to borrow large sums of money—beyond what they could afford. Taking out large mortgages without a deposit was allowed on the assumption that housing prices would continue going up. Investors and homebuyers forgot or ignored the fact that real estate values are cyclical. According to a white paper issued by the Federal Reserve (containing data from CoreLogic), housing prices in the U.S. declined by about 33 percent from 2007 to 2009 as compared to their peak in early 2006.

Declining home prices alone would have strained the U.S. economy, but the actions of the banking and investment industry exacerbated the problem. The high-risk mortgages (termed "subprime") were bundled into "collateralized debt obligations" (CDOs), were rated (absurdly) as double A and triple A by major rating agencies in the United States, and were sold to unsuspecting investors in the United States and abroad as safe, low-risk investments. Greed was in full swing, and the investment firms decided to use excessive leverage to buy and sell more CDOs. (See "The Meaning of Leverage" in Chapter Seven).

Consumers with big mortgages began to default on their loans. The monthly payments were more than they could afford in good times, but when their house declined in value, suddenly they owed more for the house than it was worth. If the homeowner lost their job or had unexpected medical expenses, there was not enough money to cover all the bills. Many homeowners quit making monthly payments or walked away from their mortgages, causing a collapse in the housing market. Meanwhile, CDOs (which contained bundles of mortgages that were now delinquent) lost value quickly. Banks and investment firms were forced to write down the value of the CDOs.

There is one more layer in this mess. When banking and investment firms started using leverage to buy and sell CDOs, firms such as AIG (a huge insurance firm) saw an opportunity to sell "credit-default swaps" (CDS), which were basically insurance policies to protect the banks and investment firms in case the CDOs lost value. The CDS were comprised of derivatives.

In March 2008, U.S. investment bank Bear Stearns failed and was purchased at a bargain price by J.P. Morgan Chase. On September 7, mortgage giants Fannie Mae and Freddie Mac were placed directly under government control. On Monday morning, September 15, 2008, we learned that investment bank Lehman Brothers had filed for bankruptcy and Bank of America had purchased Merrill Lynch. These deals were arranged very quickly during the prior weekend.

It was reported later that Lehman Brothers CEO Dick Fuld had rebuffed buyout offers. The U.S. government refused to bail out Lehman Brothers, and it was allowed to go into bankruptcy. By Friday, September 12, 2008, Merrill Lynch's stock price had declined to $17.05 (from $50 in May 2008 and $90 in January 2007), and it was losing billions of dollars due to excessive leverage and the downward spiral of the CDOs. In a frenzied weekend prior to September 15, Merrill Lynch CEO John Thain reluctantly agreed to sell the firm to Bank of America.

In late September 2008, AIG failed. The U.S. government bailed it out with a $180 billion loan. Next, Washington Mutual bank failed and was seized by the U.S. Treasury. Shortly after, it was purchased by J.P. Morgan Chase. When Wachovia bank failed, it was purchased by Wells Fargo, again at a bargain price. On October 3, 2008, the U.S. Congress agreed to provide U.S. Treasury Secretary Henry Paulson with $700 billion, in a bailout program titled TARP for Troubled Asset Relief Program. It was doled out to Wall Street investment firms such as Citigroup, Morgan Stanley, and Goldman Sachs, as well as many of the nation's banks. Within a few months, the U.S. government decided to buy bad subprime mortgages directly from banks, which resulted in transferring over a trillion dollars' worth of bad investments from big Wall Street firms to U.S. taxpayers. Firms such as General Motors and Chrysler also received a bailout from the U.S. government.

Michael Lewis, author of *The Big Short*, believes that the underlying problem within the financial industry began when the CEO of Salomon Brothers decided to turn what had been a privately held partnership into a publicly traded Wall Street firm in 1981. He states:

The moment Salomon Brothers demonstrated the potential gains to be had from turning an investment bank into a public corporation and leveraging its balance sheet with exotic risks, the psychological foundations of Wall Street shifted from trust to blind faith. No investment bank owned by its employees would have leveraged itself 35:1, or bought and held $50 billion in CDOs. I doubt any partnership would have sought to game the rating agencies, or leapt into bed with loan sharks, or even allowed CDOs to be sold to its customers. The short-term expected gain would not have justified the long-term expected loss.

In Lewis' earlier book *Liar's Poker*, he revealed the corruption and lack of morals that were insidious in Wall Street firms in the 1980s. In *The Big Short* he notes that many of the firms tried to clean up their act in the years after *Liar's Poker* was released. He states: "The changes were camouflage. They helped to distract outsiders from the truly profane event: the growing misalignment of interests between the people who trafficked in financial risk and the wider culture. The surface rippled, but down below, in the depths, the bonus pool remained undisturbed."

Michael Lewis is not alone in his criticism of Wall Street and the toxic effect its bonus programs have on investors. Andy Serwer and Allan Sloan wrote an article for *Time* magazine in which they describe the behavior of folks on Wall Street leading up to the 2008 financial crisis:

They couldn't help behaving the way they did because of Wall Street's classic business model, which works like a dream for Wall Street employees (during good times) but can be a nightmare for the customers. Here's how it goes. You bet big with someone else's money. If you win, you get a huge bonus, based on the profits. If you lose, you lose someone else's money rather than your own, and you move on to the next job.

Where Are We Now?

In some areas, there has been progress. The majority of the TARP money has been repaid to the U.S. Government. Unemployment has declined, and the U.S. housing market is showing signs of recovery.

Several Ponzi schemes have collapsed since 2008, many hedge funds have been dissolved, and huge fines have been levied on large banks. The tendency for large investment firms and banks to assume far more risk than would ever be considered prudent continues to be a huge concern for our economy and for individual investors.

Some regulators are trying to provide more oversight of the banking and investment industry, but progress has been very slow. Their efforts are repeatedly challenged by lobbyists representing banking and financial industry firms that spend millions of dollars to persuade Congress to *not* make changes that may limit their freedom.

Another financial crisis could easily occur. Some say it's not a matter of *if*, but a matter of *when*. Congress should take lessons from the average U.S. citizen to learn how to live within their means (or *below* their means), and to save for a rainy day. American investors are not asking for favors. They simply want a level playing field. When they invest their hard-earned dollars, investors should know that the odds are not rigged against them.

Despite the endearing advertisements in which the financial industry tries to make you think they are giving you advice that is in your best interest, in many cases, financial professionals simply want to sell you something. Far too often, their profit motive is a much higher priority than what is best for you. It is imperative that you protect yourself as an individual investor. Three steps that will help protect you are:

1. Work only with a fiduciary.

2. Insist on full disclosure on fees and terms.

3. Maintain control of your finances.

Work Only with a Fiduciary

A *fiduciary* is a legal term that means the financial advisor is required by law to put the needs of his or her customers first. In addition, a fiduciary is required to make "full and fair disclosure of all material facts, especially when the advisor's interests may conflict with those of his clients." This means that profit motives (such as recommending a product that pays the advisor a high sales commission or a product that is very profitable for the firm) cannot be placed before the customer's best interests. You may assume this should be expected, but that would not be correct. Registered Investment Advisors (RIAs) are *required* to be fiduciaries. They are independent financial advisors registered with the Securities and Exchange Commission (SEC) or state securities regulators. Surprisingly, most stockbrokers, insurance agents, and bank financial representatives are *not* fiduciaries. Reportedly, 80 percent of the financial professionals who describe themselves as financial advisors, investment advisors, brokers, and insurance agents are not fiduciaries.

Whether your financial advisor or broker is serving you as a fiduciary or not may seem like a technicality, but it is an important distinction. Here's how it works. From a legal standpoint, there are two levels of responsibility within the financial and insurance industries. One is being a fiduciary, in which the financial advisor is required, by law, to put the customer's interest first—always. This is a high level of responsibility, and clearly this person serves you rather than their own self-interest.

The second level of responsibility is called *suitability*. It means that the financial professional must determine if the investment or insurance product he or she is recommending is *suitable* for the investor. In some cases, suitability can be met if the investor can simply *afford* a product or if the investor has the risk tolerance to justify purchasing a product. This is a much lower standard than the fiduciary level of responsibility that requires that the product truly be in the investor's best interest.

The suitability standard applies to most stockbrokers, insurance salespeople, and bank investment representatives. Their role in providing service to a client is similar to a salesperson. If they are only *selling* you a stock, bond, mutual fund, life insurance policy, or an annuity (and you understand they are serving you in a sales role), then having them working as a salesperson may be appropriate. However, the consumer should be aware that their financial representative is not serving as a fiduciary.

A survey released in 2010 by the Consumer Federation of America, AARP, and North American Securities Administrators Association reported that "about 90 percent of investors said that a stockbroker and an investment advisor who provide the same kind of investment advisory services should have to follow the same investor protection rules."

Let's dig a little deeper into the distinction. The Investment Advisors Act of 1940 is the law that governs investment advisors who are registered with the SEC. States have adopted similar statutes to apply to state registered advisors. It states that an investment advisor has a fiduciary duty to his or her customers. That much is clear. However, broker-dealers are excluded from the definition of investment advisor where investment advice is *incidental* to the conduct of one's business as a broker or dealer and when the broker-dealer receives no special compensation for the advice. Herein lies an enormous problem. Who determines that a broker's investment advice is incidental to their conduct as a broker? Brokerage firms claim to provide extensive service, and it is difficult to understand how their investment advice can be categorized as incidental to their conduct as a broker. The SEC has tried to provide some clarity to the Investment Advisors Act in recent years, and everyone acknowledges that much has changed in the investment industry in the past 70-plus years. Brokerage firms attempt to distinguish between *advisory* clients and *brokerage* clients. Sadly, these distinctions are rarely clear to the investor.

Section 913 of the Dodd-Frank Wall Street Reform and Consumer Protection Act (signed into law in 2010) gave the SEC the authority to adopt a uniform fiduciary standard of conduct for both broker-dealers and investment advisors when providing personalized investment advice about securities to retail customers. The SEC is currently reviewing (in late 2013) whether a uniform fiduciary standard should be imposed. Many brokerage firms and banks do not *want* their employees to be classified as fiduciaries. Presumably, this is for several reasons. First, a fiduciary standard may raise the liability for large firms. Second, financial advisors would likely need to spend more time on due diligence to ensure the advice they are giving investors is truly in their best interest, and third, the fiduciary standard may reduce the sales for profitable products such as annuities. Several large brokerage, insurance, and banking firms continue to spend millions of dollars in lobbying efforts to persuade Congress and the SEC *not* to require that all persons providing financial services have a fiduciary duty to their customers.

No doubt, individual investors will benefit if a uniform fiduciary standard is established. Recognizing that most financial professionals are not currently serving their customers as a fiduciary, what can you do? In a *New York Times* article by Tara Siegel Bernard in 2010, a Fiduciary Pledge was provided (see Figure 9.1). Bernard encouraged people to keep a copy of the pledge accessible and have it handy when they meet with their financial advisor, stockbroker, bank representative, or insurance representative. Ask them if they are a fiduciary. If they say "yes" with conviction, ask them to sign it. If they hesitate, you should assume they are not a fiduciary. *You want someone who understands that they are responsible for putting you first and providing advice that is truly in your best interest.* Working only with fiduciaries is one way to help protect yourself from the sales tactics within the financial industry.

FIGURE 9.1

The Fiduciary Pledge

I, the undersigned, pledge to exercise my best efforts to always act in good faith and in the best interests of my client, _____, and will act as a fiduciary. I will provide written disclosure, in advance, of any conflicts of interest, which could reasonably compromise the impartiality of my advice. Moreover, in advance, I will disclose any and all fees I will receive as a result of this transaction and I will disclose any and all fees I pay to others for referring this client transaction to me. This pledge covers all services provided.

X _____

Date _____

Another way to tell if you are working with a fiduciary is to read the disclosure document (often called a *brochure*) that all financial advisors are required to provide their clients. If the advisor is a fiduciary, that fact should be clearly stated in the disclosure document. These documents may be very long, so it is imperative that you read the fine print.

Insist on Full Disclosure

The financial industry has earned its tarnished reputation. From 2002 until 2006 several large brokerage firms, banks, mutual fund firms, and insurance companies were fined by the SEC for a variety of allegations, including internal sales contests, late-market trading, and other alleged conflicts of interest. Eliot Spitzer, New York attorney general at the time, led many of the inquiries, and he seemed to have a personal vendetta for cleaning up the financial industry to make it a safer place for individual investors. Most of the firms paid the fines quietly without admitting guilt, in an attempt to minimize the media coverage and negative publicity. As a result of the SEC's efforts following the 2008 financial crisis, $2.7 billion in fines have been collected from firms within the financial and mortgage industries.

Unfortunately, just like there is not a fiduciary standard throughout the financial industry, there is also not a law requiring full disclosure. You may have noticed that the Fiduciary Pledge in Figure 9.1 also includes a requirement of full disclosure regarding conflicts of interest as well as fees. The Fiduciary Pledge is a powerful tool for an investor!

Maintain Control of Your Finances

Do *not* give a broker or a financial advisor *custody* of your investments. Custody is a legal term that has many meanings. In some cases, it simply means that a person's stocks or bonds have been given to a bank or brokerage firm for safekeeping. However, Ponzi schemes and scams, such as the Bernie Madoff scandal, have rattled the confidence of investors. The SEC has strict definitions for determining when a financial advisor has custody of their clients' money, and the financial advisor must undergo additional scrutiny to show he or she is handling the clients' money properly. For example, when a financial advisor has custody, the client's money may be co-mingled with other clients' funds. The advisor may have the authority to withdraw money or invest money without the client's consent. (Note that the clients who invested with Bernie Madoff had given him custody. This gave Madoff *carte blanche* to do whatever he chose. He provided the investors with fraudulent statements showing consistently high returns.) In my view, someone who has custody has too much control over your money.

It is not necessary to give a financial advisor or a broker custody of your money. Financial advisors and brokers typically ask a client to sign a *Limited Power of Attorney* document. This form originates with the firm where your account will be held (such as Charles Schwab, Vanguard, TD Ameritrade, T. Rowe Price, or Fidelity), and it provides the financial advisor or broker the authority to place trades on your behalf. It does not allow the financial advisor or broker to take custody of your money, and the financial advisor's access is limited to protect the investor.

Next, stay involved in the investment decisions for your accounts, and be very cautious about giving someone the right to place trades within your investment accounts without your approval. You should have an agreement with your financial advisor or broker as to when he or she can place trades in your accounts. Some financial advisors want to be able to rebalance their clients' accounts and make investment changes without asking for permission. There is nothing wrong with this, but you should understand the terms of the agreement. If you have this arrangement with your financial advisor, it is still not giving them custody because their ability to act without your permission is limited.

You should look upon your financial planner, financial advisor, or stockbroker as a partner. Their job is to help you achieve your goals. You should meet with your financial advisor on a regular basis. This may be once a year or several times each year. I meet with my clients twice each year, and more when necessary. Each year we cover the following topics: updating and reviewing their net worth statement, their investment accounts and performance, their saving or withdrawal rates, retirement projections, tax planning, and issues such as their estate planning documents and insurance. All meetings include discussions about their families, their goals, and any concerns they may have.

Fees and Conflicts of Interest

To protect yourself and become an educated consumer, ask questions about fees and conflicts of interest when you meet with your financial advisor. Whether you are interviewing potential financial advisors, brokers, or insurance agents, or learning more about your current advisors, below are questions you should ask.

What Are Your Fees?

You need to understand how your financial advisor is being paid and what fees you are paying. There are three primary fee models used widely within the financial industry:

- Commissions
- Fee-Based
- Fee-Only

Commissions

The majority of the financial industry still works on commissions, which has been the mainstay for many years in brokerage firms. If you are working with a broker who is earning commissions, you are probably aware that you pay commissions when your broker buys or sells an asset in your investment account. Typically, the amount of the commission will appear on your trade confirmation or your monthly statement. However, you may be paying other fees as well. Sometimes brokerage firms charge a *wrap* (bundled) fee for investment management when they are outsourcing the investment management function to a separate account manager. There may also be annual account fees. There are often multiple fees, and it is important to ask how your broker or financial advisor is being compensated.

Also, often the commissions are not disclosed. Let's assume you buy an annuity for $250,000, which may be sold by someone in the financial, insurance, or banking industry. The commission may be as high as 8 to 10 percent (or even higher with bonuses and trips), but that is rarely disclosed. If there were a full disclosure law, the salesperson would be required to disclose all commissions. If the sales commission is 8 percent, the salesperson would receive $20,000 in commissions. If you were to convey surprise at the $20,000 commission, the salesperson recommending the annuity may respond by saying, "But your $250,000 investment is not reduced by $20,000—therefore, you should not be concerned about the commission."

I would argue that even if the $20,000 is not subtracted *directly* from the $250,000 you are investing, a savvy investor realizes that the $20,000 commission paid to the salesperson comes *indirectly* from your investment. It is paid by the insurance company, which may recoup that expense through high surrender penalties attached to your annuity; from high annual fees that reduce the investment gain you receive; or from paying out less to you than would be possible if the steep commission were not present. Whether directly or indirectly, the investor is paying the commission.

A few years ago I received an email from a well-known national insurance company. The email described how to win a trip to Rome for selling a large amount of life insurance policies or fixed annuities. The trip included six days in Italy for the top 80 *producers* (producers is the industry's term for salespersons) and their guests, with virtually all expenses paid by the insurance company. The email also described another sales promotion called "Cash is King," which provided additional cash payouts (above the standard commissions) for selling indexed annuities. I do not sell annuities, so I received this email in error. Clearly, the insurance company used a mass email list to contact financial advisors.

Should there be a law prohibiting sales contests without disclosing the potential conflict of interest to the consumer? In my view, yes. The rules for earning the trip to Italy stated that *variable* insurance products are not eligible in accordance with a ruling by the National Association of Securities Dealers (NASD), effective January 1999. It seems the NASD created a rule to prevent firms from offering trips for selling variable annuities. However, the NASD did not specify that the firms cannot provide trips to their salespeople based on *fixed* annuity or life insurance sales, so the contests are still allowed.

Fee-Based

A fee model called *fee-based* combines fees on some products with commissions on others. In my view, the term "fee-based" is deceptive, because most consumers assume this is fee-only. Another source of fees are *trails* (sometimes called residual compensation or residual trails), that are paid each year to the salesperson for an annuity or insurance product sold many years ago. As long as the investor continues to own the asset, the salesperson is paid an ongoing trail.

Mutual funds have *expense ratios*, which are fees charged directly by the mutual fund company to each investor who owns that mutual fund. These fees are used to pay the fund's expenses and managers. Often, a portion of the annual expense ratio is paid back to the broker each year you own the fund. These are called *12b-1* fees. Much like a trail from an insurance product, the 12b-1 fees are like an ongoing commission that goes back to the broker every year.

I have heard the argument that a fee-based model works well because the client can choose to work on a fee arrangement for investment management and financial planning services, but if an insurance product is needed, the advisor can sell it to the investor and earn a commission. In some cases this may be true, and the advisor may be serving the client as a fiduciary. However, this argument has two serious flaws. Working on commissions is generally more lucrative for the advisor than working on a fee arrangement. Therefore, the conflict of interest in earning a commission when an insurance product is sold is still present. This conflict of interest may entice the advisor to recommend an annuity to an investor rather than leaving his money in a diversified investment portfolio, which is less lucrative for the advisor. The second flaw is that the amount of the commission is rarely disclosed to the client, and the client has a right to full disclosure of all fees.

Fee-Only

The third fee model is call *fee-only*. I believe this is the best fee model for investors. Clients know exactly what fees they are paying, and there are no commissions or other forms of compensation. The client typically pays a fee for financial planning or asset management services. Often, fee-only financial advisors work on an annual retainer for their clients, providing extensive service throughout the year. When calculating the annual retainer, the fee is often based on the amount of assets managed (termed *assets under management*), although the fee may also include a component that is based on the financial planning services provided. The investment services provided by financial planners typically include designing investment portfolios, placing trades, monitoring investments, providing performance reports, and making recommendations for changes. In addition, financial planning services often include retirement planning, tax planning, college funding, goal-setting advice, and insurance advice.

In some cases, fee-only advisors may work on an hourly or project basis with clients. When working on an hourly basis, the advisor may recommend specific investments, but the client is usually expected to implement the recommendations and place the investment trades. This business model has been compared to a dental practice, where the client is encouraged to come in for an annual or semi-annual financial review. It is best suited for people who do not need full-service financial planning on an ongoing basis. These may be *do-it-yourselfers* who want an objective opinion from a financial advisor on whether they are making wise financial or investment decisions, or for folks who only have a few questions or issues they want to discuss.

Fee-only financial planning often receives favorable media attention because of the transparency and full disclosure it provides. Although the commission model is still very common within the brokerage and insurance industry, there is a shift towards charging based upon assets under management in some of the large financial firms. If this fee model is combined with 12b-1 fees (back-end commissions) from mutual funds or trails from insurance policies, this would be termed a fee-based model because it combines fees with commissions.

Are There Any Conflicts of Interest?

As a financial advisor, it is impossible to avoid all conflicts of interest. However, you should understand the common conflicts of interest in the financial industry.

The most common conflict of interest is when commissions are involved. When an advisor works on a commission basis, there is a built-in conflict of interest. If an annuity pays an advisor an 8 percent commission, but mutual funds pay 4 percent, there is a tendency to recommend the customer buy the product with the higher commission.

What Is Good for the British...

Effective January 1, 2013, financial advisors in Britain are no longer allowed to earn commissions when they sell financial products. A new system called "Advisor Charging" is being implemented, which requires that advisors charge for their advice and service, rather than being paid commissions for selling a product. This new system is analogous to the fee-only model in the United States. According to a report issued by J.P. Morgan Asset Management in the U.K., "Advisor charging aims to refocus the investment industry away from selling products and toward providing an advice service with its own intrinsic value."

Australia is implementing a similar (no commission) policy (in mid-2013), and the Netherlands is planning a similar ban on commissions effective January 1, 2014.

We can only hope that Congress and the SEC decide that a transparent, fee-only model in the investment industry would be best for consumers in the United States, just as the authorities have determined in the U.K, Australia, and the Netherlands.

The fee-only financial planning model avoids conflicts caused by commissions, but it does not avoid all potential conflicts of interest. For example, if a client is considering buying a new home, the issue of taking out a mortgage will be discussed. Similarly, clients often decide to pay off a mortgage early. These are both potential conflicts of interest if the annual retainer fee is based on the total of the investment accounts (assets under management). Whether someone chooses to pay off a mortgage early or decides to take out a mortgage rather than pay cash for a home, these decisions impact the investment accounts. Other potential conflicts of interest include the decision to take a lump sum pension rather than monthly payments, when to begin receiving Social Security benefits, and Roth IRA conversions. Potential conflicts of interest should be disclosed to the client, and then advice can be provided that fits best into the client's overall goals.

Although I favor the fee-only model because of its transparency for the client, the fee model is actually not the most important consideration. There are many ethical financial advisors, brokers, and insurance representatives who work hard on behalf of their clients, and they may charge their clients using any of the three fee models. *The issue is that the consumer has a right to full disclosure.* Financial professionals should have to disclose the source of all their income, including commissions, referral fees, management fees, trails from insurance products sold to the client in prior years, and 12b-1 fees from mutual funds. Financial advisors should also be required to disclose all conflicts of interest. You—as a consumer and an investor—have a right to know!

Services and Benefits of a Financial Advisor

If you choose to work with a financial advisor, realize that there are many different types of financial professionals, and they provide a wide range of services. Following are sections that describe how to select a financial advisor, the services provided, potential benefits, and a discussion regarding who needs a financial advisor.

Selecting a Financial Advisor

Many different titles are used in the financial industry. The terms *financial planner* and *financial advisor* can be used by anyone, regardless of their credentials. Often, financial planners have a *big-picture* focus on helping clients achieve their goals, and the services may include investment management *plus* retirement planning, tax

planning, insurance advice, estate planning, and education funding. Financial planning services may be customized for each client.
For example, a client who owns a small business may receive services that include establishing a small business retirement plan.
Alternatively, a client who is retired may receive services geared
toward retirement withdrawal strategies and legacy planning.

Sometimes, a person who uses the title *financial advisor* will offer
extensive financial services, much like a financial planner. However, in some cases a financial advisor may only provide investment
services. The title *wealth manager* often signifies a financial advisor
who works with high net-worth clients. The title does not indicate
whether that person will offer full-service financial planning services or only investment services. It is important to ask!

If you seek someone who *only* works with investments, that person may use the title investment advisor, money manager,
investment representative, or investment consultant. If you are
working with a stockbroker, ask what services are provided.

If you are seeking someone who only sells insurance, look for
an insurance agent, although annuities and life insurance policies
are also often sold by stockbrokers, banks, and registered representatives.

Be aware that some brokers and financial planners will be limited in what they can recommend to a client. The large firms have
traditionally directed their brokers to sell certain investment and
insurance products to their clients, which may not be in your best
interest. Recognize that the broker is an agent of the firm, so the
firm's objectives often come first.

In addition to the large, well-known national brokerage firms,
there are also brokerage firms that have *independent contractors*
located across the country. Often, these folks are not as independent as they claim, and they are limited in the products they can
recommend. One way to distinguish between a broker and a (truly)
independent advisor is to ask the person if they are a *registered rep-*

resentative. If they say yes, then they are affiliated with a brokerage firm (even if they are classified as an independent contractor). Typically, an independent financial advisor (who is verifiably independent) is required to be a Registered Investment Advisor (RIA). Being classified as an RIA also carries the requirement of being a fiduciary.

You will notice that many financial advisors, brokers, and insurance salespeople have many initials (credentials) following their name. Do not be swayed. Many of the certifications require very little training, and some can be earned by spending a day in a seminar. Just like the accounting profession has one certification that holds high esteem (CPA), the financial industry has one also. Earning the right to be a Certified Financial Planner™ professional requires extensive coursework and passing a 10-hour exam. Before a person can use the mark after their name, they must have a bachelor's degree and a minimum of three years of experience in the financial industry. In addition, CFP® professionals are required to complete 30 hours of continuing education every two years to maintain the mark. Other designations that hold esteem include the ChFC (Chartered Financial Consultant) from the insurance industry and the PFS (Personal Financial Specialist) from the accounting industry. Another highly regarded mark is the CFA (Chartered Financial Analyst), although it is indicative of extensive training in investment analysis rather than comprehensive financial planning.

If you decide to work with a financial advisor (or financial planner, stockbroker, insurance agent, bank representative, etc.), you should interview several potential financial professionals and ask lots of questions about their services, fees, investment philosophy, education, experience, expertise, and typical client. If you prefer to meet your advisor face-to-face, limit your search to advisors near you. However, with today's technology tools, most advisors find it easy to provide service and interact with clients across the country. Ask for a copy of the advisor's disclosure brochure, and read it carefully. You can search the SEC's website (www.sec.gov) for information on the advisor you are considering hiring. It is also a good idea to review the advisor's website, which is often very informative.

Services Provided by a Financial Advisor

Below is a list of potential services that may be offered by a financial professional.

- Investment management
- Retirement planning and projections, including multiple scenarios and withdrawal strategies
- Tax planning
- Estate planning (in collaboration with an estate attorney)
- Insurance issues, including homeowner, auto, umbrella, life, disability, long-term care
- Budgeting and cash flow
- Developing a savings plan
- Employee benefits review
- Advice on 401(k) and other qualified plan accounts
- Stock option planning
- Small-business services (for business owners)
- Social Security planning
- Transition planning (marriage, divorce, death of a spouse)
- Legacy planning
- Advice on purchasing homes, mortgages, and cars
- Education planning
- Career evaluation and planning
- Charitable giving planning
- Clarifying and attaining goals

Who Needs a Financial Advisor?

There is no clear-cut answer. Some say that once your assets total $250,000 or $500,000, you should hire a financial advisor. I disagree with this. A young person who is early in their career and is planning for the future (but has much less than $250,000) could benefit greatly by working with a financial advisor. Many people (of all ages) do not have large investment portfolios, but they could still benefit from working with a financial advisor.

Some people assume that if have a financial advisor, you cannot manage your own finances. This is a myth. Many of my clients are highly educated and extremely savvy when it comes to investments and financial matters. Yet they understand the benefits of a financial advisor who can be very objective. They consider me as a partner in helping them achieve their goals and increase their net worth. Other clients are extremely busy (with careers or family), and they do not have the time to devote to managing their finances.

Another reason to consider a financial advisor is if you know you tend to be compulsive, or you may not be able to stick to your plan if the stock market takes a nosedive. A financial advisor can help you formulate a long-term plan and maintain it in times of uncertainty.

A major reason many folks decide to work with a financial advisor is that they are going through a major transition. The most common is retirement, but others include getting married, starting a family, getting divorced, or the death of a spouse.

I recommend that you determine the services you need (from the list above) and whether a financial advisor may be helpful to you. Although many financial advisors want to develop a long-term, ongoing relationship with a client (and they may have minimum levels of investment assets or annual fees), there are financial advisors who will work on an hourly or project basis. This can work well if you have specific issues you need addressed, such as whether you have adequate insurance, or advice on choosing investments within your 401(k). This is also a good route for young persons who are eager to start saving and investing for their future.

The Benefits of Working with a Good Financial Advisor

What value does a good financial advisor provide? The benefits will vary from person to person, but below are a few potential benefits.

- Your finances will be in good order

- You will have a financial plan designed around your goals

- You have an objective partner (your financial advisor) that you can trust to help you make financial decisions

- You will know you are on track for retirement

- You have someone who will help you "stay the course" when you become fearful due to economic or stock market volatility

- You won't need to worry that you do not have time to manage your finances

- Your investments will match your tolerance for risk and your time horizons for your goals

- If working with a full-service financial planner or financial advisor, you will receive advice on estate planning, tax planning strategies, insurance issues, college funding, etc.

- You can build a team of professionals to work on your behalf, including your financial advisor, your tax preparer, and your estate attorney. This is beneficial when designing financial, legal, and tax strategies

- You will have current retirement projections that are customized to your situation

- Your financial advisor may have access to institutional share classes of mutual funds (with lower annual expense ratios) for your investment accounts

- You will receive performance reports for your investment accounts

- Your investment accounts will be rebalanced on an annual or semi-annual basis

- You will avoid costly financial mistakes (such as buying the wrong insurance product)

- You will likely have stronger investment performance than if you managed your investments yourself (per the research from Dalbar discussed in Chapter Ten)

Invest in Yourself

- Become comfortable with terms such as *fiduciary*, *full disclosure*, and *custody*.

- Below are questions you may want to ask your financial advisor, bank representative, stock broker, or insurance salesman:

  - Are you a fiduciary? If they say yes, ask them to sign the Fiduciary Pledge provided in Figure 9.1. If they say no, discuss the issue.

  - Will you put all your fees in writing? This should include all fees, commissions, referral fees, trails, and 12b-1 fees. Ask them to mail the list of fees to you.

  - What conflicts of interest do you have when providing financial advice? Will you disclose any conflicts of interest on an ongoing basis? (This could include being limited by management to recommending specific products, being involved in sales contests, paying referral fees, having higher commissions on some products over others, etc.)

- What types of financial services do you want? For example, do you have specific issues, such as whether you should convert a traditional IRA to a Roth IRA, or how to minimize taxes? Maybe you need a financial advisor who works on an hourly or project basis. Decide whether you can implement investment trades yourself and then monitor those investments. Or, would you benefit from a financial advisor that offers extensive, ongoing services?

- Decide how you would like the financial advisor to be paid and whether having them serve as a fiduciary is important to you.

CHAPTER
TEN

■ ■ ■ ■

Investment Strategies

Rule No. 1: Never lose money.
Rule No. 2: Don't forget rule No. 1.
— WARREN BUFFETT

Can someone become a wise investor? Most definitely! You can become a wise investor. It is a learned skill. If investment advisors or folks touting their financial advice on TV suggest that investing takes special knowledge, they are wrong. Using complicated tactics, such as *shorting the market* or investing in hedge funds and other alternative investments, is not required for wise investing.

Wise investing is based on two requirements: having a plan and using discipline to follow the plan. The investment plan does not need to be complicated.

In this chapter, you will learn about different asset classes and the risks that are inherent in investing. You will learn basic investment strategies that are used by wise investors, and you will be encouraged to determine the asset allocation that is right for you. This chapter is not intended to address all investment issues. There are many excellent investment books and online resources that can provide additional details. Refer to the Resources section at the back of the book or on the website *www.joyoffinancialsecurity.com*. Specific mutual funds and other investments are not recommended in the book. The investment world is constantly changing, and every investor has individual needs and goals. It is up to you to determine which investments are best for you. If you work with a financial planner or financial advisor, he or she will provide specific investment recommendations.

Wise investing is a learned skill. Informed investors follow these 10 rules:

1. Have a plan. Know why you are investing and what your goals are.
2. Use discipline to follow the plan.
3. Have an emergency fund—a safety net.
4. Live below your means.
5. Know yourself. Honestly assess your tolerance for risk and select an appropriate asset allocation strategy.
6. Try not to lose money. (This is drastically different than trying to make money.)
7. Stay diversified.
8. Do not neglect your finances.
9. Keep your investment costs low.
10. Pay attention to taxes.

An Emergency Fund

An emergency fund is a critical part of an investment portfolio. If you do not have an emergency fund, establish one before investing in equities, bonds, real estate, or other investments. The amount of money in your emergency fund should match your estimated expenses for a six-month period.

The emergency fund should be in a *cash-equivalent* form, such as a money market account or a savings account. It is important that the fund is totally liquid, so you can access it quickly and easily if necessary. It will have a very low return, or possibly no return at all. This money is not meant to grow. I recommend that it not be included in the same account you regularly use to pay bills or for funding your next vacation. It is in reserve *only* for emergencies.

When is an emergency fund needed? It may never be needed, and that would be great. The emergency fund is for large, unexpected expenses and emergencies. Let's assume your car needs to be repaired, and the expense is $1,000. This expense may have a minor impact on your finances, but not a devastating impact. You can likely pay for the repair by using money in your checking account. However, let's assume you are in an auto accident. No one is hurt, but you need to buy another car quickly. This may exceed the amount you can pay from your checking account, so your emergency fund could be used.

Unfortunately, multiple emergencies can occur at the same time. Perhaps you lose your job, and the loss of income causes you to miss some mortgage payments. The credit card bills start to pile up. There may be a severe illness in the family, and the roof needs to be repaired. Suddenly, it may feel like you are falling into a black hole with no income and too many unpaid bills. This scenario led to a large number of home foreclosures in recent years, and it has been devastating to many families. In all these examples, having a six-month emergency fund can provide the financial safety net needed to work through the difficult times.

If you do not have a six-month emergency fund, then saving this money should be a top priority. However, there are instances where folks can *graduate* to needing less than six months in reserve. This applies to many of my clients. Let's assume a couple's living expenses are $6,000 per month. A six-month emergency fund would require having $36,000 set aside. If they are excellent savers and investors and they have a taxable investment account of $500,000 or more, they may choose to keep only $20,000 in the money market portion of their account or in a separate savings account. In this case, we know we can liquidate some of their investments within one or two days, and the proceeds are then easily accessible.

For folks who have a large taxable investment account, they may also consider using their credit card in the case of an emergency, or they may have a home equity line of credit, which would allow them access to cash in an emergency. These exceptions to the six-month emergency rule do not mean they do not have the necessary cash available in case of an emergency. It simply means they have invested wisely so they have more options for accessing cash quickly when an emergency occurs.

Asset Classes

Before describing how you determine your tolerance for risk, choose your asset allocation, or design your investment portfolio, we should define several terms that will be used throughout the chapter.

An *asset class* is a category that contains investments with similar characteristics. The two most common asset classes are *equities* (investments in the stock market) and *bonds* (fixed income assets that may include a variety of bonds, CDs, money market funds, and cash). Some financial advisors consider cash to be a third asset class. I prefer to include it with fixed income. The terms *equities* and *stocks* are often used interchangeably, and the terms *bonds* and *fixed income* are also used interchangeably.

Equities

Whenever you see the term *equities*, think *stock market*. This asset class can include many different types of investments. You can invest in individual stocks (equities) such as Exxon, Microsoft, or Coca-Cola, or you can invest in an equity mutual fund. A mutual fund provides you with diversification because it is a pool containing many individual stocks. An equity mutual fund is either managed by a computer (such as an index fund that mimics the S&P 500) or by a manager who is actively researching individual stocks and is selecting which stocks to include in the mutual fund. Mutual funds are available for equities as well as bonds, real estate holdings, and other asset classes.

When you own a stock, you are an *owner* in the company. You may own a very small fraction of the company, but you are an owner. The share price of a stock can fluctuate significantly. If you purchase 100 shares of a stock for $10 per share, you are investing $1,000. If the share price increases to $15 per share, your investment will grow to $1,500, which is a 50 percent return (from $1,000 to $1,500). Likewise, the share price could decline to $5 per share, and your investment would decline to $500, for a loss of 50 percent (declining from $1,000 to $500). Of course, the value of your stock could decline much more than 50 percent and can conceivably become worthless. This can happen when a company goes bankrupt.

Two prime examples of stocks increasing and decreasing significantly in value are Google and Bank of America. If you had been very fortunate (in hindsight) and had invested in Google stock on December 31, 2008, you would have paid approximately $307 per share. As of June 30, 2013, the share price was $880 per share. You would be feeling very smart, indeed!

Alternatively, if you had invested in Bank of America stock on September 28, 2007, you would have paid roughly $50 per share. The share price declined drastically during the economic crisis in late 2008, eventually dropping to less than $4 per share by February of 2009. The share price fluctuated between $4 and $20 from 2009 to 2012. Investing in individual stocks is not for the faint of heart!

I recommend that my clients use no-load (in other words, no commissions) equity mutual funds rather than individual stocks. Mutual funds offer several benefits over individual stocks, the greatest of which is the diversity they provide because there are many different stocks in the mutual fund pool. This is analogous to "not having all your eggs in one basket," which is the practical definition of diversification. This is discussed in greater detail below.

Dividends

The primary reason investors purchase equities (or equity mutual funds) is for the potential growth. Stocks have historically provided a higher average annual return than bonds. However, in addition to potential growth, some stocks pay dividends, which are a payback from the company to the shareholders. Traditionally, a company will either reinvest its earnings in the company (hire more employees, buy more equipment, build more buildings, spend more money on research or advertising—all done with the objective of helping the company grow), or pay its earnings to the shareholders in the form of dividends. Since the recession of 2008-2009, we have seen a third strategy appear as many corporations accrue large amounts of cash. Presumably, the corporations want the cash available to protect them in the event of another economic downturn or to reinvest in their company or acquire other companies when they choose.

An investor should not invest in a company only based on a high dividend. This mistake was apparent in the 2008 financial crisis when the financial sector within the S&P 500 declined 84 percent from its peak in 2007. Although banks have historically paid attractive dividends, investors were stunned as the value of their investments in major U.S. banks plummeted. To make matters worse, the companies reduced their dividends.

When investors own individual stocks or equity mutual funds, they are given a choice whether they want the dividends reinvested or to receive the dividends paid out in cash. I recommend that my clients have the dividends reinvested. Because my clients own primarily mutual funds (and not individual stocks), when dividends are paid, the proceeds are used to buy more shares of the equity mutual fund.

Reinvesting dividends has a powerful effect on the long-term performance of an investment portfolio. The S&P 500 index had an average annual return of 6.1 percent for the 20 years from 1993 to 2012 when dividends were not reinvested. When dividends were reinvested, the average annual return was 8.2 percent.

Exchange-Traded Funds

Another form of equity investment is called an *exchange-traded fund*, or ETF. Equity ETFs are very similar to equity mutual funds, in that they own a pool of many different stocks. ETFs are also available for bonds and other asset classes. They differ from mutual funds because their value fluctuates like an individual stock during the day. Conversely, a mutual fund is priced at the end of each trading day, based on the closing prices of all the individual stocks the mutual fund owns in its pool. Some investors prefer buying ETFs because they like the constantly fluctuating value, and ETFs may have a lower transaction fee than a comparable mutual fund.

I prefer mutual funds over ETFs for three reasons. The first reason involves computerized trading, which has become prevalent in recent years. There is the possibility of a severe decline in the market caused by unexpected technology glitches at any time. This occurred on May 6, 2010, in what was termed a "flash crash." During a 10-minute period in the afternoon, the Dow Jones Industrial Average declined 9.8 percent. A follow-up story in the *Wall Street Journal* compared the flash crash to the Black Monday crash on October 19, 1987, in which the Dow lost over 22 percent in one day. Both declines involved a major decline in the pricing of future contracts, which then led to rapid declines in stock prices. Journalist Scott Patterson wrote: "Perhaps the most troublesome parallel between the May 6 plunge and Black Monday was that buyers pulled out at the worst possible time." He continued: "Some of the key changes in the market helped magnify the selling pressure on May 6, rather than helping to cushion the market. This time around, many investors rushed to sell exchange-traded funds, which didn't exist in the 1980s. Heavy selling of ETFs spread losses to other parts of the stock market like a virus."

The second reason I do not like ETFs is that, in my view, their fluctuating share price encourages day trading (buying and selling very frequently). John Bogle, the founder of Vanguard, is not a fan of ETFs. He prefers index mutual funds. He concedes that some ETFs, like those that mimic core Vanguard index funds, are fine if used carefully by buy-and-hold investors or by institutional investors for specific purposes. However, he warns that ETFs can be dangerous because some ETFs track relatively obscure sections of the market and all of them encourage the propensity to trade rapidly—"to speculate rather than invest."

A third reason is that the vast majority of ETFs are clones of mutual funds. Very few of them provide any unique qualities that are not available in a mutual fund. To be fair, there is one benefit that ETFs provide over mutual funds. It involves tax-efficiency. Because of the way ETFs are structured, they rarely distribute taxable gains. In a taxable investment account, this may be a benefit, but only if an investor chooses an ETF that mimics a large index. Mutual funds are required to distribute taxable gains to their shareholders each year. However, an investor who invests in a large index equity mutual fund will also experience a high level of tax efficiency. Tax efficiency is not a concern in a traditional IRA, a Roth IRA, a 401(k), or any other retirement account.

ETFs are being marketed aggressively in the investment industry and have become very popular in recent years. If you choose to use them, the recommendations below (for designing your portfolio using mutual funds) still apply.

Equity Mutual Funds

Let's review the types of equity mutual funds available. There are thousands of mutual funds and ETFs to choose from. Often, equity mutual funds are categorized by the size of the companies they contain. The categories are based on market capitalization, which is simply the number of shares outstanding multiplied by the current share price. The category values shift occasionally. In 2012, the size of stocks categorized as large-cap were over $8 billion, mid-cap stocks ranged from $1 billion to $8 billion, and small-cap was less than $1 billion.

Equity funds are often divided into several categories:

- Large U.S. Stock Funds

- Mid-Cap U.S. Stock Funds

- Small-Cap U.S. Stock Funds

- International Stock Funds

Another common categorization is based on whether the mutual fund contains primarily value stocks or growth stocks. Typically, value stocks trade at low prices relative to earnings, or low P/E ratios (see P/E Ratio). Growth stocks tend to have higher prices because they have increasing earnings and revenues, and the investor expects that growth to continue. Each of the categories listed above can be further divided, depending on whether they contain primarily value stocks or growth stocks. For example, the large U.S. stock fund category could be divided into large U.S. value stock funds and large U.S. growth stock funds.

Equity mutual funds are available that focus on specific sectors, such as health care, energy, technology, financial, consumer cyclicals, telecommunication, utilities, natural resources, and precious metals.

The international stock fund category can be further divided into large international stock funds, small international stock funds, and emerging market stock funds. These can then be further divided into large value international stock funds, small value international stock funds, etc. Often, international funds focus on developed markets within specific continents, such as Europe. Funds that focus on specific countries such as Germany, France,

What is a P/E Ratio?

A P/E ratio is short for price-to-earnings ratio. It is the current share price for a stock (the price) divided by the earnings per share during the past 12 months (the earnings). If a stock has a current share price of $20 and the earnings-per-share during the past 12 months was $1.25, then the P/E ratio is 16 percent.

The P/E ratio is an indication of investors' expectations for a company. If a company has a P/E ratio of 30, but other firms in the same industry have an average P/E ratio of 18, then this would indicate that investors are expecting the firm's share price to grow at a more rapid pace than other firms. The P/E ratio is compared with recent growth rates and projected growth rates to determine if the current price per share seems fair, or if it may be low or high as compared with the growth prospects of the company.

or Spain are also available. Emerging market funds may focus on less developed countries, such as Brazil, Russia, India, China, Indonesia, or Colombia.

In my financial planning firm, I use mutual funds that focus on many different categories, and I believe diversification among many types and sizes of equities increases performance while decreasing risk within an investment portfolio. Before you start feeling overwhelmed by too many choices, recognize that it is possible to keep the selection process very simple.

Fixed Income

While the equity portion of your investment portfolio is intended to provide growth, the fixed-income portion is intended to provide income and stability. The assets that are termed *fixed income* may contain bonds, CDs, money market accounts, or cash. Let's begin with bonds.

Bonds

When you buy a bond, you are *lending* money to an entity, such as a corporation (corporate bonds), the U.S. government (treasury bills, notes, and bonds), or states and municipalities (municipal bonds). Because you are lending your money, you are a *loaner*. Bond holders are typically paid interest for lending their money to the entity. The interest rate is called the *yield*. Bonds are considered to be lower in risk (and volatility) than stocks. This is true for high-quality bonds, but there can be exceptions. If the company that issued the bonds goes bankrupt, the bonds may become worthless. This happened to investors who owned Lehman Brothers bonds when they went bankrupt on September 15, 2008. Barclays purchased most of the assets of Lehman Brothers, and the bondholders received only 21 percent of the original value of their bonds almost three years later.

A shortcut for remembering the definition of stocks and bonds is to understand that if you invest in stocks, you are an *owner*, and if you invest in bonds, you are a *loaner*. This is a bit simplistic, but it may be helpful in keeping the two definitions straight.

Many investors do not understand how bonds work. This is because bond prices and bond yields move in opposite directions. Articles about bonds are often confusing. The best way to keep it all straight is to remember that if an article says bond *prices increased*, then you need to recognize that bond *yields decreased*. Likewise, if you read that bond *yields increased*, then you will know that bond *prices decreased*. This yin and yang is a cardinal rule for understanding bond fluctuations.

Bond prices and yields fluctuate daily. Within the bond market, if interest rates rise, then bond prices decline. If interest rates decline, then bond prices increase. In the United States, interest rates have been declining since the early 1980s. As a result, bonds have performed extremely well during the past 30 years through the end of 2012. Due to the high volatility of equities, bonds occasionally outperform equities. This was evident during the five years ending December 31, 2012, as well as the thirteen years from 2000 through 2012.

Fluctuating bond prices and yields are an issue if someone sells a bond before its maturity date, or if they invest in bond mutual funds. However, if you invest in an individual bond and you hold it until maturity, you do not need to worry about the fluctuations in bond prices or interest rates. If you hold it until maturity (and assuming it does not default), you will receive the *par* value of the bond as well as the yield stated at the time of your original purchase. (Par value is simply the *face* value, or the price when originally issued. Most bonds have a par value of $1,000.)

You may recall that as recently as 10 years ago, most retirees purchased CDs and lived off the interest. Or they owned individual stocks, and the stock dividends provided their monthly cash flow. This dynamic has changed in recent years. CDs currently have extremely low interest rates so they do not provide sufficient interest for retirees. Individual stocks have been very volatile in recent years, and many have lost money, making their dividends unreliable. Bond ladders, as a part of a balanced portfolio, are a viable alternative. This strategy is discussed in Chapter Eleven.

Individual bonds are often categorized based on their maturity date. FINRA (the Financial Industry Regulatory Authority) defines a short-term bond as being between one and three years, an intermediate bond as between four and 10, and a long-term bond as over 10 years.

As stated earlier, rising or falling interest rates impact the price of bonds. Short-term bonds have less interest rate risk than longer-term maturities. If you are expecting interest rates to increase, then you may want to purchase high-quality short-term bonds. These will be impacted the least by the rise in interest rates. The down-side, however, of using only short-term bonds is that the yields tend to be very low as compared with the yields for high-quality inter-mediate-term bonds.

In early 2008, the Federal Reserve began lowering short-term U.S. interest rates in an effort to stimulate the economy after the housing market collapse in 2007 and 2008. The rates continued to be low for over five years, and the 10-year treasury bill had a yield below 2 percent in early 2013. Bonds have performed extremely well for the past 30 years, but there is concern that interest rates must go up in the near future. When interest rates go up, bond prices will come down. This will cause the values of bonds that investors own to decline.

Yet, in my view, this conundrum (the current low yields and the risk of declining bond prices if interest rates increase) does not jus-tify moving a higher percentage of a client's investments into equities or alternative assets. That would greatly increase the risk. Rather, it is important to maintain the bond portion of a portfolio, and to diversify it among many different types of bonds.

In addition to the maturity date, the quality of a bond (called the *rating*) also impacts the risk level. A high-quality municipal or cor-porate bond may be rated as double-A or triple-A. A low-quality bond may be rated as B or below. A rating of BBB or below is con-sidered to be *junk*, which indicates a much higher risk level. Once again, this demonstrates the relationship between risk and return. Investments that are lower in risk (such as high-quality short-term bonds) have lower returns. Investments that are perceived as higher risks (such as low-quality bonds or bonds with long-term maturity dates) will typically offer higher returns.

Certificate of Deposits

Often called CDs, certificate of deposits are issued by banks and are insured by the FDIC (Federal Deposit Insurance Corporation).

When an investor buys a CD, he or she knows what the interest rate is and that the investment is safe. If the bank goes out of business, the FDIC will pay the investor for the CD. The maximum amount of insurance provided by the FDIC was $100,000 for many years, and it increased to $250,000 in 2008. The amount of insurance coverage may change again in the future. (See the FDIC website at www.fdic.gov for details). There is always a very small risk that the FDIC could go bankrupt, so no investment is 100 percent insured or guaranteed. Yet the FDIC going bankrupt is very unlikely, which is why CDs are considered to be very low risk.

Credit unions also issue CDs, and they are typically insured by NCUA (National Credit Union Administration). Always request a written document from a bank or credit union that the CD you are purchasing is insured.

A CD does not provide any potential growth. It merely provides a stated interest rate, which is income for the investor. This is why a CD is categorized as fixed income.

Cash and Cash-Equivalents

Cash is another form of fixed income, used primarily to pay living expenses or to serve as an emergency fund. In its purest form, cash is a checking account, a savings account, or a money market account. Typically, folks who use checking and savings accounts do not need to worry about their balance declining. However, the SEC has been debating whether some money market funds may *float* in the future, which would mean the value may drop below $1 per share.

Short-term CDs and treasury bills (maturing in less than 12 months) are often considered cash-equivalents. Cash investments are considered very safe, but the return is very low, hovering near zero in recent years.

Real Estate

Although not one of the two main asset classes (equities and fixed income), real estate is a common asset class. It includes the equity in your home, and may also include rental property, commercial property (such as an office building), and vacant land that you own. A personal residence is often considered as a hedge against inflation, especially if the homeowner has a fixed rate mortgage. (If inflation increases, the fixed-rate mortgage rate is fixed, and therefore is not exposed to inflation). A personal residence also offers the added benefit of providing personal enjoyment. Within an investment account, there are pools of real estate assets that investors can purchase. These are called REITS, which stands for Real Estate Investment Trusts.

Other

There are many asset classes other than equities and fixed income. These are often referred to as alternative assets, and they may include commodities, real estate, hedge funds, private equity investments, and structured products. Commodities include precious metals (gold, silver, platinum), oil and gas, and agricultural products, such as sugar, corn, and wheat. Often, alternative assets are not liquid, which means you cannot withdraw your money from the investment on short notice.

Many companies that sell alternative assets to investors employ a strategy of exclusivity. They make investors feel that they are special if they can access these investments. This exclusivity strategy was used very successfully by Bernie Madoff. He made the investors feel like they were a part of an exclusive club, but it all turned out to be an enormous scam.

This exclusivity strategy is often used by hedge funds and private equity firms. Typically, investors must be *accredited*, meaning they have over $1 million in investable assets or an annual income exceeding $250,000. Hedge funds and private equity firms like to convey the impression that they make excellent investments. In fact, many studies have shown that hedge funds have very disappointing results. In 2011 Daniel Goldie and Gordon Murray reported in their book *The Investment Answer* that "the median life of a hedge fund is only 31 months. Fewer than 15 percent of hedge funds last longer than six years, and 60 percent of them disappear in less than three years."

This finding seemed alarming at the time, but in recent years many hedge funds have performed poorly. An article in *The Economist* in December of 2012 reported: "The S&P 500 has now outperformed its hedge fund rival for 10 straight years, with the exception of 2008 when both fell sharply."

Investors in hedge funds typically pay annual fees that include 2 percent of the amount they have invested, plus 20 percent of the profits. This is shortened to "2 and 20" in investment parlance, and it is excessive. In years where there are losses, the hedge fund managers do not receive the 20 percent (because there is no profit), but they still receive 2 percent in management fees. In addition, many of the hedge funds have restrictions that prevent investors from withdrawing their money.

Another problem with firms that sell alternative assets is that the performance of the investment is often not transparent. A hedge fund often owns assets that are similar to an equity mutual fund. The main difference is that the hedge fund manager is not required to report performance and earnings on a consistent basis, whereas a mutual fund manager has stricter reporting requirements. Although the SEC has tried to increase the oversight of hedge funds, it has not been successful.

Great investors, such as Benjamin Graham and Warren Buffett, did not get wealthy by investing in alternative investments. They used discipline and smart investing strategies to earn their wealth. They used what I term "plain vanilla" investment strategies.

Whether you have a financial advisor or you decide to manage your own investments, becoming educated about the financial industry is always wise. By educating yourself, you will not be at the mercy of salespeople in the investment industry who are much more interested in their sales than your financial security. Remember the adage "Plain vanilla tastes great!"

Your Tolerance for Risk

You have probably heard many times that your investments should be designed around your risk tolerance. First, we need to clarify that the issue is not really tolerance for *risk*. It should be called tolerance for *loss*. Risk, by some definitions, is "the probability that an investment's actual return will be different than expected." Morningstar defines risk as "the extent to which an investment is subject to uncertainty." These definitions imply that risk should cause anxiety if a return is significantly *above or below* what is expected.

Let's assume we want to measure the risk of overperforming or underperforming in an investment portfolio. If the expected long-term average annual return (before taxes and inflation) for a balanced portfolio is 8 percent, would you feel stressed if your investments return 12 percent for the year? By definition, you *should* feel stress because 12 percent significantly exceeds the expected performance. Yet investors only feel stressed or panicked when they experience significant losses in their investments. Therefore, it is your tolerance for loss that is important.

There are questionnaires that attempt to measure a person's risk tolerance, but they are often inadequate. A good measure is to look at how you reacted when the U.S. stock market dropped over 42 percent in the six months between September 15, 2008, and March 9, 2009. During this period, the nightly news reports were stating that no one knew when the economy would start to recover, and fear was rampant that the stock market and investment accounts would continue to plummet. It was definitely a "doom and gloom" attitude.

How did you respond to the economic turmoil during that time? Were you calm, knowing our economy (and your investments) would stabilize and recover? Or did the fear and uncertainty jolt you emotionally, causing you to lie awake at night? These are important clues to how much risk you should have in your investment portfolio.

A person's risk tolerance can change significantly over time. This is apparent in my clients' behavior. If the economic news is frightening or there has recently been a natural disaster or the stock market has been declining, their risk tolerance tends to be low. They may want to reduce the equity percentage in their portfolio because they are fearful. Conversely, if the media reports have been positive, the stock market has been climbing for the past two years, and the horizon looks sunny, they will question whether they should take more risk (have more equities) in their portfolio. It is important to realize that your risk tolerance is based on your current emotions, and your emotions can change at any time. Having a plan—and sticking to it—is essential.

Volatility

There are other factors to consider when you are attempting to determine your tolerance for risk. One factor is whether you mind large increases and decreases in your portfolio, depending on what is happening with the stock market. This is termed *volatility*, but I prefer to think of it as a roller coaster ride (see Figure 10.1). Do you mind watching your portfolio soar and then plummet in value, or would you prefer a steadier ride with less volatility?

In the investment industry, volatility is generally measured by standard deviation. Goldie and Murray, authors of *The Investment Answer*, define standard deviation as "a statistical measure of the degree to which numbers in a series (such as the annual returns of an investment) differ from their average." Equities typically have a much higher standard deviation than bonds. This means they

Don't Try to Time the Market!

Timing the market refers to investors who jump in and out of the stock market based on how they expect the stock market to perform in the short term. It may seem that if the stock market has been increasing, one could assume it will continue increasing. This may imply that it is a good time for an investor to move money out of their bank account or out of bonds and into the stock market. This is extremely dangerous and is not recommended.

Conversely, by the end of 2008, after the stock market had declined very quickly, many investors moved money out of the stock market. Their expectation was that the market would continue to drop, and by moving out of the stock market, they would avoid further decreases.

When the market is increasing (as in the first example), it is important to understand that the short-term performance of the stock market is impossible to predict. In the second example involving the financial crisis in late 2008, the U.S. stock market proved this strategy wrong when it hit its low point on March 9, 2009, and then started climbing. The investors who pulled out of the stock market at the end of 2008 "locked in" their losses by selling their stock market holdings at a low point. They had their money in cash (in a low-interest money market or bank account) while the stock market was rebounding. If they had stayed invested in the market, they would have had a chance to recoup their losses when the stock market started climbing.

Wise investors do not try to time the market. This is why having your plan (and selecting an asset allocation that you can stick with through good times and bad) will serve you well.

· FIGURE 10.1

The Stock Market Roller Coaster

The stock market roller coaster.

have greater volatility and greater risk. A portfolio with 50 percent equities and 50 percent bonds will have a lower standard deviation (and therefore lower risk and lower volatility) than a portfolio with 80 percent equities and 20 percent bonds. This simply means that a portfolio with a higher percentage of equities (and therefore a higher standard deviation, higher volatility, and higher risk) will tend to have larger swings between positive and negative returns than a portfolio with a lower percentage of equities and a lower standard deviation.

Figures 10.2, 10.3, and 10.4 pertain to volatility. They reflect historical data provided by Morningstar, Inc. Remember the classic line used when investment performance is discussed: *Past performance is no guarantee of future results*. It is true that we cannot assume that the past will repeat itself. Yet most investors believe there is value in looking at volatility and historical performance.

Figure 10.2 shows the volatility of the S&P 500 index during the 25 years between 1988 and 2012. (The S&P 500 index is a commonly used index of 500 large U.S. companies. It represents a portfolio that is 100 percent in equities.) You can see that an investor would be euphoric with the over 20 percent increases in 1989, 1991, 1995-1999, 2003, and 2009. Investors would be frightened during the 9 percent decline in 2000, the 12 percent decline in 2001, and the 22 percent decline in 2002. Recently, the 37 percent decline in 2008 rattled the nerves of investors. The volatility of the S&P 500 feels very much like a roller-coaster ride. However, for investors who can stomach the risk and volatility, they were rewarded during those 25 years with an average annual return of 11.34 percent.

In contrast to a portfolio that contains 100 percent equities, Figure 10.3 shows the volatility of a portfolio that contains 100 percent bonds (intermediate-term U.S. government bonds). The bond portfolio is represented by the gray line. You can see that the performance from year-to-year was much less volatile for the bond portfolio than for the equity portfolio. However, it also had a lower return. The average annual return over the 25 years was 7.01 percent.

Figure 10.4 adds a dotted line to the graph, which reflects the 25-year performance of a portfolio that combines 50 percent equities (the S&P 500) with 50 percent bonds (intermediate-term U.S. government bonds). This represents a balanced portfolio (between equities and bonds) and would be termed a 50-50 portfolio. The graph shows that the 50 percent in bonds eliminates the high peaks and low valleys of the 100 percent equity portfolio. This may help an investor worry less and sleep better at night. Over the 25-year period, the average annual return for the 50-50 portfolio was 9.18 percent per year.

In summary, the three portfolios had the following average annual returns from 1988-2012:

100 % equities	11.34 %
50 % equities, 50 % bonds	9.18 %
100 % bonds	7.01 %

A *balanced* portfolio does not need to contain 50 percent equities and 50 percent bonds. The term balanced portfolio is typically used to describe a portfolio that contains between 40 and 60 percent equities. It is up to the individual investor to decide what asset allocation is appropriate.

Looking at volatility—and deciding how much you want in your investment portfolio—is not the whole picture. You also need to decide what types of assets you want in your investment accounts. Looking at historical returns of portfolios with different combinations of equities and bonds will give you some insight, and examples are provided later in this chapter under "Asset Allocation."

Limit the Downside

At the beginning of this chapter is a quote by Warren Buffett: *Rule #1: Don't lose money. Rule #2: Don't forget Rule #1.* Although this may seem like a comical quip, it is filled with wisdom. Exposing your investments to significant losses can have devastating consequences to your financial security.

Trying to recoup losses in your investments is much more difficult than not losing money in the first place. Let's assume you had a portfolio that contained $100,000 in October of 2007, and it was all invested in the S&P 500 (100 percent equities). The S&P 500 declined 54 percent between October 2007 and early March 2009. Your account would also have declined by 54 percent, and you would have watched your $100,000 decrease to $46,000 by March 9, 2009. To recoup the $54,000 you lost (the 54 percent), would you assume you need to have a return of 54 percent? No! You would need to have a return of 118 percent just to return to your original $100,000!

FIGURE 10.2

Equity Volatility

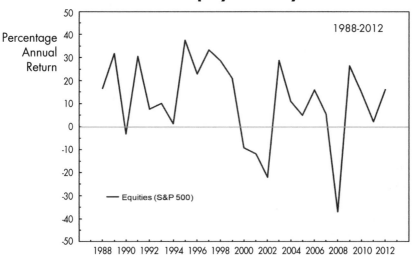

FIGURE 10.3

Equity and Bond Volatility

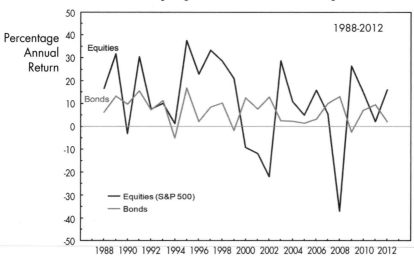

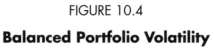

FIGURE 10.4

Balanced Portfolio Volatility

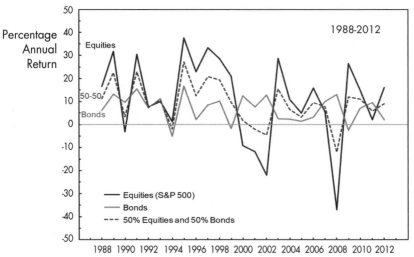

An easier way to demonstrate that the percentage increase required to recoup losses is far greater than the percentage lost is with a simple example. If you lose 50 percent of your investments (which was very common in the 2008 to 2009 recession and could easily happen again), you must have a 100 percent return just to get back to your previous level. (You can do the math: $100,000 → $50,000 = 50 percent loss. $50,000 → $100,000 = 100 percent gain.)

People who think investors should have an aggressive portfolio (with a high percentage of equities) may argue that if you are many years away from retirement, you should accept a high level of risk (volatility) because you have a long time to recover. This attitude is dangerous. It can be very difficult to "dig out" after a large loss to your investments. This is precisely why I recommend a balanced portfolio to my clients, and why I do not want them on a roller coaster ride with extreme highs and lows from year to year. A balanced portfolio is designed to provide growth, income, and stability. A smoother ride is better for your emotional health and your financial security.

Some folks will point out that maintaining a balanced portfolio will result in lower returns when the stock market is performing well. This is true. You will not have the big gains or the severe losses. But your long-term investment performance will be steadier than aggressive portfolios, and it will not feel like a roller coaster ride.

A mutual fund company has used the story of the tortoise and the hare as its marketing message for many years. Keep in mind the slogan "slow and steady wins the race" when you are tempted to buy a "sexy" investment. Have reasonable expectations, don't reach for the stars, and limit the downside.

Many investors are constantly searching for the next big winner. They feel compelled to win big, and they continue to search for the perfect investment. However, the perfect investment does not exist. Carl Richards, founder of *BehaviorGap.com* states:

> *This widespread notion that there exists somewhere an investment that outshines all others simply doesn't make sense. No single investment is right for everyone. The best investments for you depend on personal factors—your goals, your personality, your existing holdings, your credit card balance ... the list is endless.*

Investing with a focus on not *losing* money does not mean you will not *make* money. The two are not mutually exclusive. The key is to limit losses during an economic downturn so that your investments can grow more over the long term. As stated in the section on volatility (and Figure 10.4), a 50 percent equity and 50 percent bond portfolio averaged a 9.18 percent return over the past 25 years.

The balanced approach works quite well for my younger clients. They are still saving and investing each year. Although they may have 15 to 20 years before retirement, they do not want to see their hard-earned investments decline drastically. It also works nicely for my retired clients, who are taking withdrawals from their investments. The balanced portfolio strategy does not *prevent* losses

Speculating vs. Investing

In the investment industry, an important distinction between speculating and investing exists. Speculating is looking for the next big winner—hoping to "win big." This may involve acting on a stock tip from your neighbor (which is usually bad advice) or buying the hedge fund that is getting lots of media attention. Speculating typically happens when investors don't have a plan. They do not know what their goals are, and they haven't selected an asset allocation for their investments. As a result, they end up with a chaotic mix of risky investments. In most cases, these investments "lose big" rather than win big.

during a major downturn in the stock market. However, during recent downturns, it has significantly reduced the loss, thereby allowing the investment accounts to recover more quickly and start growing again.

Over the past 15 years, my financial planning clients have held portfolios that are well diversified and balanced. They contain no-commission, low-cost mutual funds. Many of my retired clients have bond ladders going out 6 to 10 years to provide cash flow each year (bond ladders are discussed in Chapter Eleven). Most of my clients are retired or within 10 years of retirement, and they maintain an asset allocation of 50 to 55 percent in equities with the remaining 45 to 50 percent in bonds. A few of my clients maintain an equity percentage as high as 65 percent, and a few have chosen to have their equity percentage as low as 30 percent.

Did my clients appreciate their balanced portfolios when the stock market crashed in the fall of 2008? Yes. Did they lose less than many investors? Yes. Shortly after the downturn, it was fascinating to talk with them about whether they wanted to adjust the equity percentages in their portfolio. Some clients wanted to "stay the course" and keep their equity percentage within their investment accounts at 50 to 60 percent. Others wanted to reduce the equity percentage slightly, to 45 to 55 percent. Some clients were very fearful, wanting to sell out at the low point and stay in cash (in a money market account or bank account). I was able to persuade these clients to stay invested and maintain a balanced portfolio. Selling after a major decline (at a low point) can be devastating to the long-term performance of an investment portfolio. This is where discipline to follow the plan is essential.

What was impacting my clients' varying reactions to the downturn? Why did they not all react the same? There are many reasons, including the way their brains are "wired" (discussed in Chapter Two), their experiences with money throughout their lifetime (Chapter Three), and their feelings about the future of the U.S. economy and the stock market.

The most common statement I heard from my clients in late 2008 was that they were fearful that this downturn was different from downturns in the past. This is a common reaction during a frightening time, although there have been many crises during the past 100 years, and the stock market has always recovered.

As you contemplate your personal risk tolerance, consider the following:

- Reflect on your reaction to the economic turmoil and losses in your investment portfolio between September 2008 and March 2009. If you had a very relaxed attitude, and you were not worried about the losses, then you likely have a high tolerance for risk. If you were not sleeping well during the downturn, and you found yourself worrying about the future, then you have a low tolerance for risk. Most investors are somewhere in between, which is why a balanced approach is often wise.

- Think about whether you tend to make rational financial decisions or emotional decisions. Like Harry Markowitz (in Chapter Two, "How Your Brain is Wired"), think through how you will react if the market goes into another tailspin. If you may sell out in a panic, then you should have a conservative portfolio.

The Relationship Between Risk and Return

Figure 10.5 shows a simple graph that illustrates the relationship between risk and return. A low-risk investment (such as a savings account or a CD) will have a very low return. A high-risk investment (such as an emerging market equity fund or a private equity fund) *should* have a high rate of return. Note that I said *should* have a high rate of return.

FIGURE 10.5

Relationship Between Risk and Return

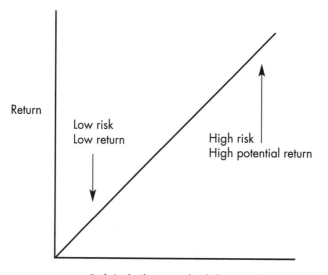

Risk (volatility, standard deviation)

The theory of the stock market is that if you are willing to take additional risk, then you should be rewarded with additional return. In real life, it does not always work out. Investors who had very aggressive investment portfolios full of technology companies were not rewarded for the risk in years 2000 to 2002 when the technology sector plummeted.

Investors who own CDs can sleep well at night, knowing their CDs are insured by the FDIC. However, the return on a CD is extremely low. Let's contrast a CD with a stock. If you buy shares in a large, well-established U.S. company (often called a "blue-chip stock"), such as Coca-Cola or IBM, you may assume your investment is safe and your investment will grow. However, the share price of a stock can be very volatile and risky. This was apparent for investors who owned Fannie Mae stock, which declined from $39.98 per share on December 31, 2007, to 76 cents per share on December 31, 2008.

Because of the high risk, investing in the stock market provides the *potential* of a high return. Although there are no guarantees with the stock market, the potential return is what entices an investor to take more risk. I recently heard a financial planner make the comment: "It is an investment—not a guarantee." This is important to remember when you buy any investment, such as an equity, a bond, an alternative asset, or real estate. If you want a guarantee, it is best to buy a CD, but then you will have an extremely low return.

Once an investor understands the relationship between risk and return, this leads to the realization that *there is no such thing as a low-risk, high-return investment.*

Another issue that affects the risk of an investment is liquidity. Liquidity is how quickly an investor could sell the asset and withdraw the proceeds. The vast majority of stocks and mutual funds can be *liquidated* (sold and turned into cash) within two or three days. In contrast, some hedge funds, private equity funds, and real estate funds do not allow their investors to liquidate their holdings or withdraw the proceeds. Some private real estate investment trusts have not released investors' money since 2008. Clearly, the managers of these real estate investment trusts are hoping the real estate industry recovers so they can return investors' money, but preventing or limiting access to the initial investment is a sure sign of very high risk.

Risks to Investors

Investors face many risks. Some are obvious; others are not. Arguably, the biggest risk for investors is allowing our brains to make impulsive decisions that do not follow logic. This ties into the discussion in Chapter Two on how our brains are wired, and how greed and fear originate in the amygdala. If the prefrontal cortex of our brain can quiet down the strong emotions from the amygdala, then rational thinking and logic can prevail. However, in a frightening economy when the stock market is dropping rapidly, fear often leads to unwise investment decisions.

Dalbar, a financial services market research firm, releases an annual study called the *Quantitative Analysis of Investor Behavior Study*. It reported that individual investors have, for much of the past 20 years, significantly trailed market benchmarks, including the S&P 500 index. In 2011, when the S&P 500 had a total return of about 2 percent, the average equity mutual fund investor lost 5.73 percent. In 2010, when the S&P 500 rose 9.14 percent, the average equity investor experienced an annual return of 3.83 percent. Sometimes investors have trailed the benchmark by as much as 10 percent.

One reason that most individual investors underperform the benchmark is that people tend to buy when prices are high and sell when prices are low. This may seem surprising, but one needs to realize this is what the media encourages, and it may also be influenced by human nature. When the stock market is rising, the media reports on the gains (the market went up again today), and the tendency to follow the herd motivates investors to buy. When the stock market is declining rapidly, the media encourages fear, and the amygdala is shouting at the investor to sell and run for cover.

The Dalbar study also found that individual investors do not stay in the stock market long enough to qualify as long-term investors. They hold stock mutual funds for an average of 3.27 years.

In addition to the risk caused by how our brains are wired (discussed in Chapter Two), there are other risks investors face.

- *Overconfidence:* After an investment increases in value, an investor may start feeling overconfident, thinking he or she is a great stock picker and investor. This is similar to the "Lake Wobegon" effect made popular by Garrison Keillor, in which "all the women are strong, all the men are good-looking, and all the children are above average." The more likely cause of the increase was simply a wise investment choice or possibly a good year for the stock market in general. Becoming overconfident can lead to taking more risk than is prudent or neglecting the potential downside of investments.

- *Herding:* As humans, we do not like to go against the crowd. We tend to follow the herd, which can be dangerous for our investment accounts. Herding is common in the financial industry, as financial firms watch the recommendations of other financial firms very closely. Herding is also prevalent in the media, in which numerous financial articles and news stories all give the same advice. When the message in the media is that the stock market is soaring, there is a human tendency to not want to be left behind. If an investor has excess cash, there may be a tendency to invest it in equities, often at the worst possible time.

- *Loss aversion:* This may cause investors to be too conservative in their choices. Research has shown that we feel losses two and a half times more strongly than gains. This means that when an investor experiences a significant loss in his or her investment account, the reaction will be two and a half times more severe than if the investor has experienced the same increase. This makes sense intuitively. Gains in our investments do not make us concerned; losses do.

- *Lack of research:* Very few investors carefully research investments before deciding to buy. Seeing an equity mutual fund featured in an investment article may be a first step, but then you should do careful research to see if that fund is appropriate for your investment account. Researching the historical performance of the fund (in good times and bad) is a good place to start. Next, review the stocks that the fund owns, the fund manager's investment philosophy, how often the manager buys and sells stocks within the fund (called the turnover ratio), and the longevity of the manager. If possible, read the commentary written by the fund manager in the most recent annual or quarterly report. Always review the costs and how the fund would fit in with the other funds you are holding. A mutual fund should have to earn a right to be included in your portfolio.

- *Short-term focus:* I often see this risk in new clients. Let's assume I have a new client who is 60 years old and is planning to retire at 65. He or she may say to me, "My time horizon is five years." I will respond by saying, "From my perspective, your time horizon is 30 to 35 years. Your finances do not need to carry you only until retirement. They need to carry you throughout your entire life, and I would assume you may live to be 95." I recall many years ago having a client tell me that I could not buy their bond ladder out longer than five years because she didn't think she and her husband would live that long. It is now 15 years later, and they are both still alive.

- *Hindsight bias*: This risk often involves regret—looking back on a situation and feeling like it was predictable. An example is if someone said that investors should have known that the drastic downturn that began on September 15, 2008, was going to occur. After all, the investment bank Bear Stearns failed in March 2008, and Fannie Mae and Freddie Mac were nationalized in early September 2008. There were clear signs that housing prices were dropping quickly, beginning back in 2007. Yet government officials were telling the American public that everything was fine and the economy was resilient.

In addition to the above risks (which I consider "risks of being human"), there are risks to specific asset classes.

- U.S. equities face *stock market risk* (fluctuations within the stock market), *sector risk* (as when financial stocks dropped in late 2008), *manager risk* (the manager changes at a mutual fund), and *investment-style risk* (as when growth stocks are in greater favor than value stocks, or when a manager moves from one investment style to another). They also face industry/company risk, such as a medical company that has a major recall or an oil company that experiences an oil spill.

- International equities face the risks listed above for U.S. equities, as well as *currency risk* (negative fluctuations in the country's currency as compared with the U.S. dollar), and *country or regional risk* (such as countries in Europe that are still facing financial hardship, or emerging market countries that may experience civil wars or takeovers).

- Bonds have very different risks from equities, including *interest rate risk* (increasing interest rates cause bond prices to decline), *inflation risk* (if inflation increases, the income from the bond may be less than inflation, causing the bond price to decline), *call or prepayment risk* (many bonds can be called early, which causes the investor to lose the future income), *default risk* (corporate bonds or municipal bonds can default if the corporation or municipality files for bankruptcy), and *credit risk* (when a bond's rating is downgraded, causing the bond's value to decrease).

In addition to the "risks of being human" and the "risks of asset classes," there are risks that all investors face. These include market volatility, economic uncertainty, and inflation. And last, there are three risks that directly impact retirees.

- *Solvency* pertains to reductions in payments from pension plans, Social Security, or Medicare.

- *Longevity*: Americans are living longer. For a couple aged 65, there is a 25 percent chance that one spouse will live to age 96.

- *Medical expenses*: This risk impacts everyone, but especially retirees. It is difficult to know what health care problems may arise in the future and to know whether the expenses will be covered by Medicare or supplemental insurance. It is also difficult to know whether you will need long-term care in a nursing home facility.

Strategies for Minimizing Risks

The best approach for minimizing the "risks of being human" is to have a plan and to use discipline to follow it. Following the rules in "A Balanced Approach" in Chapter Two can prevent you from making an impulsive decision that does not support your long-term plan. Financial planners often use an *Investment Policy Statement* with clients to document their investment objectives and asset allocation. Retirement projections often include a list of a client's goals, along with an estimated spending plan, savings plan, and withdrawal plan during retirement.

Setting a rule that you will not invest in any new investment for at least three days can also prevent a bad decision. This gives you time to think about whether that investment fits into your long-term plan and for your prefrontal cortex to apply logic to your decision. You may also want to quit listening to your friend who has the hot stock tips. Simply say, "I have a long-term plan, so I am not interested in stock tips."

The best way to minimize the risk caused by asset classes is to use a balanced asset allocation and keep your investments diversified. The last three risks (solvency, longevity, and medical expenses), which impact retirees most, can be minimized by preparing very conservative retirement projections. For example, if you are concerned that your pension may be reduced, this should be reflected in your retirement projections. Adequate funding should be included in the plan for health care, assuming that Medicare and supplemental insurance may not cover all the expenses. You may want to consider buying a long-term care policy, and the premiums would need to be included in the retirement projections. Also, include dental expenses, because these are rarely covered by insurance.

Preparing retirement projections with several scenarios works well. One scenario may be your best estimate of the future—assuming Medicare and supplemental insurance cover your medical expenses, you live to age 85 or 90, and your pension and Social Security payments are not reduced. With retirement projections, you also need to make assumptions for the average annual return in your investments and the average rate of inflation. You may choose to assume a 7 percent average annual return (assuming you have a balanced portfolio with low costs) and 4 percent for inflation. Some financial advisors will think these assumptions are overly conservative, but with retirement projections, I prefer to be conservative.

You should then prepare at least one more scenario (you may have several scenarios, but you need at least two)—a "worst-case scenario." Assume you will live to be 95 or 100. Your investment accounts will average a return that is much less than 7 percent per year (maybe 4 percent), and inflation will average 6 percent. Also, assume that your pension is reduced by 50 percent and you need to pay for additional medical expenses. No doubt, the projections will look very different (much worse) than in the first scenario.

Asset Allocation

Asset allocation refers to the percentage you have in equities (the stock market), fixed income (bonds), real estate, and other assets. The literal interpretation would be how much you have *allocated* to different asset classes.

For the sake of simplicity, we are going to limit the asset classes to equities (which includes many different types of equity mutual funds) and fixed income (which may include different types of bonds or bond funds, CDs, money market funds, and cash). If you have a large investment portfolio, you might include a small portion of real estate, commodities, or other alternative assets. If you do, I recommend you place these in a retirement account (such as a tax-deferred IRA or tax-free Roth IRA), and keep the total at less than 10 percent of all your investment accounts combined.

There are many ways to determine what your asset allocation should be. A rule that became popular in the early 1990s was "subtract your age from 100," and that is the amount you should have in the stock market. I do not recommend using this rule for three reasons. First, the rule does not take into account your tolerance for risk, which should be a primary factor. Second, the rule completely ignores your personal goals. Third, the rule results in a portfolio for young investors (under age 30) that, in my opinion, is too aggressive.

Throughout this book I have mentioned many times the benefits of a balanced portfolio. A portfolio with 50 percent in equities and 50 percent in fixed income is certainly balanced. However, within the financial industry, the balanced category typically allows for as little as 40 percent equities or as much as 60 percent equities. There-fore, portfolios with an asset allocation that range from 40 percent equities and 60 percent bonds, up to 60 percent equities and 40 per-cent bonds would all be categorized as balanced.

Figures 10.6 and 10.7 show the average annual return for several portfolios containing different allocations of equities and bonds. The data was provided by Morningstar, Inc.

Figure 10.6 reflects data from 1926 through 2012. Note that as you increase the percentage of stocks (and move to the right on the table), the average annual return increases. This reflects the fact that over the long term, the stock market has provided more growth than bonds. There are no surprises in the results.

Now refer to Figure 10.7. It is very similar to Figure 10.6, except that it only covers 13 years (January 1, 2000, until December 31, 2012). The results are drastically different than the results from 1926 to 2012. Notice that the portfolios that contain a higher per-centage of stocks had a lower performance than the portfolios that contained fewer stocks. In fact, the portfolio with the highest annual return for the 13-year period was one with no stocks at all. This is because of the major U.S. stock market declines that occurred between years 2000 and 2002 and again from late 2008 through early 2009.

Figure 10.7 shows the danger of being overly aggressive with an investment portfolio, and it creates a dilemma. Do you assume that the next 20 or 30 years for the U.S. stock market will mimic the past 86 years? Or do you assume that the next 20 or 30 years may more closely mimic the past 13 years? This will have a major impact on your decision about the percentage of equities you want in your investment portfolio. Recognizing that the future will not mimic the past, what should be your starting point when looking at historical data? Only you can decide, but the contrast between the data for the long-term (1926 to 2012) and the shorter term (2000 to 2012) is thought-provoking.

FIGURE 10.6

Average Annual Return for Portfolios with Different Asset Allocations (1926-2012)

0% Stocks 100% Bonds	20% Stocks 80% Bonds	40% Stocks 60% Bonds	50% Stocks 50% Bonds	60% Stocks 40% Bonds	80% Stocks 20% Bonds	100% Stocks 0% Bonds
5.5%	6.7%	7.8%	8.3%	8.7%	9.4%	10.0%

FIGURE 10.7

Average Annual Return for Portfolios with Different Asset Allocations (2000-2012)

0% Stocks 100% Bonds	20% Stocks 80% Bonds	40% Stocks 60% Bonds	50% Stocks 50% Bonds	60% Stocks 40% Bonds	80% Stocks 20% Bonds	100% Stocks 0% Bonds
6.3%	5.7%	5.2%	4.9%	4.6%	4.0%	3.5%

The asset allocation decision is very important. A classic 1986 study within the financial industry estimated that 91.5 percent of portfolio performance is based on the asset allocation decision, with 4.6 percent based on security selection, 1.8 percent on market timing, and 2.1 percent on other factors. A study by Daniel Wallick and colleagues at Vanguard, released in 2012, confirmed the findings from the earlier study and concluded that the asset allocation decision determined 88 percent of a diversified portfolio's return.

I recommend you decide what you want your asset allocation to be. The decision is solely up to you. Study Figures 10.6 and 10.7. If you choose an asset allocation that is not overly aggressive (meaning not too heavy in equities), you can consider your asset allocation to be a "hedge against turmoil." Many of my clients have chosen a balanced 50 percent equity and 50 percent fixed-income portfolio. This is consistent with the story about Nobel Laureate Harry Markowitz (see "How Your Brain is Wired" in Chapter Two).

There is a theory within the financial industry that was created by Markowitz called the "Efficient Market Frontier." It is shown in Figure 10.8 for the period 1970 to 2012. The theory addresses the relationship between risk and return. It suggests that a *minimum* risk portfolio has approximately 30 percent in the stock market. This may seem strange because one might expect that having 100 percent in fixed income would be less risky. The reason is that fixed-income investments carry significant risk when exposed to inflation. Although fixed-income investments do not have market risk like equities, inflation can exceed the fixed interest rates on bonds, CDs, and money market funds. This causes the investor to lose money (buying power) on the fixed-income assets. This is the risk you face if you keep all your money in a bank, CDs, or bonds. This is also why approximately 30 percent of equities are recommended in a minimum risk portfolio.

FIGURE 10.8 EFFICIENT MARKET FRONTIER

Stocks and Bonds: Risk vs. Return
1970–2012

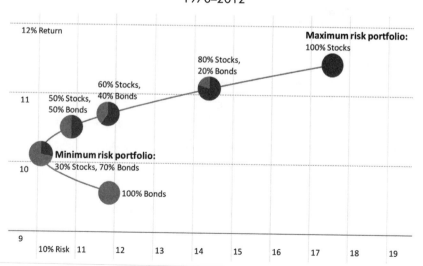

The asset allocation you choose should be a long-term decision. You may decide to adjust it in a few years if your circumstances change. "Life happens," which is why you need to be able to adjust your portfolio accordingly. Perhaps you are closer to retirement (or simply older), and you want less risk in your investments. Maybe you are financially responsible for an elderly parent or an adult child, and you need more of your money in short-term, liquid investments for monthly living expenses. Perhaps your risk tolerance has declined because you are uncomfortable with global events or the U.S. economy. Or you have decided to start a company and need more of your money in liquid investments. Maybe you received an inheritance and have decided to take more risk with your portfolio.

In light of the above changes that may cause you to shift your asset allocation in future years, I encourage you to consider your asset allocation as a long-term decision for several reasons. First, if you are not overly aggressive in your asset allocation, then you will not feel the need to "run for cover" (and sell your equity investments) during the next economic downturn. Your portfolio will experience a smaller decline than an aggressive portfolio, providing some assurance that you can stay the course. Conversely, when the stock market is performing well, you should avoid following the herd and increasing your equity percentage simply because your neighbors are all jumping into the stock market. Trying to time the market and move in and out of the stock market has proved to be very dangerous. You want to have an asset allocation that you can stick with during good times and bad.

Your asset allocation needs to be a personal decision. Take into account your age, goals, current financial situation, and tolerance for risk. Think about the way you reacted to the rapid decline of the U.S. stock market in late 2008. Also, keep in mind that if you are on track to achieve all of your goals, you may not need to assume much risk. A financial advisor colleague tells his clients,

"If you have already won the race, stop running." In other words, take less risk. This is often wise advice. However, there is a conflicting viewpoint as well. I have several retired clients who do not take withdrawals from their investments. They have sufficient income from Social Security, pensions, and other sources to cover their living expenses. In this case, I often recommend that they maintain a balanced asset allocation because they want to grow the assets for their children and grandchildren.

The asset allocation you have selected is:

_____ percent equities and _____ percent fixed income.

Active or Passive Investing?

Another important distinction when designing an investment portfolio is whether you want to use mutual funds that are actively managed, passive funds that track an index, or a combination. This is an ongoing debate within the financial industry. Let's start with some definitions.

An actively managed mutual fund typically has a team of managers who are continuously analyzing companies and determining which stocks they want to own in their mutual fund. They are buying and selling stocks in an effort to maximize the fund's performance for their investors.

Conversely, a passive investing strategy means you will use index funds. These are run by a computer, and there is not a human (an active manager) making buy or sell decisions for the fund. Many folks, such as John Bogle (the founder of Vanguard), are strong supporters of index funds.

I have followed this debate closely because it is important in terms of the investment recommendations I give my clients. For many years, the debate was contentious. Some investors felt strongly that passive was a better strategy, and others felt equally strong about the actively managed approach. There was very little collaboration between opposing viewpoints. Fortunately, this is changing.

Recent studies in the financial industry show that cost is a key factor in whether an actively managed fund can beat an index. An actively managed fund with a high expense ratio is at a huge disadvantage. Similarly, there are index funds with high fees that are also at a disadvantage. Don Phillips, president of Morningstar's Investment Research Division, stated the following:

Not all index funds are good. Not all active funds are bad. The focus instead should be on low cost versus high cost. The cause of passive's collective advantage over active is not manager ineptitude; it's essentially just cost. Lose the cost benefit, and you lose the advantage. Active versus passive is largely a smokescreen; it's low cost that matters most. Intelligent investors should feel free to fish in either the active or passive ponds, but they should be vigilant in avoiding high-cost options from either.

I realized several years ago that the best indicator for my financial planning firm is to compare the specific actively managed funds that I recommend to my clients against a select group of their peers (similar actively managed funds that have passed my due diligence process) and also against their corresponding index. Software and data from Morningstar assists me in this process. This allows me to analyze a very small and select group of actively managed funds using many different metrics and to monitor whether those funds are outperforming their indexes. If they are not, then I may consider replacing that fund with a different actively managed fund or with an index fund. This methodology—comparing and contrasting only the funds I am recommending with their index—is a more useful gauge than the massive studies used in the debate between passive and active.

The Vanguard Group released information in 2012 that supports using a combination of index funds and actively managed funds within an investment portfolio. The rationale is to take advantage of the low index-fund costs for much of the equity portion but to supplement the equity portion with some actively managed funds in an attempt to outperform the market. This is called a *core and satellite* strategy.

After monitoring the debate between active and passive investment management for over 15 years, I believe index funds work great for individual investors who are managing their own portfolios and who do not want to devote much time to analyzing actively managed funds on an ongoing basis.

Within my financial planning firm, I use many actively managed equity funds. I am willing to devote the time to perform the necessary due diligence, and I am convinced that carefully selected actively managed mutual funds can outperform the index. However, I closely monitor the expense ratios of the equity funds I recommend, and I often use bond index funds for the fixed-income portion of my clients' portfolios.

In summary, if you are going to design and manage your own portfolio, then I recommend using index funds. They are simple to use and they do not require excessive time to research or monitor. It is important that you select an index fund family with very low costs and do not assume that all index funds have low costs. Vanguard (www.vanguard.com) offers index funds for large-cap stocks, small-cap stocks, international stocks, and bonds. Although I am not recommending any specific Vanguard fund, I believe Vanguard currently has the best offering of index funds (with very low costs) available in the financial industry.

If you are working with a financial advisor, your advisor will provide you with specific recommendations.

Diversification

The saying "don't put all of your eggs in one basket" explains the concept of diversification.

Consider the following examples. If your portfolio contains stock in five technology companies (and nothing else), the five investments will likely move up and down together over time because there is very little diversification. Alternatively, let's assume you invest in an S&P 500 index fund, a small-cap U.S. fund, an international equity fund, a corporate bond fund, and an intermediate-term bond index fund. The combination of many different asset classes provides diversification, which should also result in lower volatility.

Now that we have covered asset classes, asset allocation, the relationship between risk and return, the debate between passive and active, and diversification, let's move to how to design an investment portfolio.

Designing Your Own Portfolio

Equity Portion

As stated earlier, I recommend equity mutual funds rather than individual stocks. Equity mutual funds are simply a pool of many individual stocks. If an equity mutual fund combines 100 stocks into a fund, then it is much more diversified than if you only own one stock.

Earlier in this chapter, you were encouraged to select your asset allocation. For the sake of simplicity, we will assume you chose 50 percent equities and 50 percent fixed income. If you chose an asset allocation that is different, you can adjust the percentages below.

Index funds are an excellent choice for this purpose. If you want a very simple portfolio, there are index funds with names such as the Total Stock Market Index. Vanguard has a fund by this name, and it is designed to contain approximately 70 percent U.S. large-cap stocks, 20 percent U.S. mid-cap stocks, and 10 percent U.S. small-cap stocks within one fund. Index funds like this work well as a primary holding for the equity portion of a portfolio. By adding a few more funds (see below), you can design a diversified portfolio that matches your personal preferences.

Let's focus on the 50 percent that you plan to invest in equities. You need to decide how much of that 50 percent will be large-cap, mid-cap, small-cap, or international funds. I am purposely keeping the three hypothetical examples provided below very simple. Keep in mind that the remaining 50 percent will contain a variety of fixed-income investments. For now, we are only focusing on the equities.

50 Percent Equity Portion

Portfolio A

35 % Total Stock Market Index Fund
(includes large-cap, mid-cap, and small-cap U.S. stocks)

15 % International Fund

Portfolio B

10 % Large-Cap Growth Fund

10 % Large-Cap Value Fund

10 % Mid-Cap Fund

10 % Small-Cap Fund

10 % International Fund

Portfolio C

14 % Large-Cap U.S. Fund

 8 % Mid-Cap Fund

 8 % Small-Cap Fund

10 % International Fund

10 % A combination of alternative assets or sector mutual funds, such as a utility, a health care, an energy, a technology, a financial services, a telecommunication, a precious metals, a real estate, or a commodity fund

From the above examples, you can see that the possibilities are endless. If you are designing your own portfolio, you should choose the combination that you prefer. If you want your portfolio to contain a higher percentage of international stocks, then increase the international percentage. If you want a higher percentage of small-cap stocks, then increase the small-cap percentage. If you are working with a financial advisor, he or she will prepare specific recommendations for you.

Fixed-Income Portion

I consider the fixed-income portion of my clients' portfolios to be just as important as the equity portion. Many of my clients have bond ladders in their accounts, which are designed to provide the cash flow needed for their yearly living expenses or the amount that is required that they withdraw from an IRA each year after age 70½. Some of my younger clients have bond ladders that are designed to begin maturing around the time they plan to retire. Other clients have an assortment of bond funds in their investment accounts, which may include an intermediate-term bond fund, an inflation-protected bond fund, a short-term corporate bond fund, an intermediate-term corporate bond fund, and a foreign bond fund.

If a client is in a marginal tax bracket that is 28 percent or above, I often recommend some municipal bonds or municipal bond funds in a taxable investment account. Municipal bonds are usually federal tax-free, and if they are issued in the state in which you live, they are often state tax-free. However, they may be subject to the alternative minimum tax (AMT). Also, the key is to compare the after-tax yield of various types of bonds. In a taxable account for a client in a high-income tax bracket, I do not recommend municipal bonds exclusively. I want the diversification offered by many different types of bonds.

Buying individual bonds takes a significant amount of research and skill (there are many factors to consider), so I recommend that you hire a financial advisor if you want to invest in individual bonds. Alternatively, you can use bond funds.

Other Considerations for Fixed-Income Portion

As you begin designing the 50 percent for the fixed-income portion of your portfolio, consider several factors. First, do not forget the importance of your emergency fund. It was discussed earlier in this chapter and should contain enough cash (in a savings account or a money market fund) to pay for six months of normal living expenses.

Next, consider the amount of money you will need for living expenses over the next eight to 10 years. If you are young and retirement is at least 10 years away, then this is not a major concern. You would likely assume that you will not need to withdraw from your investment account while you are still working. Alternatively, if you are retired and are taking withdrawals from your investment account, then the amount you plan to withdraw must be available when you expect to need it. This is where a bond ladder (consisting of CDs or individual bonds) works well. The concept of a bond ladder is covered in Chapter Eleven. The bond ladder can be designed to match the estimated withdrawals each year, and it also works well for Required Minimum Distributions (RMDs) from an IRA for investors over age 70½. If you choose to use bond funds instead of a bond ladder, then you need to plan how you will liquidate the funds to cover the needed monthly or annual withdrawals or the RMDs.

Rebalancing Your Portfolio

I recommend that you rebalance your account once or twice a year. Often, investors follow a strategy they call "buy and hold." This strategy often works very well, but it is not analogous to "buy and neglect." Your investment account does not require you to watch it every day, or even every week. I recommend you review your monthly statements when they arrive, and then look at your asset allocation once or twice each year. Some investors rebalance their investments each year during the week of their birthday. This can be a good rule to follow, along with changing the batteries in your smoke alarms at home. If you work with a financial advisor, semi-annual or annual rebalancing should be a part of the services provided.

If you are using an asset allocation of 50 percent equities and 50 percent fixed income, and the equity percentage has shifted to 55 percent, then sell enough equities to bring the percentage back to 50 and invest the proceeds in fixed income. Likewise, if your equity percentage has declined to 45 percent, then you should sell enough of your fixed-income holdings and buy enough of an equity mutual fund to bring your equity percentage back up to 50. This is the concept of rebalancing.

Rebalancing not only pertains to asset allocation but to the diversification within your portfolio as well. Here is an example: I recommend small-cap mutual funds for my clients' portfolios. The balance between large-cap, mid-cap, and small-cap can shift and become out of balance when one asset class outperforms another. This can happen in any one year, or it can happen over the course of several years.

According to research from Morningstar, during the 15-year period from 1998 to 2012, small-cap stocks outperformed large-cap stocks for 12 of the 15 years. (In addition to better performance than large-cap stocks, small-cap stocks also have higher volatility.) Due to the stronger performance of small-cap equity funds, I have rebalanced my clients' accounts several times (over the 15-year period) to reduce the small-cap exposure back to the original percentage. This requires liquidating a portion of those small-cap funds and purchasing a different asset class that has become underweighted due to recent underperformance. This is counterintuitive, because rebalancing requires reducing the amount of a fund that has had very strong performance, but it is necessary. The rebalancing strategy supports the golden rule of "buy low, sell high." The overweighted asset class is sold at a high point, and the underweighted asset class is purchased when it is low.

If you work with a financial advisor, he or she will recommend rebalancing strategies. Prior to my semi-annual meetings with clients, I carefully review each of their investment accounts. I look for areas that need to be rebalanced, and I use my due diligence data to decide if I want to replace any mutual funds with other mutual funds. For taxable accounts, the tax consequences are always considered. I also consider upcoming cash flow needs. I then present the recommendations to the client during our meeting. Once they approve the changes, I place the necessary trades for them.

Weeding Your Garden

The previous sections cover how to design your portfolio to match your goals and risk tolerance, as well as how to rebalance your investments. Another strategy I recommend is called "weeding your garden." It can be done at the same time you rebalance your investments, but the concept is slightly different.

Everyone knows that gardens need to be weeded. Cleaning out the weeds and the old growth clears the way for new, healthy flowers and vegetables. The same strategy applies to your investment accounts. By getting rid of the clutter—the assets that have dropped significantly in value or that are not appropriate for your goals and risk tolerance—you can eliminate the weeds and let the flowers bloom.

Weeding your garden was especially important in response to the downturn in the U.S. stock market during 2008 and early 2009. Many people never weed their investment accounts and just hope their investments will recover from the losses.

Human nature tells us to leave it alone so it can recover.

I encourage you to think of the *opportunity cost* when deciding if you want to sell a stock or equity mutual fund. If an asset in your investment account has lost value, the first step is to acknowledge that the fair market value of the investment is the value *today*. It is not worth what it was prior to the loss. The opportunity cost is simply defined as the cost of passing up an opportunity. For example, if you sell a stock that has dropped in value and you use that money to buy a no-load, diversified equity mutual fund that is appropriate for your goals and tolerance for risk, would you expect your investment to grow faster in the mutual fund or in your current devalued investment? This is the concept of opportunity cost.

How do you weed your financial garden?

After determining what you want your asset allocation to be, you should review your current investment accounts. Determine if the current investments are appropriate for you. If you decide that a stock or mutual fund is appropriate for you for the long term, keep it. If you determine some investments are not appropriate, then sell them (weed them out) and replace them with better choices.

If you want to research your current investments, a website such as www.morningstar.com can be helpful. In addition, the brokerage firm or custodian for your retirement accounts will have performance data on their websites.

Invest in Yourself

- If you have not yet established a six-month emergency fund, make that your first priority. Start saving!

- Ponder your tolerance for risk. Think about how you reacted when the U.S. economy seemed to be in a downward spiral in late 2008. Decide what your asset allocation should be for your investments. You should select an asset allocation that you will be able to stick with in good times and in bad.

- If you already have investment accounts, review them using the information you learned in the asset allocation and diversification sections. Determine if they fit your goals and your tolerance for risk. If they do not, make the necessary changes. If you are building a new investment portfolio, decide whether you want to use passive or active funds, whether you want to do it yourself or work with a financial advisor, and the types of funds you want to own.

- If you have investment accounts that have been neglected, review them to see if the assets are appropriate, rebalance them, and eliminate any assets that are performing poorly.

- If you are working with a financial advisor, make an appointment to discuss changes you would like to make to your investment portfolio after reading this book.

Retirement Strategies

It is better to live rich than to die rich.
— SAMUEL JACKSON

reparing for retirement includes two distinct components; the psychological preparation and the financial
preparation. Both are essential, and both deserve your
attention. Let's start with psychological preparation.

Preparing Psychologically

Retirement is a big deal. Moving from your working years into
retirement is a major transition, especially considering your retirement "season" may last 30 or more years. Retiring can be stressful,
but preparing wisely can make the transition much easier.

The old idea of retirement was to simply stop going to the office
one day at age 65. Often, a gold watch was given to the retiree, and
co-workers wished him well. Until 40 years ago, few women
worked outside of their home, so the stereotypical retiree was male.
Often, very little planning occurred, and it was not unusual to hear
that the retiree died within a few years. Who would look forward
to that future? It is no wonder people were often fearful of retiring!

Thankfully, retirement has evolved into a much healthier process. In his book *The New Retirementality*, Mitch Anthony talks about the fact that many retirees want to stay engaged in their work:

> *People have often referred to retirement as "getting out of the race."*
> *The fact is that we no longer want out of the race. We simply want*
> *to run at our own pace. We want to make the decision whether we*
> *run, jog, or walk. We want to be able to sit out once in a while and*
> *re-enter the race at our own choosing.*

Retirement is a *process* rather than an *event*. Retirement should be flexible, allowing you to work part time, full time, or not at all; work within the same industry as your career; or work in a totally different field. It can include devoting more time to hobbies, focusing on volunteer work, and allowing additional time for friends and family, exercise, or travel. Retirement should provide the freedom to live the lifestyle you choose.

Several factors have led retirees to continue working. In many cases, the economic downturns during the past 15 years have led folks to realize they *must* keep working because they need the income for their monthly expenses. Their retirement nest eggs are not sufficient to allow them to fully retire. *New York Times* journalist Joe Nocera wrote an article titled "My Faith-Based Retirement." As he was approaching his 60th birthday, he wrote poignantly about not being able to afford to retire. He began saving in retirement plans in the late 1970s. His investments performed well until year 2000, when his technology-heavy portfolio declined 50 percent. A few years later, he divorced—and his portfolio was cut in half again. He then bought a house, and borrowed from his retirement plan to pay for renovations. The recession in 2008 and 2009 further reduced the value of his retirement nest egg. He now realizes his investments are woefully inadequate to support him in retirement, so he plans to continue working indefinitely. Unfortunately, this situation is very common.

According to the Employee Benefit Research Institute's *2012 Retirement Confidence Survey* (RCS), a *retiree* is an individual who is retired or who is age 65 or older and not employed full time. Based on this definition, a person over age 65 who continues to work full time is not retired. However, working part time at age 65 or older would categorize a person as retired.

The *2012 Retirement Confidence Survey* includes:

Almost all retirees who worked for pay in retirement in the 2010 RCS gave a positive reason for doing so, saying they did so because they wanted to stay active and involved (92 percent) or enjoyed working (86 percent). However, the percentage who report working solely *for nonfinancial reasons is small. Ninety percent identify at least one financial reason for having worked, such as wanting to buy extras (72 percent), a decrease in the value of their savings or investments (62 percent), needing money to make ends meet (59 percent), or keeping health insurance or other benefits (40 percent).*

Even if you need income and *must* continue working, you can still build more flexibility and more freedom into your week. Making some minor changes can have an enormous impact on helping you enjoy your retirement.

Retirees may continue working for reasons other than income. Research has shown that interaction with other people is extremely important to maintaining our health as we age. In fact, maintaining strong relationships with family and friends is often considered the most important determinant of well-being for retirees. When we step back and take an objective view, we realize that our jobs offer us many rewards such as camaraderie with co-workers, challenges, laughter, friendships, and a sense of purpose. For many of us, much of our identity and self-worth is tied to our jobs. This is another reason why planning for retirement is so important.

Employers are becoming more flexible and are often eager to keep good employees. Working part time (such as three days a week), working from home, or taking on projects rather than a full-time workload are options. I have had clients who discussed various options with their employers and arrived at a favorable solution for everyone. Prior to making proposals to your employer, explore strategies that would be appealing to you as well as your employer. For example, if you are great at mentoring young people, offer to be more involved with training new hires. If you are the key employee for a certain function, offer to continue with that role but let other responsibilities be passed to other employees. You may offer to train your replacement or work part time over several months to complete some important projects.

If you want to continue working during retirement, consider finding a job in a new field. Allow yourself the freedom to explore new interests and be open to new opportunities.

Another option—if you do not need the income—is to use your skills to give back through volunteer work. Many of my clients are volunteers, and I see their faces light up as they talk about their volunteer work. This is an excellent way to meet new friends and find a sense of purpose. Giving back can do wonders for your happiness and well-being, and it is discussed in greater detail in Chapter Four.

Retirement is a time to reassess your schedule and add more flexibility to your daily routine. Frequently, when we work full time, we settle into a rigid routine that allows very little time for fun or spontaneity.

In the Retirement Activities exercise below, you will choose activities for a sample week of retirement. Going to work Monday through Friday will likely not be required, so you will have more discretionary time in your schedule. This is where planning is important. In my experience, building structure into your daily routine is helpful. You may decide to leave a few mornings free to stay home and not have anything planned, but you do not want every day to be unplanned.

Exercise is very important for retirees because your health is your most valuable asset. Exercise should be the first activity you fill in on your sample week of retirement. Maybe that will be going to a health club, but it may also be morning walks, meeting a friend for a tennis match, biking, hiking, swimming, etc. Build variety into your exercise choices.

Retirement provides an opportunity to add more leisure time and relaxation in your schedule. Meet friends for lunch or dinner. Do not assume that you will suddenly spend all day and every day with your spouse. The saying "for better, for worse, but not for lunch" pertains to married couples and the transition into retirement. Plan some time away from your spouse and some alone time for you. If you love to read, put time for reading on your schedule. Sitting down with a good book in the afternoon is a treat for avid readers.

Decide to be a lifetime learner. Read daily newspapers, attend lectures, register for classes on topics you enjoy. Most communities have a variety of free services available, and now you will have the time to explore new subjects. Online courses are also a great way to expand your horizons.

If you enjoy traveling, plan some trips. These may be extensive trips that require planning airplane flights and hotels, or they may be driving trips that only last two or three days. We often neglect wonderful destinations that require only a few hours of driving from our homes. Hotels, resorts, and bed and breakfast inns often have special discounts for retirees, local residents, or last-minute bookings. Never hesitate to ask for discounts. Adding a sense of adventure to your plans will open you to new experiences and surprises.

Add hobbies to your schedule. If you enjoy gardening, set some time aside each week and get your hands dirty. If you want to cook some special meals each week—and experiment with some of the recipes you never tried when you were working full time—put that on your schedule. Grocery shopping will need to be on your schedule or going to a farmer's market to get fresh fruits and vegetables.

Think about activities you enjoyed in the past or ones you have always wanted to do. Now is your chance.

Think about how you would like to fill your days once you retire. Fill in your exercise and hobbies first. Next, include some "must dos" such as grocery shopping, doing your laundry, cooking, and cleaning. Fill in other activities, such as attending church or community events. Do not forget fun time to meet friends or family.

If you are many years away from retirement, this exercise may provide insight on some activities you want to start including in your schedule now. (Even though you may work Monday through Friday, you can still fill in fun activities on evenings and weekends.) The exercise is also on my website (*www.joyoffinancialsecurity.com*). You may want to print blank copies for your family and friends since this is a fun exercise to complete and share with others. It can lead to great discussions about what you would like to do during retirement as well as generate new ideas that you may choose to start now.

How Much Money Do You Need in Retirement?

"How much money do I need to retire?" This is a common question. Some people think there is a magic number, and if you reach that amount, you can afford to retire. Maybe it is $250,000, $500,000, $1 million, $2 million, or more. Unfortunately, there is not a magic number. The only accurate answer to the question is "it depends."

It depends on how much you expect to need each year for living expenses and how this amount may increase or decrease throughout retirement. It depends on whether you will have other income sources, such as a pension, Social Security, or a salary from a part-time job. It depends on how your investment accounts are invested

Retirement Activities Worksheet

	SUNDAY	MONDAY	TUESDAY	WEDNESDAY	THURSDAY	FRIDAY	SATURDAY
6:00 a.m.							
7:00 a.m.							
8:00 a.m.							
9:00 a.m.							
10:00 a.m.							
11:00 a.m.							
12:00 p.m. (noon)							
1:00 p.m.							
2:00 p.m.							
3:00 p.m.							
4:00 p.m.							
5:00 p.m.							
6:00 p.m.							
7:00 p.m.							
8:00 p.m.							
9:00 p.m.							
10:00 p.m.							
11:00 p.m.							
12:00 a.m. (midnight)							

and the estimated average annual rate of return you expect in future years. It depends on what you estimate for inflation, and what your estimated tax rate will be. It depends on what age you are planning to retire and the mortality age you select.

By now, you are probably tired of hearing "it depends."

All the variables listed above are considered in thorough and customized retirement projections. One of the services that my clients enjoy is the annual update of their retirement projections. We work on these together so they can select the assumptions, and sophisticated software allows us to look at many different scenarios. They can see the ramifications of retiring earlier or later, reducing their living expenses now or during retirement (by paying off their mortgage, downsizing to a smaller home or apartment, or moving to a less expensive community), retiring early but planning to work part time, and increasing their saving percentage now. We also look at other issues, such as paying for children's or grandchildren's college educations, replacing cars every 10 to 12 years, funding extra vacation expenses for the first few years of retirement, expecting medical expenses to increase, and funding major goals, such as a family reunion.

If you do not have access to sophisticated retirement projection software, there is one good shortcut that avoids the complex analysis. It involves establishing a reasonable withdrawal rate from your investment accounts. By applying that withdrawal rate to the amount you have saved for retirement, you will arrive at the amount you can withdraw each year from your retirement nest egg. This figure can then be compared with the amount you estimate you will need during retirement, and you will see whether you have saved enough.

A Sustainable Withdrawal Rate

Everyone agrees they do not want to outlive their money. With so many uncertainties about the future, it is not a surprise that retirees are concerned about their retirement nest eggs. Fortunately, several financial advisors and analysts have been studying this issue to try to determine a sustainable withdrawal rate.

There is a short answer and a long answer to the question, "What is a sustainable withdrawal rate during retirement?" Let's start with the short answer because that leads to the shortcut you can use to estimate how much money you need to retire.

The Short Answer

The short answer is approximately 4 percent. This means if you have a $1 million nest egg, you can plan to withdraw $40,000 during the first year of retirement. If your investments total $500,000, then you can withdraw $20,000 each year. Each subsequent year you can increase the withdrawal amount by an inflation factor such as 3 percent (or the consumer price index for the prior year). Therefore, if you withdraw $40,000 in year one, your withdrawal in year two will be $41,200 ($40,000 x 1.03).

This shortcut resulted from statistical analysis conducted by William Bengen, CFP®, published in 1994 in the *Journal of Financial Planning*. Bengen has devoted his career to statistical analysis on sustainable retirement withdrawal rates. Using stock market returns from 1926 until 1993, he determined that a 4.15 percent withdrawal rate would have sustained a portfolio for 30 years during the worst-case scenario. This quickly became known as the *4 Percent Rule*, and it is still widely used today.

Bengen later released additional analysis that raised the initial withdrawal rate to 4.5 percent, although he warned against using the higher rate, which requires that the income (outside of investments) increases at the same rate as the expenses (see notes for details).

That leads us back to his original 4 Percent Rule. It requires that the portfolio contain at least 50 percent equities, and the portfolio must be diversified. If you have a portfolio heavily weighted with technology stocks, the 4 Percent Rule may not apply. If you have mutual funds with extremely high expense ratios and high commissions, it also won't apply because too much of your money will be going toward expenses each year, rather than growing and compounding for you. If your investments are heavily weighted in one stock or in one industry, it won't apply. The reason at least 50 percent of the portfolio must be in the stock market (preferably in no-load mutual funds) is that, historically, the stock market has provided the growth that a portfolio needs to sustain itself over many years of retirement. Portfolios that contain only fixed-income investments have not fared well over the long term and have often been depleted due to taxes and inflation exceeding the fixed rate of return.

Applying the 4 Percent Rule

The 4 Percent Rule can be used to determine how large your nest egg should be when you retire.

1. Estimate how much you expect to need each year during retirement for living expenses. Let's assume you estimate you will need $80,000 per year, not including taxes and inflation. (The $80,000 is the amount you estimate you would need if you were retiring this year).

2. Next, you need to estimate your average annual tax rate while you are retired. (To calculate your average tax rate for the prior year, take the figure from the "total tax" line from your federal 1040 tax return and divide it by the figure on the "adjusted gross income" line. Do the same calculation for your state tax return, and add the federal and state tax rates together. This is your "average" tax rate, and it is typically significantly lower than your marginal tax rate.) For this example, let's assume your average tax rate for federal taxes is 16 percent and your average tax rate for state taxes is 4 percent for a combined total of 20 percent. Many of my clients have average tax rates well below 20 percent during retirement. (Do not get side-tracked

by trying to estimate how taxes may change in the future. These calculations are only estimates. Sophisticated retirement projections can estimate changes in your tax rate when you start drawing Social Security or when you turn 70½ and are forced to begin taking Required Minimum Distributions from your retirement plans. However, retirement projections cannot predict how Congress may change tax rates in the future, which is why estimates are adequate.)

3. The $80,000 you estimate you will need each year during retirement (for living expenses) needs to be "grossed up" to include taxes. This will then allow you to have $80,000 to spend after taxes are paid. To do this, divide $80,000 by 0.80 (that is, 1.00 – 0.20 = 0.80) for a 20 percent average tax rate.

$$\$80,000 \div 0.80 = \$100,000$$

Based on these assumptions, you would need approximately $100,000 each year during retirement to provide you with $80,000 after taxes are paid.

4. Next, you need to consider all income sources. Let's assume you will have Social Security benefits of $24,000 per year (using today's dollars from your Social Security benefit estimate), and you have a pension that will provide approximately $20,000 per year. These total $44,000. You would then subtract the Social Security and pension from the total amount needed to determine how much you will need to withdraw from your investments each year.

$$\$100,000 - \$44,000 = \$56,000$$

$56,000 is the amount you have estimated you will need to withdraw from your investments each year.

5. Now you can apply the shortcut. If you estimate you will need $56,000 from your investment portfolio each year, and you do not want to withdraw over 4 percent from the portfolio, how

large does the portfolio need to be? Divide $56,000 by 4 percent.

$$\$56,000 \div .04 = \$1.4 \text{ million}$$

In this example, you would need an investment "nest egg" at retirement of $1.4 million or more.

Before you apply the 4 Percent Rule, consider the following warnings. First, it is based on a retirement portfolio lasting for 30 years. Many financial planners elect to use an estimated mortality age of 95, so the rule is intended for persons retiring at age 65. Yet many people retire at 60 or 62, or even 58. When the retirement period is longer than 30 years, the risk is greater that the portfolio will run out of money, so you may decide to use a withdrawal rate less than 4 percent.

There are many issues to consider when discussing withdrawal rates during retirement. For example, spending does not stay constant throughout retirement. Several studies have shown that new retirees tend to spend more, especially if they want to travel during the first few years of retirement. Yet, at some point they tend to reduce their traveling, eat out less, and buy less clothing.

Health care expenses during retirement are always a factor, although in recent years this has not been a major concern for my clients who are over age 65 because Medicare and their supplemental policies pay most of their medical expenses. However, dental expenses can have a major impact on annual spending. You may want to include an allowance in your budget for medical and dental expenses that will not be paid by Medicare or supplemental policies. Also, persons planning on retiring before age 65 should include a significant amount in their budget for health insurance prior to becoming eligible for Medicare. For my clients who are retiring at a young age (and who do not have access to their employer's continued health insurance coverage), we often assume between $1,000 and $2,000 per month for a couple. Private policies with generous benefits are very expensive. Alternatively, retirees can buy a high-deductible plan, but then the high deductibles need to be included in the budget. The future of health care for retirees is unknown at this point. It is likely that the rules for Medicare may change, and the price for Medicare coverage may increase significantly.

Not surprisingly, not everyone agrees with the 4 Percent Rule. Some industry experts have speculated that much lower withdrawal rates should be used because the United States has had two declines of over 50 percent in the S&P 500 between 2000 and 2012. Other financial planners think 4 percent may be too low.

If the 4 Percent Rule is the short answer, what is the long answer?

The Long Answer

The topic of a sustainable withdrawal rate continues to be debated, and some excellent research has been conducted in recent years. In 2004, financial planner Jonathan Guyton added *decision rules* and *guardrails* to the concept of withdrawal rates. He focused his research on whether applying flexibility to the withdrawal rate could allow for a rate higher than 4 percent. The flexibility would be based on the recent performance of the retiree's investment portfolio. His initial guardrails were that if the retiree's portfolio lost money in any given year, then the next year's withdrawal would not include an adjustment (an increase) for inflation. Next, if the size of the withdrawal, in dollars, in any year amounted to an actual percentage rate of the remaining portfolio that was at least 20 percent more than the initial withdrawal rate, retirees would have to take a 10 percent cut in their annual allowance that year. The increase for inflation would build on that new base the following year.

Guyton also used a prosperity rule that would allow for an increase of 10 percent in withdrawals if the portfolio had performed very well. In essence, he was requiring his clients to agree that if the stock market performed poorly (which would cause the retiree's nest egg to decline), then the retiree may have to reduce the withdrawal the next year. Clearly, this does not work if the money is being used to pay a mortgage or other fixed expenses. However, he surmised that his clients would be willing to cancel or delay a trip one or two years if they knew their nest eggs were more vulnerable to being depleted. Or they could delay replacing a car or be more conservative with dining out or holiday gifts for family members. His theory was tested in 2008 and 2009 when the U.S. stock market plummeted over 50 percent (from the peak value in October 2007).

The conclusion of his research is that if the retiree is willing to be flexible and reduce withdrawals when the stock market performs poorly, then a higher withdrawal rate than 4 percent can be used. In fact, his research suggests that a withdrawal rate as high as 6 percent *may* be sustainable.

Another financial planner, Michael Kitces, researched withdrawal rates from another perspective and released his findings in 2008. He suspected that the price-earnings ratio (P/E) of the U.S. stock market could be used to adjust the withdrawal percentage. He assumed that if the P/E ratio was high (above 20), then this signified the stock market was overvalued and a correction may be on the horizon. In this situation, he would recommend a withdrawal rate of 4.5 percent. However, if the P/E ratio is between 12 and 20 (the historical median is approximately 15.5), then he would recommend raising the withdrawal rate to 5 percent. If the P/E ratio is below 12, he surmised that the stock market may be undervalued and may perform well during the next few years. In that case, he would recommend a withdrawal rate of 5.5 percent. (Kitces calculated the P/E ratio by taking the current price of the S&P 500 index and dividing it by the average inflation-adjusted earnings for the past 10 years.) This strategy requires that the client agree to flexible withdrawal rates, as well as a high degree of confidence that the P/E ratio is an accurate indicator of upcoming stock market returns.

David Blanchett, head of retirement research for Morningstar, and professors Michael Finke and Wade Pfau are researching how the current low interest rates on bonds will impact sustainable withdrawal rates for retirees. A 2013 article summarizing their research suggests a much lower withdrawal rate of only 2.8 percent per year would allow for a 90 percent success rate for a portfolio that contains 40 percent equities. No one knows for certain how the stock and bond markets will perform in the future, but many economists expect the bond market to provide lower yields than in the past. This concern is reflected in the lower 2.8 percent recommended withdrawal rate.

Let's summarize the research. Bengen's earlier research suggested a withdrawal rate of 4.15 percent (termed the 4 Percent Rule). Kitces recommends a withdrawal rate between 4.5 percent and 5.5 percent, depending on the current P/E ratio. Guyton recommends a withdrawal rate of 5 to 6 percent if the retiree is willing to accept guardrails. And Blanchett, Finke, and Pfau's research suggests a withdrawal rate of 2.8 percent.

Undoubtedly, the range of 2.8 to 6 percent is very broad. For a $1 million retirement nest egg, the annual withdrawal would range from $28,000 to $60,000! What are the risks involved if you choose a withdrawal rate that is too high or too low? First, you will likely not know for certain until many years into retirement if the withdrawal rate you chose is too high or too low. At that point, you will have the clarity provided by knowing how your investment accounts performed in recent years, whether your annual spending was as you predicted, and whether the assumptions you made were close to what actually occurred.

The risk of running out of money before you die is high if you withdraw too much early in retirement. If your withdrawal rate is too low, that can lead to leaving a large estate when you die and possibly regretting that you did not spend and enjoy the money during retirement. Some investors want to leave an estate for their children, grandchildren, or a charity. Others want to spend all the money and enjoy it during their lifetime.

All the variables in retirement income planning are just assumptions, but projecting you will live to age 95 has a significant impact on the analysis. The average mortality age is significantly less than age 95. If retirement projections are based on living until age 95, and a person dies at age 85, they may leave a large estate, which could have been spent. Alternatively, what if the person lives to be 103? Clearly, we don't know the age when we will die, and most people want to base projections on a long life.

So how do you determine what withdrawal rate you want to use when you retire? There are a few safeguards that will reduce the risk of running out of money before you die. One that I use is that we do not automatically increase the withdrawal each year based on the inflation factor from the prior year. I have found that if a client decides to withdraw $4,000 per month for living expenses (and that is a safe withdrawal percentage for them), then the $4,000 tends to remain constant for several years. I have conversations with my clients about whether their cash flow is working well, but I do not assume the withdrawal amount needs to increase each year due to inflation. After several years, we may adjust the amount (up or down), depending on changes in their lifestyle, expenses, and income.

Next, I agree with the guardrails that Guyton adds to the strategy. I have conversations with my clients that if the stock market declines significantly, then they may need to forgo a trip the next year or delay replacing their car. They have all agreed to these adjustments. I calculate their withdrawal rate each spring, based on the prior calendar year. Ongoing monitoring is essential. I tend to follow Bengen's 4 Percent Rule with my clients, with the understanding that the 4 percent may be adjusted lower or higher depending on the future performance of their investment accounts.

One other warning is needed. The 4 Percent Rule (as Bengen applied it) establishes the withdrawal amount based on the value of the investment accounts at the time of retirement. This can cause serious problems, both from the perspective of the client and the financial planner. From the client's perspective, he or she would like an investment account to have had strong performance prior to retirement so the 4 Percent Rule is based on a high investment total. If their initial 4 percent withdrawal is calculated immediately *after* a major stock market correction, the annual withdraw allowance will forever be reduced.

A financial planner would be very concerned if the stock market declined drastically *after* the annual withdrawal amount is established. A frightening scenario would be that the client's portfolio has strong performance, so the initial withdrawal (based on the 4 Percent Rule) is calculated using a high starting point. Then the stock market nosedives, causing the portfolio to decline significantly in value.

As an example, let's assume a couple has an investment portfolio that totals $1 million when they retire. The 4 Percent Rule is applied, and the first year withdrawal is $40,000. Let's further assume that later that same year the stock market experiences a major correction and the investments decline to only $600,000. For the second year, the $40,000 withdrawal will be increased by an inflation factor (say, 3 percent), so it becomes $41,200. However, when checking the withdrawal rate, the $41,200 would be applied to a $600,000 portfolio total, and the withdrawal rate is actually 6.87 percent! This is the reason that Bengen back-tested the 4 Percent Rule against every 30-year period since 1926 (when standardized stock market data became available). It is also why he reported that a person retiring in 1969 would have run out of money in the 30th year if they used a withdrawal percentage as high as 4.5 percent. Guyton's guardrails would help in this case, causing the withdrawal in year two to be reduced due to the stock market correction.

This example shows why building flexibility and reassessment into a sustainable retirement withdrawal rate is very important.

None of the recommended withdrawal strategies come with guarantees. You need to select the withdrawal percentage that feels right to you, taking into account the age you are retiring, other income sources, estimated mortality age, desire to leave an inheritance to your heirs, expectations regarding health care expenses when you are older, and the level of your concern about running out of money.

It is also important that you update your net worth statement annually (to monitor the impact that your withdrawals are having on your net worth), update your retirement projections annually (to see if you are on track to achieve your goals, or whether your budget needs to be reduced), and monitor your withdrawals at least once a year to make sure you are not exceeding your withdrawal percentage. This calculation involves taking your total withdrawals for the prior calendar year and dividing them by the total value of all your investment accounts. In a year when your investments have grown significantly, your net worth may increase. In a year when the stock market has performed poorly and your investment accounts have lost value, you may need to trigger the guardrails to reduce the withdrawals in the next year.

Applying the Safe Withdrawal Rate

Let's assume you are 10 years from retirement, and you want to see if you are on track for retirement. There are savings and retirement calculators offered on many financial websites (*www.joyoffinancial security.com* provides a list of current online savings and retirement calculators). If you input your current investment account totals, the amount you are saving each year, and your estimated annual return, the calculators will estimate how much you will have when you retire.

Now, assume you will have $800,000 by the time you want to retire in 10 years. Yet you would like to save $1 million by the time you retire. You have several options.

- *Increase the amount you are saving each year.* Use online savings calculators to determine how much additional money you should be saving each month to accumulate the extra $200,000 by the time you plan to retire. If you are 10 years from retirement and you assume an average annual return of 7 percent, this would require saving $1,165 per month. If this seems unrealistic, consider other strategies (below) or a combination of strategies.

- *Delay retirement for a few years.* This may allow you to delay starting Social Security benefits, allowing the benefits to accrue to a higher monthly benefit at a later date.

- *Decide to work part time during retirement.* In the above example, if you were to work part time during the first five years of retirement and earn $25,000 ($20,000 after taxes), you would only need to withdraw roughly $36,000 from your investment portfolio during the first five years. If you are following the 4 percent withdrawal rule, that would require a nest egg of $900,000, which may be more reasonable. In addition to reducing the amount you need to withdraw each year, working part time also allows your portfolio time to grow and compound during those five years.

- *Reduce your expenses, either now or during retirement.* You may decide you do not need to live in a big house. After all, the size of your house has nothing to do with your happiness. Or you may choose to keep your car much longer than before. Eliminating cable TV, shopping for a less expensive cell phone plan, getting rid of lots of "things," and deliberately not replacing them can all significantly impact your expenses. Simplifying your life has many benefits, including reducing your stress, freeing up time, and reducing your expenses.

- *Pay off debt now to reduce your expenses during retirement.* All credit cards and car loans should be paid in full, and you may want to consider paying off your mortgage (see "Should I Have a Mortgage in Retirement," below). Or refinance your mortgage to reduce your monthly payments. Then save and invest the amount you are saving on your mortgage payment each month.

- *Revise your investment accounts to reduce the expenses.* Investors are often surprised to learn that the assets in their investment accounts have high expenses caused by commissions, mutual fund expense ratios, or annual fees. The expenses all reduce the net amount that is available to grow and compound over the years.

- *Pull equity out of your home.* In many cases, retirees are "house rich and cash poor." This means they have large amounts of equity in their homes, but they have very little money accessible to pay for basic living expenses, unexpected medical bills, etc. In some cases, you can refinance your mortgage to pull out some of the equity to provide cash flow. *Note: This should only be done after careful consideration because you would have to include your monthly mortgage payment in your budget.* Refinancing may also result in a lower interest rate. However, if the house is completely paid off, this may not be an option. Sometimes, a reverse mortgage is a viable option. This is typically reserved for people over 62 who own their home outright or who have a very low mortgage balance. Reverse mortgages can have detrimental terms and high fees, so talk with a financial advisor and do careful research before deciding if a reverse mortgage is appropriate for you.

- *Consider charitable gifting strategies.* In some cases, gifting your home to a charity in a way that allows you to live in the home for the remainder of your life can be an alternative. In this situation, the charity may pay you a specific amount each month, thereby providing cash flow in exchange for gifting the house. When you die, the charity owns the home. There are other charitable gifting strategies that may work well, such as a charitable lead trust or a charitable remainder trust. *Note: These arrangements can be very complex. If you are interested in this concept, work with a reputable charity, an attorney, and a tax advisor on charitable gifting strategies.*

- *Create additional income streams using immediate fixed (or inflation-indexed) annuities.* Again, tread with caution. Annuities are discussed later in this chapter.

Should You Have a Mortgage in Retirement?

In "Good Debt vs. Bad Debt" in Chapter Seven, we discussed why having a mortgage (rather than paying cash for a home) is often a wise financial decision. But does that advice hold true during your retirement years as well?

Should you have a mortgage in retirement? The answer, again, is "it depends." For many people, it is not a good idea. Let's start by reviewing why having a mortgage during retirement is *not* a good idea. If you answer "yes" to any of the following three questions, having a mortgage during retirement is *not* recommended.

- Do you have credit card debt that you carry forward from month to month?

- Do you ever have trouble paying all your bills during the month?

- Would having a mortgage payment during retirement cause you increased stress because you would worry about having enough money to pay the mortgage?

Many people do not want a mortgage during retirement for two reasons. First, if you are not financially secure, then the risk of losing your home if you cannot make your mortgage payment for a few months is too high. Second, many people were taught that all debts should be paid off by the time a person retires. These money messages are deeply ingrained, and the thought of a mortgage during retirement may cause unnecessary stress. (Minimizing stress leads to greater happiness!)

Of course, not having a mortgage during retirement has the added benefit of significantly reducing your monthly living expenses. However, for some folks, having a mortgage during retirement is a wise strategy. There are several reasons.

First, our current tax code allows a tax deduction for mortgage interest if you itemize on your tax return. Let's assume you have a combined federal and state tax rate of 33 percent (28 percent federal and 5 percent state). If you have a mortgage rate of 4 percent, your *after-tax* mortgage interest rate is roughly 2.7 percent. (Note: The tax law changes effective January 1, 2013, may cause some deductions to be phased out for high-income earners.) If you are averaging a long-term annual return of 7 to 8 percent for your investments, then you are exceeding the after-tax mortgage rate.

If you are a retiree with a mortgage during retirement, the monthly mortgage payment is included in your annual budget and in your retirement projections. In many states, the mortgage can be paid off early with no penalties. That means if you decide you want to eliminate the mortgage, you can pay it off early by using your investment assets.

Pension: Lump Sum or Annuity?

Defined benefit pensions are "going the way of the dinosaur." They are becoming very rare, as corporations, states, and cities search for ways to reduce their expenses. Many are turning to 401(k) plans for newer employees, which are far less lucrative to the employee than the old defined benefit pensions.

Defined benefit pensions provide a guaranteed income stream for your lifetime and the lifetime of your spouse if a spousal benefit is selected at the time of retirement. Pensions act as a monthly annuity. They typically do not have a cost-of-living adjustment, but they provide a high level of assurance that the monthly benefit will be there for the remainder of your life. Defined benefit pensions are quite valuable.

Recently, several corporations (Ford, General Motors, Sears, and the *New York Times*) have offered retirees an option of taking a lump sum that is based upon the present value of the future pension benefits, rather than the monthly annuity. Corporations are doing this to reduce their long-term liabilities and because the IRS issued rules in 2012 making the calculations more attractive for corporations (in essence, making the lump-sum payout smaller than the previous calculations). It is likely that more corporations will follow, offering the lump sum as an option for retirees.

How do you decide between a lump sum or the traditional monthly annuity over your lifetime? This is a very difficult decision, and there is no right or wrong answer. However, there are a few issues to consider.

- *How long do you (and your spouse) expect to live?* Although a pension will provide monthly benefits for your lifetime, when you die, there is no further benefit to your children or grandchildren. Conversely, if you take a lump sum, manage it wisely, and you die at a relatively young age, the lump sum will be in your estate for your children or grandchildren to inherit. A related question is, "Do you want to leave an inheritance for your children or grandchildren?" If not, then the monthly benefit (the annuity) may be more appealing.

- *What other assets do you have?* If you have large investment accounts that would provide money as needed (for dental expenses, health care expenses not covered by Medicare or supplemental insurance, living expenses, and emergencies), then the annuity option may be your best choice. Having a guaranteed income stream for the rest of your life is an enormous benefit. Conversely, if you have very limited investment accounts, you may want to take the lump sum because you need access to cash flow during retirement.

- *How confident are you that you could manage the lump sum wisely?* You will need to look very objectively at how you have managed your investments in the past. Have you used a disciplined approach, staying the course when the stock market became volatile? Have your investments performed well over the past 10 to 20 years? Ellen Schultz, journalist for the *Wall Street Journal* writes: "Though lump-sum payouts transfer all the risk—investment, inflation, interest, and longevity—to the retirees, many nonetheless find the prospect of receiving a large sum of money seductive and are tempted to forfeit what is essentially a guaranteed monthly paycheck they and their spouse can't outlive."

- *Would having more guaranteed income each month provide you more security during retirement?* You likely already have Social Security as a guaranteed income stream, and it includes a cost-of-living adjustment. The monthly pension benefit would increase this.

- *Do you trust your employer's financial condition?* If a corporation becomes bankrupt, the future monthly benefits will likely be covered by the Pension Benefit Guaranty Corporation (PBGC). The maximum annual benefit covered by the PBGC is approximately $56,000. Many folks are concerned about the future of pensions for government employees. In an effort to reduce expenses, many states, cities, and government agencies are attempting to reduce cost-of-living adjustments, change the formulas for calculating pension benefits, and require higher employee contributions. These changes will likely impact future retirees. If you are concerned that future pension benefits may be reduced, then the lump sum may seem more attractive.

- *Have you considered the tax consequences?* If you choose the monthly payment for life, the amount you receive each year from the pension is taxed as income on your tax return. If you elect to take a lump sum, you would roll it into an IRA. This would not trigger any taxes at the time of the rollover, but when you withdraw the money, you would be taxed on the amount withdrawn. If you roll the lump sum into an IRA, the IRA rules would apply. At age 70½, you would be forced to withdraw a Required Minimum Distribution (RMD) from the IRA, even if you do not need the money. Based on today's IRS rules, the amount of the first year RMD is slightly less than 4 percent of the total in the IRA. It increases very slightly each year as you get older. Rolling the money into an IRA also provides the opportunity to convert a portion (or all) of the money to a Roth IRA. A Roth IRA triggers taxes on the amount converted each year, but it is then tax-free going forward. Roth IRAs also provide attractive estate planning benefits for passing down tax-free assets to your children or grandchildren.

- *Have you considered a hybrid plan?* Some plans may allow you to choose a hybrid plan, which would allow taking a lump sum for a portion of the benefit and a monthly benefit for the remainder. You may also be able to do this on your own, by taking the lump sum and then buying a lifetime annuity using a portion of the funds. This gets very complicated, and it is imperative that you research the choices. Annuity terms (monthly payouts, costs, and penalties) vary drastically among different insurance companies.

The decision between taking a monthly payout for life or a lump sum can be complex. Each person will react differently to the issues discussed above. Review each one objectively, and you will likely find that one or two are most important to you. That will help you make your decision.

Annuities

Annuities may be a good option as a part of an overall retirement plan, but buying one requires caution. First, let's review the dangers. Annuities often have high (hidden) fees, and they may have steep surrender penalties for many years. They often pay high commissions to the salesperson, so they are highly recommended by insurance agents, brokers, and financial advisors who work on commission. For many annuities, the consumer needs to realize they are giving up control over their money to the insurance company.

There are many different types of annuities. A *variable annuity* functions much like a traditional IRA. You invest money in the variable annuity and select among the insurance company's investment choices. The money can grow tax-deferred over the years, and if you never *annuitize* the variable annuity, you maintain control over the funds and can withdraw it at any time after age 59½. Upon withdrawal, the *gain* (the amount the variable annuity has grown since the initial investment) is categorized as taxable income. Once the gain is completely withdrawn, the *basis* (the initial investment) can be withdrawn tax-free.

I consider a variable annuity to be more like a retirement account rather than an annuity, because you retain control over how the money is invested. (*Note: This is only true if the consumer never annuitizes the variable annuity.*) If you die, the value of the variable annuity is included in your estate, and it will be inherited by the beneficiary you selected. However, upon your death it will not receive a *step-up in basis*. (This is one of the negative features of a variable annuity from an estate planning standpoint. A taxable investment account would receive a step-up in basis, but a variable annuity does not). One warning is that the variable annuity should be purchased from a low-cost provider, so the fees charged each year by the insurance company are kept to a minimum. This allows you to maximize your investment gain on the variable annuity. Also, it is important to only buy annuities that do not have surrender penalties.

The types of annuities most often used for retirement are *single-premium immediate* annuities (you purchase an annuity for a specific amount, and the insurance company guarantees you will receive a monthly check for the rest of your life) and *deferred* annuities (you purchase an annuity, and the insurance company guarantees you will receive a monthly check starting at a predetermined point in the future). With both types, you can elect to receive payments over your lifetime, over your lifetime and the lifetime of your spouse, or over your lifetime and a certain period (such as 10 years or 15 years). The payments can be *fixed* (the same amount throughout your lifetime), or they can be increased over time based on inflation.

Annuities create a monthly income stream, much like a pension or Social Security benefits. The "guaranteed income stream for life" is the primary selling feature because retirees want to know they will not outlive their money. The drawbacks are that the fees are frequently high (which reduces the monthly payout), they often have high surrender penalties for many years (preventing the consumer from changing their mind), and the money is not accessible in the event of a medical emergency or unexpected expenses. (Sometimes, a set amount, such as 10 percent, is accessible if needed). Also, when you die, nothing will go to your heirs. In other words, the insurance company benefits when an annuitant dies at a relatively young age. If you expect to live a very long life, then an annuity may be a good choice.

What are the conclusions for annuities? In some cases, annuities are a nice supplement to other parts of a retirement plan. If you have a large investment portfolio, you can supplement it with an immediate annuity. The annuity simply creates another income stream—one that is guaranteed for life. Also, a single premium immediate annuity is not exposed to the risk of the stock market fluctuations.

So why do I rarely recommend annuities to my clients? The primary reasons are that the money invested would not return to their estate when they die, and the money cannot grow over time (as an investment account can). I prefer that they keep control of their money and that it will pass down to their heirs when they die.

When buying annuities, it is critical that an investor does ample research. The payouts can vary significantly from one company to another because of the annual fees. If you decide to purchase an annuity, search for low fees, a high payout, and a very financially stable insurance company.

Create Your Own Pension from Your Investments

One of the biggest fears about managing your finances during retirement is uncertainty. As mentioned in Chapter Four, we have to accept that certain things are beyond our control (such as the economy or stock market fluctuations), so we focus on "controlling the controllables." One area of uncertainty that many retirees mention is how to access money from their investment accounts for cash flow. Often, investors may not know how to structure their investment accounts to allow them to take monthly withdrawals. Prior to retirement, the focus was always on saving and investing. Now, distribution strategies become important.

There are multiple ways to structure an investment portfolio to provide cash flow. You can set up a structure that feels very much like a pension, Social Security benefits, or an annuity. The money can flow from your investment account directly into your checking account on the same day each month, so you can rely on it being there. This is easy to establish by working with the custodian where your investment accounts are held. The custodian can set up automatic electronic transfers between your investment accounts and your bank.

Deciding how much money you want to withdraw each month will result from preparing a retirement spending plan, looking at your other income sources, and preparing retirement projections.

This leads to the question, "How do you structure your investments to allow for the monthly withdrawals?" Financial planners and financial advisors can help you with this issue. Deciding which account to use for withdrawals is very customized, because it will depend on where your money is located. For example, if you have three tax buckets (Chapter Eight), then you have plenty of choices for whether you want to withdraw from a traditional IRA, a Roth IRA, or a taxable account. If the majority of your money is in a traditional IRA, then you have fewer choices. At age 70½ you must start Required Minimum Distributions, but until then, you can withdraw from any account.

In the past, retirees often purchased certificate of deposits (CDs) and individual stocks. They would use the interest from the CDs and the dividends from the stocks to provide their monthly cash flow. This was sometimes referred to as an *income strategy*, and the portfolio was designed primarily to produce income. This is currently not a viable strategy because CDs have such low interest rates and individual stocks can be very risky. A strategy used more frequently is referred to as a *total return strategy*. It is based on maintaining a diversified, balanced portfolio, and the investments are designed to produce growth and income. The portfolio is structured based on withdrawing a specific amount each year or each month, and the withdrawals come from the overall portfolio. One way to structure an investment account to support the monthly or annual withdrawals is by using a bond ladder.

Bond Ladders for Retirement Cash Flow

A bond ladder is a part of the fixed-income portion of a portfolio, and it can provide stability, income, and cash flow during retirement. It can be designed to provide a specific amount of cash flow each year that can be used for living expenses, or to fund the required distribution from an IRA after age 70½.

Figure 11.1 shows a diagram of a bond ladder. In this simple example, the bond ladder was designed to provide $24,000 per year for living expenses. It was created for a couple who are expecting to retire in 2016 and estimate they will need approximately $2,000 per month for living expenses at that time (in addition to the pension and Social Security benefits they will be receiving).

Earlier in this chapter (in "A Sustainable Withdrawal Rate"), I mentioned that my clients often do not increase their withdrawals each year. For instance, if they withdraw $2,000 per month, then they may withdraw $2,000 per month for several years, and we do not automatically increase the amount for inflation. However, I am aware that we will likely increase their monthly withdrawal at some point, and I typically increase the amount maturing each year in their bond ladder slightly. If the bond matures and the client does not need the entire amount, then we invest the remainder back into their investment account.

My clients often estimate the year when they may replace a car, take an expensive vacation, or do some major repair projects on their home. These extra expenses are sometimes added to their bond ladder in the year they estimate they will need the additional money. Or, we may plan to withdraw the additional money from other parts of their investment portfolio by selling equity mutual funds. Regardless, we track the goals (and the estimated amount of money to accomplish each goal) in the retirement plan that we update each year.

In many cases, my clients may have a bond ladder that extends for six to eight years, but they may also own several bond mutual funds to complete the remainder of their fixed-income investments in a balanced portfolio. The bond ladder that you design will never perfectly match the expenses each year. Being able to access additional amounts from bond funds or from the equity portion of the portfolio provides additional flexibility.

Twice each year I review my clients' accounts to see if they need to be rebalanced. If the asset allocation chosen by the client is 50 percent equities and 50 percent fixed income, but the equity percentage has increased to 55 percent, then we need to rebalance the portfolio. In that case, I would sell the excess 5 percent in equities.

The proceeds could be used to invest in the end of the client's bond ladder (by buying another year) or can be added to their bond mutual fund holdings.

FIGURE 11.1

Bond Ladder for Retirement

Year	Amount Maturing in Bond Ladder
2016	$24,000
2017	$25,000
2018	$26,000
2019	$27,000
2020	$28,000
2021	$29,000
2022	$30,000
2023	$31,000

A bond ladder can be used in a taxable account or in an IRA. With an IRA, there is no concern about income taxes. All withdrawals from an IRA are subject to income taxes in the year of the withdrawal. Therefore, there is no reason to be concerned about triggering income inside an IRA. When I build a bond ladder in an IRA, it is usually to match what we expect the RMD to be beginning at age 70½. However, there are exceptions. For example, I have a few clients who have saved their entire retirement nest eggs inside IRAs. In that case, they do not wait to take IRA withdrawals at age 70½. They start taking them as soon as they retire (but after age 59½), and the money is used for living expenses. In this case, the amount that is maturing each year in their bond ladder will match our estimate for how much they will need for living expenses.

In other cases, I have clients who are not required to withdraw money from their IRAs until age 70½, but they choose to start withdrawals in their 60s. This is done to minimize future taxes when the IRA is very large. I have one client who routinely takes $60,000 from her IRA each year, even though she is only in her mid-60s. By taking withdrawals now, she can manage the taxes and not be required to take out a much larger amount beginning at age 70½. We have recently been converting the $60,000 each year to a Roth IRA. The tax impact is exactly the same as if she had withdrawn the money outright, but she is gradually moving it over to a Roth IRA. She is also very charitably inclined, so she gifts a sizable amount each year to several charities. In this way, she minimizes her taxes, gets to make generous charitable gifts, and is building a Roth IRA. One of the many benefits of a Roth IRA is you are not required to take distributions at age 70½. The steps she is taking would definitely be considered smart tax planning!

Several different types of bonds can be purchased for a bond ladder. If the bond ladder is inside an IRA, I prefer to use treasury strip bonds. These are treasury bonds in which the coupons (semi-annual payments) have been stripped away. They are also called zero-coupon bonds. They are sold at a discount, and the semi-annual interest is added back to the bond principal rather than being paid to the investor. This is perfect for a bond ladder in an IRA because you don't have to pay full price when you purchase the bond, and you don't want income being paid out semi-annually. These can be purchased with maturity dates of February 15, May 15, August 15, or November 15. I prefer to build a bond ladder with all February 15 maturities, so the bonds will mature early each year and the proceeds are available to provide cash flow throughout the year for my client.

If the bond ladder is *not* in an IRA, then CDs may be used. Often CDs have higher interest rates than the yield on treasury strip bonds. If the client is in a low tax bracket, I may decide to use treasury strip bonds in a taxable account (the accrued interest is state tax-free but is federally taxable). If a client is in a federal tax bracket of 28 percent or above, I may recommend municipal bonds (called muni bonds). Muni bonds are federal tax-free and if you purchase them in the state in which you live, they are usually also state tax-free. Unfortunately, using muni bonds or CDs makes it difficult to build a bond ladder with consistent maturity dates, such as the February 15 dates available for treasury strip bonds. Muni bonds are discussed in Chapter Ten under "Asset Classes-Fixed Income."

Other types of bonds, such as corporate bonds or mortgage-backed securities could be used. I prefer not to buy these individual bonds because they often hold significant risk. The bond ladder is intended to provide safety for the portfolio rather than risk.

Invest in Yourself

- Take some time to prepare psychologically for retirement. Create a weekly schedule of activities using the worksheet provided in this chapter.

- Work with your financial advisor or use some of the retirement calculators available online to see if you are on track for retirement. You will need to prepare a budget for retirement and estimate the amount you will need to withdraw from your investment accounts each year.

- If you are given a choice between taking a lump sum or a traditional pension, weigh the pros and cons carefully.

- Structure your investment portfolio to provide the necessary monthly or annual withdrawals during retirement.

PART FOUR

■ ▪ ■ ▪ ■

Moving Forward

In Part One, we reviewed the relationship between money and happiness, specifically from the perspectives of psychology and neuroscience. We learned that we control roughly 40 percent of our happiness and that the way our brains are "wired" impacts our financial decisions. We also discussed how the money messages we learned as a child influence our financial decisions today.

Part Two was overflowing with happiness strategies. Many of these include a related financial component, reminding us of the complex relationship between our happiness and our money.

Part Three was all things financial. A myriad of financial planning topics were covered, including tax planning, investment planning, and retirement planning.

Throughout the book, we have emphasized that although money does not *buy* happiness, it definitely *impacts* our happiness. We have explored financial strategies that encourage managing money wisely, and making sure our finances are aligned with our values and goals. *The fact that our choices (our behaviors and attitudes) play such a large role in whether we are happy means that when it comes to our happiness—and our finances—we are truly in control.* We are not at the mercy of our genetics or our environment for happiness, just as we are not at the mercy of the next economic downturn for financial security. It is up to us to maximize our happiness and financial security.

The time has come to pull all the information together into a practical plan of action. Chapter Twelve will help you commit to making a few small intentional changes to increase your happiness and your financial security. You will select the strategies you want to implement, and you will design your plan. It is time to Move Forward!

CHAPTER
TWELVE
■ ■ ■ ■ ■

Time for a Change

And the day came when the risk it took to remain tight in the bud
was more painful than the risk it took to blossom.

— ANAIS NIN

What Does Happiness
Look Like to You?

 our idea of happiness is unique to you. Neuroscientists are finding that we each have distinct emotional styles, which reflect specific patterns of brain activity. Likewise, our perception of happiness varies from person to person.

What does happiness look like to you? Some may say it is being able to walk on the beach, climb a mountain, or spend time with family and friends. Perhaps it is being able to snuggle up with a good book, bake cookies with your child or grandchild, or take your dog for a walk.

In this chapter I encourage you to think about your personal life and what small changes you can make that may increase your happiness. The choice is yours. The number of potential changes you could make is unlimited. Yet it is important that you make some small changes. Mark Twain said: "The secret of getting ahead is getting started. The secret of getting started is breaking your complex, overwhelming tasks into small, manageable tasks, and then starting on the first one."

Making major changes in your life may seem overwhelming. Making small changes is more realistic and also more likely to result in greater happiness.

In this chapter I will share my story with you. There is nothing special about my story, and you may feel there is nothing special about yours either. But I've learned from my clients and people in my life that sharing our stories can help others determine what makes them happy or what changes they might like to make in their lives.

What Does Happiness Look Like to Me?

My definition of happiness is a loving family and good friends. I am an introvert, so it is very easy for me to become solitary and isolated. But I recognize the importance of family and friends to my happiness.

Happiness is also...

- having daughters who respect me and love me. The teenage years were difficult, and I'm enjoying our relationship more as they leave the teenage years.

- being healthy.

- being able to travel and stay in nice hotels. I am rather frugal, but I allow myself to spend money on nice hotels.

- having a successful business and loving my work. I have tremendous respect and admiration for my clients, and I appreciate their respect in return.

- having pets.

- having no commitments on a Saturday or Sunday, and spending the day with my husband. I have a busy lifestyle, so I appreciate free time.

- being able to slip away to write this book. I will be very happy if I learn that the book helped some readers increase their happiness and their financial security.

- having time to travel, enjoying downtime, and slowing down the pace.

- tackling my challenges—improving my health by getting more exercise and eating healthier, as well as spending fewer hours at the office on weekends.

Invest in Yourself

- Give yourself a few minutes to think about what happiness looks like to you.

What Does Financial Security Look Like to You?

This book contains many financial strategies, and they may seem overwhelming. The idea of getting your finances in good order may seem like an enormous project. Do not fret! The great news is:

Managing your money wisely is not rocket science!

The key points can be broken down into small steps, as shown below.

- Remember that your savings rate has a bigger impact on your financial security than the selections in your investment accounts. Focus on getting your savings rate to 15 or 20 percent of your pre-tax income.

- Live *below* your means. Teach your kids that saving is important. Don't try to keep up with the Joneses.

- Establish your emergency fund.

- Create a net worth statement. Update it once each year to track your progress.

- Estimate how much you will need to save for retirement.
- Review your investment accounts to determine whether they have the asset allocation you have selected, whether the accounts are diversified, and how they have been performing recently.
- Start building your three tax buckets.
- Discuss your finances with your family.

Your idea of financial security is unique to you. What does financial security look like to you? Maybe it is knowing you have a six-month emergency fund. Maybe it is being able to afford a vacation with your family each year. Perhaps it is sending your children to college, or knowing that you will be able to afford to retire.

Invest in Yourself

- Give yourself a few minutes to think about what financial security looks like to you.

Look at What's Working and What's Not

As you read through Chapters One through Eleven, you may have been thinking of changes you would like to make in your life. Maybe you spend too much time working and would like to have more free time. Maybe you would like to improve your relationship with a family member. Maybe you would like to make new friends, take up a new hobby, or improve your health. Maybe you want to increase your savings rate, open a Roth IRA, or see if you are on track for retirement.

Reflections: A Work in Progress

In my personal life, I have never been accused of not working hard. I am driven to succeed at whatever project I am working on, and for the past six years, I have juggled the responsibilities of running a demanding company with the desire to write this book. The priority I have always pushed aside has been my health. Leading a sedentary lifestyle (too much sitting, not enough exercise) as a financial planner and a writer took its toll on my health. I realized I was sabotaging my efforts at a healthy lifestyle by working too many hours and not leaving any energy (or time) for exercise. My health must become a very high priority for me.

What's Working?

I am strong on perseverance and resilience, and I will continue striving to improve my fitness level and my overall health until I am successful. I have begun to place my health at a much higher priority in recent months.

I have absorbed what I have learned about happiness from psychology research and the field of neuroscience, and I am deliberately making small changes.

I finally finished this book! Writing required an enormous time commitment, and I would like to redirect that time to my family, my health, and to speaking engagements pertaining to the book.

What's Not Working?

I continue to spend too many hours at my office. I have set boundaries on the number of clients I serve so my work will not consume me. Yet I still spend too many evenings and weekends at the office working on behalf of clients.

I also have not simplified my life to the degree I would like. I want to purge my house (room by room) as well as my office. I haven't found the time to do this.

Invest in Yourself

- Take a few moments and write in your journal what is working and what is not. This is a simple exercise that may take only 15 minutes. There are no right or wrong answers.

Break Out of Your Routine

We love our routines—until we take a step back and realize that our routines are often stifling, eliminating any chance of spontaneity, surprise, or joy. It is common that weeks, months, and years can go by before we recognize that changes can have such a positive impact. After reading this book, hopefully you have lots of ideas about how to change your routine.

Let's look at some examples. Perhaps you routinely go to work at 7 am each morning and you work until 6 pm, while your co-workers work from 9 am until 5 pm. It is time for a change. Start treating yourself to breakfast one or two mornings each week at a local café. Read the newspaper or write your thoughts in a journal while having breakfast. Or enjoy breakfast at home with your family before everyone departs for the day. If you arrive at work by 9 am, no one will notice that you were not there at 7 am.

Perhaps you could take a walk at noon each day, just to get out of the office and enjoy the fresh air. You could take a day trip on a weekend. Go somewhere you have never explored. If you are in the habit of turning the TV on each evening, leave it off for one night, a second night, and then an entire week. Buy yourself a magazine you don't normally read, take a hot bath, play with your dog, plan a trip, or cook a nice meal. Anything that breaks your routine will be a healthy change.

Embrace Change

In Chapter One, I encouraged you to embrace change. Commit to making changes in your life, while also realizing that change is hard. In fact, change can be *very* hard. We are creatures of habit, and the easiest path is the one that we have been following. Making changes requires intention. Pilar Gerasimo, editor-in-chief of *Experience Life* magazine, said this about the changes we choose to make: "It has to do with a deeper kind of wisdom—the little voice inside each of us that says, 'I believe life can be better than this; I am ready to try something different.'"

There are multiple theories about how to make changes. James Prochaska, a psychologist at the University of Rhode Island and author of *Changing for Good*, began researching change after his father died of alcoholism, despite his family's best efforts to help. He created the "Stages of Change" model, which defines the six stages required to change a behavior. The six stages are:

1. Precontemplation
2. Contemplation
3. Preparation
4. Action
5. Maintenance
6. Termination

Prochaska's approach is easy to use, encouraging you to find which stage you are in, and then start moving forward. Occasionally you may fall back into an earlier stage, but once you resume the strategies for that stage, you will begin moving forward again. The *WebMD* website lists the following strategies for a person creating an exercise plan. Stages Three and Four in the Stages of Change model may look like this:

Stage Three: Preparation—Make Yourself a Plan

- Think through the details: Will you walk or swim? Where and when will you exercise? What kind of clothing or equipment do you need?

- Draw up a contract with yourself. Set three goals: one for the next month, one for six months, and one for a year. Reward yourself for each goal accomplished. Set an initial goal you're sure to attain; early success will propel you onward.

- Develop a detailed contingency plan. Where will you walk if it rains? How will you exercise when you visit your in-laws? What will you do on days you're tired?

- Make a public commitment. Ask for support from your friends and have them follow up on your progress.

Stage 4: Action—Put your Plan in Motion

- Make your environment conducive to exercise. Leave notes reminding yourself to work out; have your clothes ready ahead of time.
- Reward yourself for sticking to your plan.
- Think long-term. You're forming a lifelong habit here. No need to fret about a missed day; you have the next 50 years to make it up.

Prochaska's Stages of Change model is grounded in theory and research. At the other extreme is the Nike slogan "Just Do It." This approach may work for some people, especially if a person is focused on one change in particular, such as training for a 10K run, sorting (and purging) a pile of papers, or signing up to contribute to a 401(k) retirement plan. Whichever strategy appeals to you is the one you should use. Remember, this is your customized plan.

Willpower

Roy Baumeister, a psychologist at Florida State University, has devoted his career to studying willpower. The term *willpower* is often used interchangeably with self-control and self-discipline. Baumeister's research is fascinating, with very different conclusions from what most people would expect. He has determined that our supply of willpower is limited, and it can become depleted very easily. He compares it to a muscle that can be fatigued through use. Furthermore, our willpower is fueled by glucose in the body's bloodstream. The link between glucose (sugar) and self-control became evident in studies that measured low blood sugar (hypoglycemia). Researchers discovered that "hypoglycemics were more likely than the average person to have trouble concentrating and controlling their negative emotions when provoked." This would suggest that going for a long period of time without food (which causes the blood sugar levels to drop) is not wise. Baumeister suggests eating healthy food and snacks to keep the blood sugar levels in the body steady, thereby replenishing the supply of willpower on an ongoing basis.

He also determined that our limited supply of willpower is used for many purposes. If you have a good night's sleep and a healthy breakfast, you start the day with a renewed supply of willpower. As the day progresses, you use a portion of your willpower as you battle a traffic jam on your way to work; sit through a long, unproductive meeting; answer too many emails; and feel overwhelmed by too much work. Suddenly, your supply of willpower is depleted. You need a healthy snack to carry you through lunchtime and to help replenish your willpower. Hopefully, you will not grab a doughnut. This would cause your blood sugar to spike quickly, followed by a drastic decline a short while later. It is better to eat a healthy combination of protein, complex carbohydrates (fruits, vegetables, and whole grains), and healthy fats.

Let's say you have a busy afternoon at work making decisions and working on projects. Near the end of the day you may decide what to have for dinner and whether you are going to exercise after work. These actions all pull from the same limited source of willpower. It is no wonder that by the end of the day our willpower is at its weakest.

Managing our limited supply of willpower has a major impact on whether we can successfully make small changes. Baumeister's advice is to play offense with our willpower rather than defense. He recommends finding some calm and peaceful moments to plan an offense. "Start an exercise program. Learn a new skill. Quit smoking, reduce drinking, make one or two lasting changes toward a healthy diet. These are all done during times of relatively low demand, when you can allocate much of your willpower to the task. Have an idea of what you want to accomplish in a month and how to get there. Leave some flexibility and anticipate setbacks. When you check your progress at month's end, remember that you don't have to meet each goal every time—what matters is that your life gradually improves from month to month."

His physiological approach to willpower seems to suggest multiple strategies. One is to eat healthy food throughout the day, thereby preventing your blood sugar from dropping too low. Also, start paying attention to what is depleting your willpower. If your commute to and from work is stressful, consider changing jobs, proposing to your boss that you work at home a few days each week, or moving closer to your workplace. If the hundreds of emails you receive each day are stressful, look at ways to set boundaries. Limit reviewing emails to one hour in the morning and one hour in the afternoon, or consider whether you can start directing unnecessary emails to your junk folder. Avoid looking at emails on weekends and at night. If you know your willpower is often depleted by the end of your workday, plan to exercise early in the morning. If you are aware that your willpower is a limited resource, this may lead you to make healthy changes to your daily routine.

Habits and Rituals

Establishing new habits and positive rituals can be very helpful as we make changes. Jim Loehr and Tony Schwartz, authors of the book, *The Power of Full Engagement*, define positive rituals as "precise, consciously acquired behaviors that become automatic in our lives, fueled by a deep sense of purpose." Recognizing that we are creatures of habit, we can easily fall back into our bad habits. Creating positive rituals requires intentional changes on our part. However, after about a month, the new habits become ingrained, and no longer require as much effort.

Take, for instance, brushing your teeth. Most people brush their teeth at least twice a day, and it is a habit that does not require any conscious effort. What new habits or positive rituals will help you with the changes you would like to make? If you want to get more exercise, the ritual you may want to establish is meeting a friend for a long walk every Saturday morning. Or perhaps you commit to going to the health club every Monday after work. If you want to add more laughter to your life, mention this to some friends and decide you will meet every Saturday night to watch movie comedies at someone's home. If you want to become more knowledgeable about your current investments, perhaps you decide to set aside Tuesday evenings from 7 to 9 pm each week to devote to your finances. Or maybe you set aside the first day of each quarter to review your financial goals and determine if you are making progress toward achieving them.

Rituals—such as sitting down to a family dinner each evening or reading a bedtime story to your young children every night—build healthy relationships. Rituals also create memorable family traditions, including the way your family celebrates Christmas, Hanukkah, or Thanksgiving. Rituals provide structure and a firm foundation. Establishing positive rituals is helpful as you make changes.

There is plenty of debate as to how to create habits. Research suggests it takes 21 to 30 days to create a habit. Some believe it can be done in shorter time periods, as long as the changes you are making are small. I recommend that you make small changes and that you select two happiness changes and two financial changes that you can focus on during the next month. If you prefer to only select one change, that's fine. However, do not attempt more than two per month. At the end of one month, assess your progress. If the changes you selected have become habits, then you can choose two more changes for the next month. If the changes still require a lot of effort, you may decide to focus on them for another month.

The first step in moving forward is to create a personal wish list. To do this, recognize that you are doing these exercises as a gift to yourself. You are in charge of your happiness and your financial security, and only you can decide to make small changes. As Winnie the Pooh's friend Christopher Robin said, "You're braver than you believe, and stronger than you seem, and smarter than you think."

Create a Wish List

Debbie Macomber wrote a book titled *Twenty Wishes*. In it she describes a group of women who are all widows, and they join together to add more joy to their lives. At a gathering on Valentine's Day, they challenge each other to create a list of Twenty Wishes. The book describes how difficult this is for many of the women (we are all so busy—who has the time to think about a wish list?), but the characters then set out to accomplish some of their wishes. The book does a great job of demonstrating how easy it is for us to slip into a rut. By focusing on our wishes and trying something new, we unexpectedly recapture our excitement about life.

Create a Personal Wish List

I strongly recommend that you create your own personal wish list, and write it down. You could also call it a goals list or a bucket list. I like the term wish list because, in my view, it gives you permission to include wishes that are a bit more lofty rather than just goals.

A wish list is not a to-do list. Your to-do list may be incredibly long—full of tasks that must be completed, such as responsibilities at work or scheduling a dentist appointment. In Macomber's book, the women's wish lists include items such as learn to knit, buy red cowboy boots, take French lessons, find a reason to laugh again, dance in the rain with bare feet, volunteer and become a lunch buddy, take a cake decorating class, plant a garden, and attend a Broadway musical.

You do not need to follow strict rules when selecting your personal wishes. If you were writing objectives for a strategic business plan, you would want each objective to be quantifiable and to have a completion date. These constraints are important in a business.

They are not important in your personal life. I encourage you to give yourself permission to be very lofty. Be kind to yourself. Notice that in the list above "dancing in the rain with bare feet" is not something that would require much planning, and it is certainly not quantifiable. Yet a person may need to be in a certain frame of mind before he or she would want to dance in the rain with bare feet. Likewise, "find a reason to laugh again" may sound like it should be easy to accomplish, but it may require several preliminary steps to attain increased happiness. Do not feel that your wishes must be major projects—in fact, do not feel constrained by any rules as you create your wish list.

Chapters One through Six provided many strategies for increasing your happiness. Some of these are listed on the next page as a starting point. Your personal wishes do not have to come from this list.

Happiness Strategies

- a healthy lifestyle
- freedom
- good friends
- a loving family
- focus on gratitude
- being creative
- experiencing "flow"
- giving back
- having a sense of purpose
- faith
- confidence
- a job that you love
- contentment
- free time
- a lazy morning
- going to a movie
- buttered popcorn
- a good book
- great music
- laughter
- pets
- accomplishing a goal

- financial security
- good health insurance
- sports
- enjoying nature
- a good education
- a vacation
- being able to afford to retire
- trying something new
- having peace of mind
- volunteering
- being spontaneous
- pursuing hobbies
- going on an adventure
- a home you love
- a garden
- an outdoor concert
- simplifying your life
- becoming less materialistic
- meditation
- solitude
- rich conversation

Reflections: My Wish List

I'm sharing a portion of my wish list with you. The wishes are not in any particular order.

- Focus on my health. Get consistent exercise; eat healthy foods.
- Read some books just for pure enjoyment.
- Manage my financial planning firm with boundaries.
- Schedule speaking engagements centered around my book.
- Have more free time with my husband.
- Continue to improve my relationship with my daughters.
- Start playing the piano again.
- Laugh more, become less intense, have more fun.
- Design a new home with my husband, a home that is designed for retirement.
- Slow down the pace of my life—learn to smell the roses.
- Socialize more with friends.
- Delegate more; take things off my plate.
- Run or walk a 10K race or a half marathon.
- Visit my hometown and old friends.
- Learn to say "I am a writer."
- Plan an adventure—possibly to watch sea turtles hatching on a beach or to see monarch butterflies when they migrate to Mexico. Or take a hiking vacation.
- Make my gardens a safe haven for bees, butterflies, and humming-birds.
- Purge my home of unnecessary items—room by room. Focus on simplifying my life.
- Take an online course from a great professor.
- Go to Europe or New Zealand with my husband.

Use the lines below to create your personal wish list. Keep in mind that this is *your* private list. You do not need to share it with anyone.

My Personal Wish List

1. _____

2. _____

3. _____

4. _____

5. _____

6. _____

7. _____

8. _____

9. _____

10. _____

11. _____

12. _____

13. _____

14. _____

15. _____

16. _____

17. _____

18. _____

19. _____

20. _____

Create a Financial Wish List

Next, create a financial wish list. This is very similar to your personal wish list, except it is focused on improving your financial security. Below is a list of some of the financial strategies that were provided throughout the book. This list is only meant to be a primer.

Financial Strategies

- having financial and personal goals
- saving 20 percent of your income
- having retirement projections that are customized for you
- knowing your tolerance for risk
- having an asset allocation that you can stick with through thick and thin
- paying off your credit card balance each month
- knowing your investment accounts are diversified
- having low expenses in your investments
- working with a fiduciary that you can trust
- knowing how your investments are performing
- utilizing tax planning strategies to minimize your taxes
- filling all three tax buckets
- living within your means
- not striving to keep up with the Joneses
- having sufficient insurance
- having current estate planning documents that match your wishes
- having an estate planning binder
- discussing your finances with your spouse and children
- working in a career you love
- having a current net worth statement

continued...

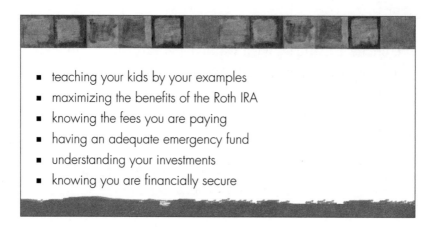

- teaching your kids by your examples
- maximizing the benefits of the Roth IRA
- knowing the fees you are paying
- having an adequate emergency fund
- understanding your investments
- knowing you are financially secure

The items on your financial wish list may be very different from the strategies listed above, and they may be much more specific. For example, one of the strategies listed above is to stop trying to keep up with the Joneses. Your financial wish list may include specific wishes that pertain to this, such as "Keep my 8-year-old car because it is perfectly fine, and I am saving money for retirement rather than buying a new car." Or "Start having family discussions about our finances, and teach our kids the dangers of trying to keep up with the Joneses." Perhaps your wish list includes researching potential vacations that stay within your travel budget or updating your net worth statement once each year. Your financial wish list may include taking your lunch to work two days a week and redirecting that money into savings or switching to a less expensive cable television or cell phone package.

My Financial Wish List

1. _____
2. _____
3. _____
4. _____
5. _____
6. _____
7. _____
8. _____
9. _____
10. _____
11. _____
12. _____
13. _____
14. _____
15. _____
16. _____
17. _____
18. _____
19. _____
20. _____

Select Two Changes Pertaining to Happiness

Until now we have been discussing lots of happiness strategies, and you have created your wish list. Now it is time to select two changes you want to make. Review the items on your wish list, and decide on two intentional changes, which must be very specific. For example, on my list was the wish "Focus on my health. Get consistent exercise; eat healthy foods." This is much too broad for a change that I want to implement. My change that supports my wish may be to exercise four days per week or to go to the grocery store on Sunday and Wednesday so I will have fruits, vegetables, and healthy food in my home. Or perhaps the change I select would be to keep healthy snacks at work.

Make your changes realistic, rather than confining. If one of the changes you decide to make is to replace your afternoon soda with a glass of water, give yourself some leeway. Consider allowing yourself to have one soda on the weekend. This will prevent you from feeling deprived, and you will have drastically reduced the amount of soda you drink while also increasing the amount of water you drink.

The two changes I plan to make to increase my happiness are:

1. _____

2. _____

Select Two Changes Pertaining to Finances

Just like for your happiness strategies, your two financial strategies will derive from your financial wish list. If, as mentioned above, you decide to use two hours each Tuesday night to focus on your finances, there may be some preliminary steps required. For example, you may need to schedule those two hours on your calendar for every Tuesday evening. You may need to discuss this with your family so they understand that not interfering with your Tuesday evenings is important. Discussing your changes with your family and friends is very helpful. It shows them that you feel strongly about making this intentional change, and it also allows them to be supportive. Building a support team to provide encouragement is always good.

The two changes I plan to make to improve my financial security are:

1. _____

2. _____

Be Prepared for Resistance

Remember that change is hard. You may be determined to make the changes you have selected, and then you will find that you are slipping back into your old habits. Prepare for the challenges. Remind yourself that you are developing positive rituals. These will serve you well if you can convert the new positive ritual from being a very intentional change to becoming an automatic behavior. As we have said, research suggests that we create habits in 21 to 30 days, so the intentional change will only be difficult for the first few weeks if you can stick with it.

When making change seems hard, remember that you can draw from your own inner strength to access perseverance and resilience. As the adage says, "Try until you succeed."

Perseverance

Perseverance is dogged stubbornness, being determined to not give in until you succeed. You can apply perseverance to any change you decide to make.

If your goal is to exercise four times a week, and after the first week you realize you didn't exercise at all, then it is time to alter your strategies. Perhaps you were planning to exercise after work and you determined that your willpower is at a very low level at that time. Next week, decide you will exercise two mornings before work and take a walk twice each week during your lunch hour. Or decide to take tennis lessons or try a class at your health club. Keep trying new strategies until you find ones that work for you. Lay out your exercise clothes the night before. Put them on as soon as you wake up, and walk out the door. (Do not have a cup of coffee and start reading the newspaper or your emails.) Most exercisers know that if you can force yourself to walk for 10 minutes, then you will likely continue for 30 or 40 minutes.

Track your progress. The act of writing down what you did is a way of holding yourself accountable. Research has shown that when dieters write down the food they eat, they lose twice as much weight as dieters who do not track their food intake. Make plans to meet a friend on Saturday morning or one evening each week for a walk. If you were going alone, you may decide not to go. However, you will not want to let your friend down, so you can hold each other accountable for showing up.

Resilience

Resilience is a powerful trait. Steven Southwick, professor at Yale University School of Medicine, said, "Resilient people are like trees bending in the wind. They bounce back."

Another definition of resilience is "the capacity to rise above adversity." Everyone faces adversity at some point, whether it is triggered by the death of a loved one, the loss of a job, health problems, or any other setback or disappointment. In a situation where you are trying to make a positive change to increase your happiness or your financial security, adversity may interfere. If you plan to go for a walk and it is raining, you must alter your plans to get exercise in spite of the rain. Perhaps you have a treadmill you can use, or you can lift weights and do stretches instead. If you plan to work on your finances on Tuesday evenings and a family commitment interferes, then you may decide to work on your finances on Thursday evening.

As mentioned in Chapter Two, resiliency is being researched by neuroscientists. Richard Davidson has conducted research that shows the left prefrontal cortex within our brains (where logic and rational thinking prevail) can send inhibitory signals to the amygdala (where negative emotions prevail), encouraging the amygdala to quiet down. This calming effect results in increased resiliency and the ability to bounce back when faced with adversity.

As you commit to making changes in your personal life (to increase your happiness) and in your financial life (to attain financial security), obstacles will appear that seem to sabotage your efforts. Remember that perseverance and resilience are your friends.

Celebrate

There is one last exercise I recommend that you do. It is to take some time to celebrate your accomplishments. We rarely take time to realize that we have much to celebrate. Tooting your own horn may be difficult. We are taught to be humble and not to brag. Even if you are not comfortable telling others about your accomplishments, you should toot your horn to yourself. Be cognizant (and grateful) for all you have accomplished, and celebrate your accomplishments. Perhaps you will celebrate that you have decided to make small changes and that you are embarking on a path with more happiness and greater financial security. Don't hesitate to celebrate that you are a good friend, mother, father, sister, or brother. Maybe you are the person who never forgets to send holiday cards to friends or you do volunteer work for those less fortunate. You may celebrate an accomplishment at work or your love of nature. It doesn't matter what you are celebrating. What matters is that you are taking the time to celebrate the wonders of your life.

If you are using a journal, write your celebration list in the journal. If you are not, write your celebrations below. Then do something nice for yourself. Buy yourself flowers or a book you have been wanting. Be adventurous; try something new. Practice self-compassion. Embrace Nora Ephron's advice: "You can order more than one dessert."

My Celebration List

1. _____
2. _____
3. _____
4. _____
5. _____
6. _____
7. _____
8. _____
9. _____
10. _____
11. _____
12. _____
13. _____
14. _____
15. _____
16. _____
17. _____
18. _____
19. _____
20. _____

Moving Forward

Throughout the book, I emphasize that you have a golden opportunity to add more happiness and financial security to your life. The choice is yours. Gerontologist Karl Pillemer asked folks who have lived long enough to gain tremendous wisdom what lessons they can share. Gretchin Phelps, age 89, said, "In my 89 years, I've learned that happiness is a choice—not a condition." She explained that taking charge of your own happiness simply must happen at some point if you are going to live a fulfilling life.

Mary Oliver, in her poem *The Summer Day* asked: "Tell me, what is it you plan to do with your one wild and precious life?" We are each fortunate to have a wonderful life. It is up to us to make it fabulous. What will you do? Will you continue down your current path, resisting making any changes and just following your current routine? Or will you commit to making small changes, expanding your horizons, allowing yourself to fail (so what!), laughing more, and being happier?

Artist Georgia O'Keefe was known for blazing her own path and not following the status quo. She said, "I decided to start anew, to strip away what I had been taught." She was definitely moving forward, and it is evident in her paintings.

When we make changes, they require very deliberate actions. Otherwise, we slip back into our old routine. We know that roughly 40 percent of our happiness is within our control. The 40 percent that we control is influenced by our choices, behaviors, and attitudes. In a sense, we need to give ourselves permission to be happy. Likewise, we need to give ourselves permission to be financially secure.

The two small changes you selected for increasing your happiness and financial security are your assurance that you are moving forward. They are your goals for the next month. Make a commitment to yourself that you will make them very high priorities this month, and you will achieve them.

In one month, review your list and see if you have made progress. If you have implemented the small changes, take the time to look objectively at the results. Did your small changes make you happier? Did your financial changes move you forward toward financial security? If they did, congratulations!

Now decide what you want to set as small changes for the *next* month. Remember, these are not long-term commitments; it is just for one month.

If you made some progress but did not fully achieve your small changes, you may decide to commit to focusing on them for another month. Perfection is not important. We simply want progress. You may even choose different small changes to try for the next month.

Review what you have written in your journal occasionally. Remember to focus on gratitude, and look for ways to nurture creativity in your life. Enjoy rich experiences, and manage your money wisely. Honor your core values, and design your lifestyle and your goals around those values.

Continue moving forward by making small changes. You will soon realize that you are becoming happier, your finances are more secure, and the relationship between money and happiness in your life has become healthier. Yes, small changes equal big rewards!

WITH
GRATITUDE
■ ■ ■ ■ ■

lthough writing a book is often a solitary endeavor, I have many people to thank. Six years ago, Joan Hunter helped me convert an idea that was percolating in my head into the first semblance of a book. My idea was to articulate the wonderful opportunity we all have to create a happier lifestyle with financial security. Joan was doggedly stubborn in her belief that the book must contain stories my clients had shared with me and personal stories from my life. She said these stories would make the book "authentic," allowing readers to relate the message to their own lives. I thank Joan for launching me on this journey.

During the next four years I gathered information, wrote, and rewrote. This was the solitary phase. I also learned a lot about psychology, neuroscience, and economics as I read books and articles written by many of the leading researchers. I honed my understanding of financial topics after realizing that writing about financial strategies in lay terms was more difficult than merely understanding the concepts. During the past year as I sprinted to the finish line, many people played an important role. My clients often nudged me to finish the book. When I saw them, they would say, "How's your book coming?" and they encouraged me to carve extra time out of my financial planning firm to fulfill the dream of writing this book. The book includes stories from several of my clients, and I appreciate that they gave me permission to share their stories. I am very grateful for my clients.

I want to thank my sister, Susan, who encouraged me throughout the entire six years. I appreciate her support and love. I also want to thank my parents for instilling in me the fortitude to write this book. Throughout the book, I share many personal stories about about growing up, and I will always be grateful for the lessons I learned from my parents and grandparents.

Near the end of the project, several clients, colleagues, and friends agreed to review the manuscript. I had no idea that so many of them would take this project so seriously, and I will forever be grateful. Their careful attention to details—what they liked about the book, what they didn't like, what they thought should be added or deleted—was incredibly helpful in countless ways. For their review and suggestions, I sincerely thank Denise Atencio, Elizabeth Barrett, Celia Cook, Gary Cygan, Heather Darby, Connie Eckert, Stephanie Eras, Robert Hammerstein, Kim Maness, Diane Nelson, Bonnie Paisley, Cathy Reese, and Richard Salmen.

In addition, I want to say a special thank you to Jason Zweig for helping me resolve some questions regarding neuroscience in Chapter Two, to Michael Kitces for providing clarification on the asset location strategy discussion in Chapter Eight, to Tom Giachettti for his legal expertise in Chapter Nine, and to Bill Bengen for reviewing the retirement strategies in Chapter Eleven. The generosity of these colleagues as they shared their knowledge and expertise was impressive and very much appreciated.

I am grateful for the members of my E3 Advanced Financial Planner's Group for their professional support and personal friendships. Author and financial planner Kathleen Rehl deserves a special thank you for sharing her advice throughout the writing process. Thanks also to Diane MacPhee for keeping me focused while I was juggling the responsibilities of my financial planning firm with writing a book and trying to find time for family and exercise. I never found the perfect balance, but her encouragement helped tremendously.

I owe a special thank you to my editor, Marla Markman. She took the manuscript and shaped and molded it into a book. Marla took ownership in the project and treated it like her own. It was a pleasure to work with her.

Thank you to Tammy Ditmore for her amazing talent as a proofreader. Special thanks to everyone at TLC Graphics for their hard work on the book, including Monica Thomas (cover design) and Erin Stark (interior design). Thank you to Tamara and Tom Dever at TLC for making it all happen.

I am especially grateful for my husband, Randy. He encouraged me to "slip away" to write during the past six years. I discovered hotels and casitas in New Mexico with quiet, outdoor patios that provided many hours of solitude and a nurturing writing environment. Randy's support and encouragement during the last hectic months seemed unlimited. He created the charts and graphics throughout the book, and he revealed his talent as a copy editor. When he retires from his scientific career, he should write a book. I promise to encourage him to "slip away" to write and to embrace the creative process.

Lastly, on a personal note: throughout the past few years, I have finally started to absorb many of the strategies for becoming happier. Increasing our happiness is not a linear process, and that's a wonderful thing. At times I would feel incredibly dense ("Why can't I walk the talk?"), but then I would realize I *was* making progress. I kept reminding myself of the adages in the book: simplify, control the controllables, ponder, small changes lead to big rewards, enjoy rich experiences, focus on gratitude, embrace change, and move forward. Now that I have completed this book, I plan to continue on this journey to a happier lifestyle. And Randy and I intend to "slip away" together more often.

DONNA SKEELS CYGAN
Albuquerque, New Mexico
August 1, 2013

RESOURCES

■ ■ ■ ■ ■

An expanded resource list is available on the Joy of Financial Security website: *www.joyoffinancialsecurity.com.*

Books

Creativity

Julia Cameron, *The Artist's Way*, Tarcher/Putnam, 2002
Anne Lamott, *Bird by Bird*, Anchor Books, 2004
Nora Naranjo-Morse, *Mud Woman*, University of Arizona Press, 1992
Keith Sawyer, *Zig Zag*, Jossey-Bass, 2013
Twyla Tharp, *The Creative Habit*, Simon and Schuster Paperbacks, 2003

Financial

Mitch Anthony, *The New Retirementality*, Dearborn Trade, 2001
Barry K. Baines, *Ethical Wills*, Da Capo Press, 2006
Sheila Bair, *Bull by the Horns*, Simon and Schuster, 2012
Eleanor Blayney, *Women's Worth*, Direction$, 2010
Warren E. Buffett, *Letters to Shareholders*, Berkshire Hathaway, 2013
Benjamin Graham, *The Intelligent Investor*, HarperBusiness, 1973
James E. Hughes, Jr., *Family Wealth—Keeping It in the Family*, Bloomberg Press, 2004
Deborah L. Jacobs, *Estate Planning Smarts*, DJ Working Unlimited Inc., 2011
George Kinder, *Seven Stages of Money Maturity*, Random House, 1999
Michael Lewis, *The Big Short*, W. W. Norton, 2011
Michael Lewis, *Boomerang*, W. W. Norton, 2011
Gretchen Morgenson, *Reckless Endangerment*, Henry Holt and Company, 2012
Wayne Muller, *Sabbath*, Bantam Books, 1999
John E. Nelson and Richard N. Bolles, *What Color Is Your Retirement Parachute?*, Ten Speed Press, 2010
Helaine Olen, *Pound Foolish*, Portfolio, 2012
Kathleen Rehl, *Moving Forward On Your Own: A Financial Guidebook for Widows*, Rehl Financial Advisors, 2010

Carl Richards, *The Behavior Gap*, Portfolio, 2012
Kenneth F. Robinson, *Don't Make a Budget*, SPS Publications, 2009
Thomas J. Stanley and William D. Danko, *The Millionaire Next Door*, Pocket Books, 1996
Bert Whitehead, *Facing Financial Dysfunction*, Infinity Publishing, 2002
Jason Zweig, *Your Money and Your Brain*, Simon and Schuster, 2007

Happiness and Psychology

Roy F. Baumeister and John Tierney, *Willpower*, Penguin Press, 2011
Martha Beck, *The Joy Diet*, Crown Publishers, 2003
Tal Ben-Shahar, *Happier*, McGraw-Hill, 2007
Joan Borysenko, *Inner Peace for Busy People*, Hay House, Inc., 2001
Marcus Buckingham and Donald O. Clifton, *Now, Discover Your Strengths*, Free Press, 2001
Dan Buettner, *The Blue Zones*, National Geographic Society, 2008
Susan Cain, *Quiet*, Crown, 2012
Pema Choden, *How to Meditate: A Practical Guide to Making Friends With Your Mind*, 2013
Pema Choden, *Living Beautifully: With Uncertainty and Change*, 2012
Mihaly Csikszentmihalyi, *Flow*, Harper Perennial, 1990
Ed Diener and Robert Biswas-Diener, *Happiness*, Blackwell, 2008
Charles Duhigg, *The Power of Habit*, Random House, 2012
Robert A. Emmons, *Thanks!*, Houghton Mifflin, 2007
Nora Ephron, *I Feel Bad About My Neck*, Alfred A. Knopf, 2006
Nora Ephron, *I Remember Nothing*, Alfred A. Knopf, 2010
Daniel Gilbert, *Stumbling on Happiness*, Alfred A. Knopf, 2006
Malcolm Gladwell, *Outliers*, Little, Brown and Company, 2008
Jon Kabat-Zinn, *Guided Mindfulness Meditation Series 3* (audio), 2012
Jon Kabat-Zinn, *Mindfulfulness for Beginners: Reclaiming the Present Moment and Your Life*, Sounds True, Inc., 2011
Daniel Kahneman, *Thinking, Fast and Slow*, Farrar, Straus and Giroux, 2011
Kate Larsen, *Progress Not Perfection: Your Journey Matters*, Expert Publishing, 2007
Anne Morrow Lindbergh, *Gift from the Sea*, Pantheon Books, 1975
Jim Loehr and Tony Schwartz, *The Power of Full Engagement*, Free Press, 2003
Sonja Lyubomirsky, *The How of Happiness*, Penguin Press, 2007
Sonja Lyubomirsky, *The Myths of Happiness*, Penguin Press, 2013
Debbie Macomber, *Twenty Wishes*, MIRA Books, 2008
Kelly McGonigal, *The Willpower Instinct*, Avery, 2012
Christopher Peterson, *A Primer in Positive Psychology*, Oxford University Press, 2006
Christopher Peterson and Martin E. P. Seligman, *Character Strengths and Virtues*, Oxford University Press, 2004
Karl Pillemer, *30 Lessons for Living*, Hudson Street Press, 2011
Anna Quindlen, *A Short Guide to a Happy Life*, Random House, 2000
Cheryl Richardson, *The Art of Extreme Self-Care*, Hay House, 2009
Sharon Salzberg, *The Force of Kindness*, 2010
Sharon Salzberg, *Real Happiness, The Power of Meditation*, Workman Publishing, 2011
Sharon Salzberg, *Guided Meditations for Love and Wisdom* (audio), 2009

Martin E. P. Seligman, *Authentic Happiness*, Free Press, 2002
Martin E. P. Seligman, *Flourish*, Free Press, 2011
Maria Shriver, *Just Who Will You Be*, Hyperion, 2008
Richard H. Thaler and Cass R. Sunstein, *Nudge*, Penguin Group, 2009
Henry David Thoreau, *Walden*, Empire Books, 1854
Laura Vanderkam, *All the Money in the World*, Portfolio, 2012
Jim Wallis, *Rediscovering Values*, Howard Books, 2010
Andrew Weil, *Spontaneous Happiness*, Little, Brown and Company, 2011

Neuroscience

Richard J. Davidson and Sharon Begley, *The Emotional Life of Your Brain*, Hudson Street Press, 2012
Daniel Goleman, *Emotional Intelligence*, Bantam Books, 1995

Simplifying, Decluttering, and Organizing

Julie Morgenstern, *Organizing from the Inside Out*, Henry Holt, 2004
Julie Morgenstern, *Time Management from the Inside Out*, Henry Holt, 2004
Laura Vanderkam, *168 Hours*, Portfolio, 2011

Websites

Happiness

Authentic Happiness	www.authentichappiness.sas.upenn.edu
A Network for Grateful Living	www.gratefulness.org
Positive Psychology Center	www.positivepsychology.org
Psychology Today	www.psychologytoday.com
Pursuit of Happiness	www.pursuit-of-happiness.org
TED: Ideas Worth Spreading	www.ted.com
Zen Habits	www.zenhabits.net

Financial

CNN-Money	money.cnn.com
Financial Planning Association	www.fpanet.org
Financial Industry Regulatory Authority	www.finra.org
IRA Information Website	www.irahelp.com
Internal Revenue Service	www.irs.gov
Morningstar	www.morningstar.com
Saving for College (529 Plans)	www.savingforcollege.com
Securities and Exchange Commission	www.sec.gov
Social Security Administration	www.ssa.gov
Vanguard	www.vanguard.com
Yahoo Financial	www.finance.yahoo.com

Financial Calculators

Bankrate Calculators	www.bankrate.com
CNN-Money Financial Calculators	cgi.money.cnn.com/tools/
Financial Calculators	www.dinkytown.net
Yahoo Financial Calculators	finance.yahoo.com/calculator/

Locating a Financial Advisor

Nat'l Assoc. of Personal Financial Advisors   www.napfa.org
(for locating a fee-only financial advisor)
CFP Board of Standards   www.cfp.net
(for locating a financial advisor who is a CFP® professional)
Financial Planning Association   www.fpanet.org
Alliance of Cambridge Advisors   www.acaplanners.org
(for locating a fee-only financial advisor)
Garrett Planning Network   www.garrettplanningnetwork.com
(for locating a fee-only financial advisor who will work on an hourly basis)

Financial Sites for Retirement Projections

Bloomberg   www.bloomberg.com/personalfinance/calculators/retirement
Charles Schwab   www.schwab.com
T. Rowe Price   www.troweprice.com
Vanguard   www.vanguard.com

Neuroscience

Neuroscience Information Framework   www.neuinfo.org
Neuroscience Online   neuroscience.uth.tmc.edu
Society for Neuroscience   www.sfn.org

Simplifying, Decluttering, and Organizing

Institute for Challenging Disorganization   www.challengingdisorganization.org
Nat'l Assoc. of Professional Organizers   www.napo.net

NOTES

Author's Note: In a few instances, quotes were edited for length, but special attention was given to not alter the meaning. Notes below are listed by chapter and page number.

Chapter One:
The Relationship Between Money and Happiness

5   As The Beatles' George Harrison wrote: The song was written by George Harrison in 1988, and it is the opening soundtrack for his posthumous album, *Brainwashed*; www.youtube.com and www.lyricsmode.com, accessed on July 6, 2013.

5   The definition I prefer is from psychologist: Martin Seligman, *Authentic Happiness*, Free Press, (2002), 261. This quote was derived from different phrases by Seligman, all on page 261.

6   Ed Diener and Robert Biswas-Diener state: Ed Diener and Robert Biswas-Diener, *Happiness*, Blackwell Publishing, (2008), 4.

7   Olivia Mellan, psychotherapist and author, states: Ellen Goodstein "Have That Money Talk—For Better, Not Worse," www.bankrate.com, (December 8, 2004).

8   Financial security is the amount of money: Definition is by author.

9   A classic essay written by John Maynard Keynes: John Maynard Keynes, "Economic Possibilities for Our Grandchildren," http://www.econ.yale.edu/smith/econ116a/keynes1.pdf, accessed on July 6, 2013.

9   Americans with full-time jobs: "United States Bureau of Labor Statistics, Household Data Annual Averages: Persons at Work in Agriculture and Nonagricultural Industries by Hours of Work," (2012), http://www.bls.gov/cps/lfcharacteristics.htm, accessed on June 11, 2013.

10   "The problem," she says: Laura Vanderkam, *168 Hours*, Portfolio, (2010), 21.

12   The goal of practitioners was to bring patients: Claudia Wallis, "The New Science of Happiness," *Time*, (January 17, 2005), A4.

13   "I realized my profession was half-baked": Ibid.

14   "I have to confess that even though I write books about children": Martin E.P. Seligman and Mihaly Csikszentmihalyi, "Positive Psychology, An Introduction," *American Psychologist*, (January 2000), 5–6.

16   The study concluded that about 50 percent of our happiness: Wallis, "The New Science of Happiness" A7.

16   They concluded that our environment: Sonja Lyubomirsky, *The How of Happiness*, Penguin Press, (2007), 22; S. Lyubomirsky, K.M. Sheldon, and D. Schkade, "Pursuing Happiness: The Architecture of Sustainable Change," *Review of General Psychology*, (2005), 9: 111–131.

18   If we accept that our happiness is on a continuum: Tal Ben-Shahar, *Happier*, McGraw-Hill, (2007), 8.

18   They developed a theory called the *hedonic treadmill*: P.D. Brickman and D.T. Campbell, "Hedonic Relativism and Planning the Good Society," in *Adaptation Level Theory: A Symposium*, edited by M.H. Appley, Academic Press, (1971).

18   Hedonic is defined as the science of how we feel: Martin Seligman, *Authentic Happiness*, Simon and Schuster, (2002), 6.

20   But, for the remainder of the study: Diener and Biswas-Diener, *Happiness,* 151–164.

21   Specifically, their research suggests that most: Ed Diener, Richard E. Lucas, and Christie Napa Scollon, "Beyond the Hedonic Treadmill, Revising the Adaptation Theory of Well-Being," *American Psychologist*, (May–June 2006), 305–314.

21   In addition, their research has shown that individuals differ: Ibid.

21   Their research has raised new issues involving adaptation: Ibid.

22   Most people have baselines: Diener and Biswas-Diener, *Happiness*, 152.

22   David Lykken (the lead researcher in the Minnesota twin study) stated: Wallis, "The New Science of Happiness," A8.

22   Csikszentmihalyi emphasized the importance of intention: Mihaly Csikszentmihalyi, "If We Are So Rich, Why Aren't We Happy?" *American Psychologist*, (1999), 54(10): 824.

23   Hierarchy of Needs Diagram: A.H. Maslow, "A Theory of Human Motivation," *Psychological Review*, (1943), 50: 370–396; A. Maslow, *Towards a Psychology of Being*, Van Nostrand, (1968); A. Maslow, *The Farthest Reaches of Human Nature*, Viking, (1971).

23   He found similar results in China and the United States: R.A. Easterlin, "Will Raising the Incomes of All Increase the Happiness of All?" *Journal of Economic Behavior and Organization*, (1995), 27: 39–40.

23   After researching 37 countries over many years: Richard A. Easterlin, Laura Angelescu McVey, Malgorzata Switek, Onnicha Sawangfa, and Jacqueline Smith Zweig, "The Happiness-Income Paradox Revisited," http://www.pnas.org/cgi/doi/10.1073/pnas.1015962107, (October 26, 2010), 1.

24   The fact that societies do not seem to become happier: Andrew Clark, Paul Frijters, and Michael Shields, "Relative Income, Happiness and Utility: An Explanation for the Easterlin Paradox and Other Puzzles," *Journal of Economic Literature*, (2008), 46(1): 95–144; John Helliwell, Richard Layard, and Jeffrey Sachs, "World Happiness Report," (2012), chapter 3, 60; Richard Easterlin, "The Economics of Happiness," *Daedalus*, (2004), 133(2): 26–33.

24   Researchers have agreed that the impact of income on happiness: Daniel Kahneman and Angus Deaton, "High Income Improves Evaluation of Life But Not Emotional Well-Being," Center for Health and Well-Being, Princeton University, http://www.pnas.org/cgi/doi/10.1073/pnas.1011492107, (August 4, 2010).

25   Even small gains in a household's income: Helliwell, Layard, and Sachs, "World Happiness Report," chapter 1, 3.

25 The fact that relatively small amounts of money: Helliwell, Layard, and Sachs, "World Happiness Report," chapter 1, 8.

25 Conversely, countries that ranked lowest: Ibid., chapter 2, 13.

25 Respondents are asked whether they experienced: Kahneman and Deaton, "High Income Improves."

26 Happiest Countries and Least-Happy Countries: Helliwell, Layard, and Sachs, "World Happiness Report," chapter 2, 52.

26 Respondents are asked to answer the question: Kahneman and Deaton, "High Income Improves."

26 Within any society, richer people: Helliwell, Layard, and Sachs, "World Happiness Report," chapter 3, 60.

27 They found that increased income: Kahneman and Deaton, "High Income Improves."

28 "It's like you hit some sort of ceiling": Jennifer Robison, "Happiness Is Love—and $75,000," , (November 17, 2011).

28 Kahneman states: "Emotional happiness": Ibid.

28 Kahneman and Deaton also suggest that poor health: Kahneman and Deaton, "High Income Improves."

28 Accomplishing goals and feeling financially secure: Robison, "Happiness Is Love"; Helliwell, Layard, and Sachs, "World Happiness Report," chapter 1, 7 and chapter 2, 2.

28 Countries such as France: David Gauthier-Villars, "For France, a Joie de Vivre Index," Wall Street Journal, (September 15, 2009), A11.

28 Great Britain is studying well-being: Ibid.

28 In his summary of recent research: Adam Davidson, "Money Changes Everything," New York Times Magazine, (February 10, 2013), 14–15.

29 In the United States, people in the top 1 percent: Timothy Noah, "The 1 Percent Are Only Half the Problem," The New York Times Opinionator, http://opinionator.blogs.nytimes.com/2013/05/18/the-1-percent-are-only-half-the-problem, (May 18, 2013).

29 A Pew Research study concluded that the top 7 percent: Pew Research Study 2009–2011, http://www.rt.com/usa/us-financial-crisis-wealth-occupy-wall-street-307/, (April 24, 2013).

29 Workers are concerned about job security: Richard A. Easterlin, "When Growth Outpaces Happiness," New York Times, (September 28, 2012), A31.

30 The tax rate in Denmark is considered: Sarah Hampson, "The World's Happiest People Share Their Lessons," Globe and Mail, www.theglobeandmail.com/life/relationships/the-worlds-happiest-people, (September 10, 2012); Timothy D. Bunn, "The Danish Way: World's Highest Taxes Buy Prosperity, Happiness," http://www.blog.syracuse.com/opinion/2010/11/the_danish_way, (November 3, 2010).

30 All citizens have equal rights: "Denmark: The Official Website of Denmark," http://www.denmark.dk/en/society/welfare, accessed on May 27, 2013; Bunn, "The Danish Way."

30 Danes have the lowest poverty level in the world: Bunn, "The Danish Way."

30 This is not happenstance; Denmark devotes: Dan Buettner, "Thrive: Finding Happiness the Blue Zones Way," "Lessons from Denmark," http://www.bluezones.com/2012/02/lessons-from-denmark/, (February 7, 2012).

30 They have a strong work ethic: Ibid.

30 Danes place a high priority on living a socially: "Denmark: The Official Website of Denmark," http://www.denmark.dk/en/society/welfare, accessed on May 27, 2013.

31 This eliminates the pressure to: Buettner, "Thrive."

31 Danes are very tolerant: Ibid.

32 Other U.S. research studies involving: Helliwell, Layard, and Sachs, "World Happiness Report," chapter 1, 7 and chapter 2, 20; David Lykken, *Happiness: The Nature and Nurture of Joy and Contentment*, St. Martin's Griffin, (1999); Jan-Emmanuel De Neve et al., "Genes, Economics, and Happiness," referenced in "World Happiness Report."

32 Cognitive scientist Hal Pashler: Sally L. Satel, "Primed for Controversy," *New York Times*, (February 24, 2013), 8.

32 The objective is to make sure the basic tenets: Ibid.

33 Researchers suggest many possible reasons: Adam Davidson, "Money Changes Everything," *New York Times Magazine*, (February 10, 2013), 14–15; Gauthier-Villars, "For France," A11.

33 Easterlin's research has been challenged: B. Stevenson, J. Wolfers, "Economic Growth and Subjective Well-Being: Reassessing the Easterlin Paradox," *Brookings Papers on Economic Activity*, (Spring 2008), 1–87; R. Veenhoven, and M. Hagerty, "Rising Happiness in Nations 1946–2004: A Reply to Easterlin," *Social Indicators Research*, (2006), 79(3): 421–436.

33 "Instead of straining to feed the illusion": R. Easterlin, "Feeding the Illusion of Growth and Happiness: A Reply to Hagerty and Veenhoven," *Social Indicators Research*, (2005), 74(3): 429–443.

33 There is a lot of evidence that being richer: British Broadcasting Company News, *The Science of Happiness*, series producer Mike Rudin, http://news.bbc.co.uk/2/hi/programmes/happiness_formula/4783836.stm, (April 30, 2006).

Chapter Two: How Your Brain Is Wired

36 Although most people tend to think of neuroscience: "What Is Neuroscience?," http://www.allpsychologycareers.com/topics/neuroscience.html, accessed on May 27, 2013.

36 Although neuroscience originally resided within the field of biology: "Neuroscience," http://en.wikipedia.org/wiki/Neuroscience, accessed on May 27, 2013.

36 Neuroscientist and professor of psychology Richard Davidson: Richard J. Davidson and Sharon Begley, *The Emotional Life of Your Brain*, Hudson Street Press, (2012), viii.

36 Loosely called *brain mapping*, researchers can see: Penelope Green, "This is Your Brain on Happiness," *Oprah*, (March 2008), 228–233.

37 All mammals have an amygdala: Susan Cain, *Quiet*, Crown Publishers, (2012), 101 and 118.

37 In addition to the amygdala: Jason Zweig, email correspondence to author, May 31, 2013.

37 Neuroscientists have discovered that the brain: Alison Gopnik, "The Brain as a Quick-Change Artist," *Wall Street Journal*, (May 4, 2013).

37 Most brain areas can also multitask: Ibid.

37 The human brain has evolved: Daniel Kahneman, *Thinking, Fast and Slow*, Farrar, Straus and Giroux, (2011), 37.

37 Psychologist Kelly McGonigal states in her book: Kelly McGonigal, *The Willpower Instinct*, Avery, (2012).

37 Researchers are learning that the prefrontal cortex: Davidson and Begley, *The Emotional Life of Your Brain*, 69–72.

38 These inhibitory signals tell the amygdala: Ibid.

38 His research showed that some people: Ibid.

38 Not everyone has a significant amount: Ibid.

39 "Pure rationality with no feelings can be as bad": Jason Zweig, *Your Money and Your Brain*, Simon and Schuster, (2007), 5–6.

42 "So I split my contributions 50/50": Ibid., 4.

43 The brain's ability to build new neural pathways: Davidson and Begley, *Emotional Life of Your Brain*, 9.

43 Although the traditional thinking was that reaching: Malcolm Gladwell, *Outliers*, Little, Brown and Company, (2008), 38.

43 It also applies to technology experts: Ibid., 50–67.

43 The brains of virtuoso violinists: Davidson and Begley, *Emotional Life of Your Brain*, 9.

44 It allows us to know what a clock is for: Kahneman, *Thinking, Fast and Slow*, 21.

45 Only System 2 can follow rules: Ibid., 36.

45 Yet, System 2 is lazy: Ibid., 31.

45 "System 1 runs automatically": Ibid., 24

45 For the physicians who were given the second statement: Ibid., 367.

46 Would you still buy it if it were described: Ibid., 88.

46 Kahneman offers some wise advice: Ibid., 417.

46 This theory states that we care more: Ed Diener and Robert Biswas-Diener, *Happiness*, Blackwell Publishing, (2008), 107, they describe this as social comparison; Jonathan Clements, "Money and Happiness: Here's Why You Won't Laugh All the Way to the Bank," *Wall Street Journal*, (August 16, 2006).

48 Figure 2.5: Carl Richards, BehaviorGap.com, (2012); this sketch is titled "Repeat Until Happy"; used with permission.

49 This suggests that it is not the *amount* of money: Diener and Biswas-Diener, *Happiness*, 111.

50 "Always wanting more, in order to keep up with whoever has more": Zweig, *Your Money and Your Brain*, 243.

51 Behavioral finance experts have shown that the pain: Jonathon Clements, "Getting Going, Why Your Lizard Brain Makes You a Bad Investor," *Wall Street Journal*, (October 25, 2006).

51 If we use an average of 2.0: Kahneman, *Thinking, Fast and Slow*, 284.

51 According to Kahneman: "Organisms that treat threats": Kahneman, *Thinking, Fast and Slow*, 282.

51 Investors may be very hesitant to sell: Veronica Dagher, "Control Yourself," *Wall Street Journal*, (June 8, 2009).

53 Physiologists are hoping that studying the biology: John Coates, "The Biology of Bubble and Crash," *New York Times*, (June 10, 2012).

Chapter Three: Your Foundation

57　Psychologist Jonathan Schooler at the University of California: Jonah Lehrer, "How to be Creative," *Wall Street Journal*, (March 10, 2012).

62　many great contributions originated from introverts: Susan Cain, *Quiet*, Crown Publishers, (2012), front inside cover flap.

62　Money Messages You Were Taught as a Child: This concept is attributed to George Kinder, *Seven Stages of Money Maturity*, Random House, (1999), 40-42.

68　Author Anne Lamott, in her book: Anne Lamott, *Bird by Bird*, First Anchor Books, (1994), 185–186.

69　She decided to fill the void by writing: Ibid., 187.

71　She then returns home to New York: Katherine Rosman, "Over the Internet, Into My Mom's Heart," *Wall Street Journal*, (September 1, 2007).

Chapter Four: Compound Benefits—
Small Changes with Big Rewards

83　"Family and friends are crucial": Ed Diener, *The Science of Happiness*, British Broadcasting Company News, *The Science of Happiness*, series producer Mike Rudin, (April 30, 2006).

84　Relationships were mentioned by 73 percent: *The Undervalued Component of Happiness*, British Broadcasting Company News, series producer Mike Rudin, http://news.bbc.co.uk/2/hi/programmes/happiness_formula/4888706.stm, (May 9, 2006).

84　One study reported that isolation triggers: Kanoko Matsuyama, "Aging Easier When Interacting," *Albuquerque Journal*, (October 6, 2012).

84　In his book *Spontaneous Happiness*: Andrew Weil, *Spontaneous Happiness*, Little, Brown and Company, (2011), 163.

84　In recent years, he came to realize: Ibid., 164.

85　Pets also provide health benefits: Mehmet Oz, "Why Keeping a Pet Is Good for You," http://www.Oprah.com/spirit/Pets-and-Health-Benefits-Why-Keeping-A-Pet -is-Good-For-You, accessed on July 26, 2013.

86　Experiences have a far greater impact on our happiness: Eliza Sarasohn, "Your Ultimate Day Off," *Experience Life*, (March 2010), 76–77.

93　"Then I have a tuna salad sandwich": "Talking with Gene Wilder," *Time*, (March 24, 2008).

93　"That's the way my parents and my family": Maria Shriver, *Just Who Will You Be?*, Hyperion, (2008), 74–75.

93　She realized that the true answer involved: Ibid., 76.

94　We have to give ourselves permission and freedom: Ibid., 78.

95　He defines flow as "the psychological state": Christopher Peterson, *A Primer in Positive Psychology*, Oxford University Press, (2006), 66; quote is by Csikszentmihalyi.

96　"Self-consciousness disappears, and the sense": Mihaly Csikszentmihalyi, *Flow, The Psychology of Optimal Experience*, Harper Perennial, (1990), 71.

96 The state of flow can be created from a creative: Peterson, *A Primer in Positive Psychology*, 66.

96 It requires "presence, a problem-solving attitude, and the conviction": Joseph Hart, "5 Ways to Practice Happiness," *Experience Life*, (July-August 2008).

96 An optimal experience for flow may be challenging: Csikszentmihalyi, *Flow*, 71.

96 "Happiness, in fact, is a condition that must be prepared": Ibid.

97 Csikszentmihalyi believes that negative emotions: Ibid., 7.

97 boredom, and anxiety may prevent the state of flow: Ibid., 75.

97 Psychologist Ken Pargament characterizes spiritualism: Jerry Lopper, "Faith and Religion Bring Benefits of Health, Happiness, Longevity," http://www.jerry-lopper.suite101.com/find-spirituality-positive-psychology-research-a113231, accessed on May 24, 2012.

97 Christopher Peterson, a psychology professor at the University of Michigan: Peterson, *A Primer in Positive Psychology*, 294.

98 "Being a member of a spiritual community provides": Diener and Biswas-Diener, *Happiness*, 119.

101 Psychologist Tal Ben-Shahar discusses the idea: Tal Ben-Shahar online course; "Foundations of Positive Psychology," Penn Liberal and Professional Studies, June 2, 2009–August 18, 2009.

102 One research study looked at several different forms: M.E.P. Seligman, T.A. Steen, N. Park, and C. Peterson, "Positive Psychology Progress: Empirical Validations of Interventions," *American Psychologist*, (2005), 60: 410–421.

102 They were told the three things could be minor: Peterson, *A Primer in Positive Psychology*, 38.

102 The researchers found that "counting one's blessings increases": Peterson, *A Primer in Positive Psychology*, 39.

102 It doesn't make life perfect: Robert A. Emmons, *Thanks!*, Houghton Mifflin, (2007), 209.

102 Psychologists Robert Emmons and Michael McCullough found: Ibid., 30.

103 Research has shown that translating thoughts into words: Ibid.,189.

105 Maya Angelou captured the spirit of giving back: Maya Angelou, *Letter to My Daughter*, Random House, (2008), 12.

107 According to Robert Putnam, professor of public policy: Jan Alexander, "Positive Yields," *Worth*, (March, 2005), 43–45.

108 Scientists in the field of neuroscience have studied: Frans De Waal, "Our Kinder, Gentler Ancestors," *Wall Street Journal*, (October 3, 2009).

108 In essence, doing good feels good: Ibid.

111 "The third generation's numerous members grow up in luxury": James E. Hughes Jr., *Family Wealth—Keeping It in the Family*, Bloomberg Press, (2004), 3.

111 To successfully preserve its wealth, a family must: Ibid., 20.

111 All work is of equal value to the growth: Ibid., 36.

113 In his book, *Ethical Will*, Baines describes: Barry K. Baines, *Ethical Wills*, Da Capo Press, (2006).

113 Sometimes, they are funded by contributions: Ron Lieber, "Borrowing From Your Family, by Design," *New York Times*, (September 28, 2012); Ron Lieber, "From Parents, a Living Inheritance," *New York Times*, (September 21, 2012).

116 However, the next highest response was contentment: British Broadcasting Company News, *The Undervalued Component of Happiness*.

116 "Happiness is when you are OK inside": Ibid.

116 This implies that we are content when the different parts: Ibid.

116 It reported that men and women tend to be happier: British Broadcasting Company News, *Happiness is Smile Shaped*, series producer Mike Rudin, http://news.bbc.co.uk/2/hi/programmes/happiness_formula/4787558.stm, (May 9, 2006).

116 This same dynamic may impact our memories: Zweig, *Your Money and Your Brain*, 256.

117 God grant me the serenity to accept the things I cannot change: "Serenity Prayer," written by Reinhold Niebuhr on July 1, 1943, for the Union Church of Heath, Massachusetts.

118 Whitehead states in his book: Bert Whitehead, *Why Smart People Do Stupid Things With Money*, Infinity Publishing, (2002), 36 of preview edition.

Chapter Five: Compound Benefits—Lifestyle Shifts

123 Research studies show that regular exercise: Jen Mueller, "Your Body Benefits from Your Hard Work," http://www.sparkpeople.com/resource/articles_print.asp?id = 413, accessed on November 6, 2011.

123 A 2010 study found that just 10 minutes of exercise: Andrew Heffernan, "Don't Skip That Workout," *Experience Life*, (October 2012).

123 Sitting at a desk or in front of a computer for long hours: Gretchen Reynolds, "Don't Just Sit There," *New York Times*, (April 29, 2012), 8.

123 Another study by the Baker IDI Heart and Diabetes Institute: Ibid.

124 Exercise provides far more than just physical benefits: P. Callaghan, "Exercise: A Neglected Intervention in Mental Health Care," *Journal of Psychiatric and Mental Health Nursing*, (2004) 11: 476–483.

124 Exercise has been called a natural antidepressant: Tal Ben-Shahar online course; "Foundations of Positive Psychology," Penn Liberal and Professional Studies, June 2, 2009–August 18, 2009.

126 Laughter triggers the release of endorphins: Elizabeth Scott, "The Laughing Cure," About.com, http://www.stresshealth/a/laughter.htm, (October 7, 2009).

130 "Giving yourself permission to take care of yourself": Kate Larsen, "Winning Lifestyles Connection," http://www.katelarsen.com/ezines/july2007.html, (July 31, 2007).

132 Our body repairs itself during sleep: Pilar Gerasimo, "Ten Acts of Healthy Rebellion," *Experience Life*, (May 2012).

133 Researchers have determined that even a short nap: David K. Randall, "Rethinking Sleep," *New York Times*, (September 23, 2012).

133 They concluded that people often sleep a few hours: Ibid.

133 Once the research subjects stopped fighting: Ibid.

134 Buying stock in Microsoft on December 31, 1986: Data is from investment research firm Morningstar, Inc.

134 After that date the "dotcom crash" began: Andrew Beattie, "Market Crashes: The Dotcom Crash," http://www.investopedia.com/features/crashes/crashes8.asp, accessed on August 10, 2013.

137 "More stuff doesn't make people happier": Mark Matousek, "Live Better With Less," *Experience Life*, (December 2007); quote is by McKibben.

137 "The idea that more is better, which has been orthodoxy": Ibid.

137 McKibben suggests that we choose to buy: Ibid.

138 "On bad days, clutter pecks away at my whole outlook on life": Pilar Gerasimo, "Clutter's Continuity," *Experience Life*, (April 2012), 7.

138 In her book *Organizing from the Inside Out*: Julie Morgenstern, *Organizing from the Inside Out*, Henry Holt, (2004), 16.

139 Morgenstern calls this "zigzag organizing": Ibid., 71.

140 To take better care of myself and spend more time: Cheryl Richardson, *The Art of Extreme Self-Care*, Hay House, (2009), 18–21.

144 When researchers look for the physiological location for creativity: Jonah Lehrer, "How to Be Creative," *Wall Street Journal*, (March 10, 2012).

145 We know a great deal about how memories are formed: Joseph LeDoux, "Why the 'Right Brain' Idea is Wrong-Headed," *Huffington Post*, http://www.huffingtonpost.com/joseph-ledoux/why-the-right-brain-idea_b_206156.html, (May 29, 2009).

145 Sure, the task may engage the activated area: Ibid.

145 The idea is to get your thoughts: Julia Cameron, *The Artist's Way*, Tarcher/Putnam, (2002), 9–18.

146 "It's Pavlovian: Follow the routine and you get a creative payoff": Twyla Tharp, *The Creative Habit*, Simon and Schuster, (2003), 18.

146 "Combining the two is the essence of the creative life": Ibid.,173.

146 If he takes a vacation , Mosley writes: Walter Mosley, "This Year You Write Your Novel," Little, Brown and Company, (2007), excerpt in *Oprah*, (August 2007).

147 For example, blue is often associated with relaxation: Jonah Lehrer, "The New Rules of Creativity," *Wired Magazine*, (May 2012).

147 Watch a short video of stand-up comedy: Lehrer, "How to be Creative."

147 Experience other cultures through travel: Ibid.

147 "He is playing for pleasure": Ibid.

149 Cognitive reappraisal therapy: Richard J. Davidson and Sharon Begley, *Emotional Life of Your Brain*, Hudson Street Press, (2012), 243.

149 Davidson states: "This type of cognitive training": Ibid., 244.

149 In his 2011 book *Flourish*, Seligman talks about: Brian Johnson, "Flourish," *Experience Life*, (November 2011), 75–76; quote is by Seligman.

149 They think, "It's going away quickly": Ibid.

149 Seligman concludes that we can learn: Ibid.

Chapter Six: Happiness—Pure and Simple

155 Start planning an "ultimate day off": Eliza Sarasohn, "The Ultimate Day Off," *Experience Life*, (March 2010).

156 At work, he reported that his stress levels: Peter Bregman, "How (and Why) to Stop Multitasking," *Harvard Business Review*, http://blogs.hbr.org/bregman/2010/05/how-and-why-to-stop-multitaski.html, (May 20, 2010).

157 The following traits (and many more) can be cultivated: Brian Johnson, "Flourish," *Experience Life*, (November 2011), 75–76; Roger Walsh, "To Give is to Receive," http://www.gratefulness.org/readings/rw_togive.htm, accessed on September 23, 2007.

159 He was curious whether a meditation practice: Richard J. Davidson and Sharon Begley, *Emotional Life of Your Brain*, Hudson Street Press, (2012), 200–205.

159 Dr. Kabat-Zinn developed a type of meditation: Ibid.

159 While referring to the benefits of MBSR: Ibid., 204.

159 In addition to the benefits that Davidson identified: Handout from lecture by Barry W. Ramo and Michelle DuVal of the New Mexico Heart Institute, Albuquerque Academy Community Lecture Series, (September 11, 2012).

160 He is a proponent of what he refers to as *breath work*: Andrew Weil, *Spontaneous Happiness*, Little, Brown and Company, (2011), 145–146.

161 To deepen breathing, practice exhaling more air: Ibid., 146.

162 The days after the day of rest become better, too: Naomi Levy, "Change Your Life … Take a Day of Rest," *Parade Magazine*, (October 11, 1998).

163 The color yellow is associated with joy: *Real Simple*, (January 2011).

163 Blue is considered to be relaxing and to induce creativity: Jonah Lehrer, "The New Rules of Creativity," *Wired Magazine*, (May 2012).

164 Spend time with your dog or cat: Ibid.

164 Author Francine Prose fell in love with a crabapple tree: Francine Prose, "The Giving Tree," *Real Simple*, (May 2012), 61–63.

Chapter Seven: The Essentials of Financial Security

171 Financial Advisor Paula Hogan describes human capital: Paula Hogan, "Financial Planning: A Look from the Outside In," *Journal of Financial Planning*, (June 2012).

172 A college degree is considered the clearest path: Ben Casselman, "The Cost of Dropping Out," *Wall Street Journal*, (November 23, 2012).

173 and jobs close to home (with short commutes): "How to 'Thrive': Short Commutes, More Happy Hours," National Public Radio, http://www.npr.org/2011/10/19/141514467/small-changes-can-help-you-thrive-happily, excerpt from *Thrive* by Dan Buettner, (October 19, 2011).

177 Many people with high incomes: Thomas J. Stanley and William D. Danko, *The Millionaire Next Door*, Pocket Books, Simon and Schuster, (1996), 15.

177 He discovered that, on average: Ibid., 11.

177 The average savings rate in the United States: U.S. Department of Commerce, Bureau of Economic Analysis, (June 1, 2013); savings rate is 4.4%.

180 Financial advisor Kenneth Robinson: Kenneth Robinson, *Don't Make a Budget*, SPS Publications, (2009), 19.

184 Financial planner Carl Richard astutely asks: Carl Richards, email June 12, 2012, with the "Repeat Until Happy" sketch.

185 A Dun & Bradstreet study found that people spend: "Guide to Credit Cards: How Credit Cards Encourage You to Overspend," http://www.seekingalpha.com/article/20333-guide-to-credit-cards-how-credit-cards-encourage-you, (November 2012).

185 McDonald's restaurants found that the average: Matthew Paulson, "Do We Really Spend More with Credit Cards?," http://voices.yahoo.com/do-we-really-spend-more-credit-cards-195486.html, (February 14, 2007).

186 George Lowenstein, a professor of economics: Jeanette Pavini, "When Using Cash is Better Than Credit," http://articles.marketwatch.com/story/when-using-cash-is-better-than-credit-2011-09-06-174820, (September 6, 2011); quote is by Lowenstein.

190 Companies use derivatives (such as swaps: Louis Chaillet, "Financial Leverage-Lights on an Elusive Concept," http://www.edhec-risk.com/latest_news/featured_analysis/RISKArticle.2008-10-10.2612?, (October 10, 2008); Kimberly Amadeo, "What Are Derivatives?" About.com, http://useconomy.about.com/od/glossary/g/Derivatives.htm, (April 2, 2013).

190 This was apparent with Lehman Brothers: Andy Serwer and Allan Sloan, "The Price of Greed," *Time*, (September 29, 2008), 37.

190 In other words, Lehman Brothers was in debt for 35 times: Ibid.

190 Other financial firms were reportedly leveraged at roughly: Alan S. Blinder, "Six Blunders En Route to a Crisis," *New York Times*, (January 25, 2009).

190 A *New York Times* article reported that "under 33-to-1 leverage: Ibid.

195 One is that he has thoroughly enjoyed living: Jonathan Clements, "How Houses Eat Money," *Albuquerque Journal* (*Wall Street Journal* syndicated article), (June 12, 2005).

199 A will typically goes through a probate process: Saabira Chaudhuri, "The 25 Documents You Need Before You Die," *Wall Street Journal*, (July 2, 2011).

Chapter Eight: Tax Strategies

209 If all of your money is in an IRA: Money withdrawn from an IRA is subject to income taxes. In the example provided, $40,000 is needed from the IRA to cover living expenses (in addition to the $20,000 in Social Security benefits). Because taxes are due on the $40,000, the amount withdrawn may need to be as high as $55,000 in order to provide $15,000 for taxes, leaving $40,000 for cash flow. The $15,000 estimate for taxes is a hypothetical example. The actual taxes may be higher or lower.

212 In March 2013 he recommended that it may *not* be wise: Michael Kitces, "Asset Location: The New Wealth Management Value-Add For Optimal Portfolio Design," http://www.kitces.com/blog/archives/479-Asset-Location-The-New-Wealth-Management-Value-Add-For-Optimal-Portfolio-Design.html, (March 6, 2013).

214 Other examples of tax avoidance or tax deferral investments: Paul Sullivan, "The 1040 Blues," *New York Times*, (February 12, 2013).

217 The backdoor Roth IRA involves contributing: Walter Updegrave, "The Other Way to Invest in a Roth IRA," *CNN Money*, http://money.cnn.com/2013/01/23/pf/expert/roth-ira.moneymag/index.html?iid = EL, (January 13, 2013).

Chapter Nine: Protect Yourself

225 "And now he's wearing stripes": Dewey Johnson, excerpt from sermon, Sandia Presbyterian Church, August 18, 2002.

226 Throughout 2007, members of the Federal Reserve: Jon Hilsenrath and Kristina Peterson, "Records Show Fed Wavering in 2007," *Wall Street Journal*, (January 19, 2013).

226 According to a white paper issued by the Federal Reserve: Letter and white paper from Ben Bernanke to Congressmen Tim Johnson and Spencer Bachus, (January 4, 2012); white paper is titled "The U.S. Housing Market: Current Conditions and Policy Considerations."

227 In March 2008, U.S. investment bank Bear Stearns: Michael Lewis, *The Big Short*, W. W. Norton, (2011), 235.

227 On September 7, mortgage giants Fannie Mae: Ibid., 259.

227 On Monday morning, September 15, 2008, we learned: Ibid., 237.

227 The U.S. government refused to bail out Lehman Brothers: Andy Serwer and Allan Sloan, "The Price of Greed," *Time*, (September 29, 2008).

227 By Friday, September 12, 2008, Merrill Lynch's stock price: Heidi N. Moore, "Is Bank of America Getting a Bargain in Merrill Lynch?" *Wall Street Journal*, (September 15, 2008).

227 Merrill Lynch CEO John Thain reluctantly agreed: Ibid.

227 In late September 2008, AIG failed: Lewis, *The Big Short*, 259–260.

228 Within a few months, the U.S. government decided to buy: Ibid., 261.

228 "The short-term expected gain would not have justified": Ibid, 258–259. This quote was altered slightly. The term "mezzanine" was removed twice. The original quote stated: "No investment bank owned by its employees would have leveraged itself 35:0, or bought and held $50 billion in *mezzanine* CDOs. I doubt any partnership would have sought to game the rating agencies, or leapt into bed with loan sharks, or even allowed *mezzanine* CDOs to be sold to its customers." CDOs are divided into three tranches, which signify the amount of risk. A mezzanine CDO is the middle level of risk.

229 "The surface rippled, but down below": Ibid., 254.

229 "If you lose, you lose someone else's money": Serwer and Sloan, "The Price of Greed."

230 In addition, a fiduciary is required to make: Thomas Giachetti, "Defining Fiduciary: What is an Advisor's True Fiduciary Duty?," *Investment Advisor*, (November 2006).

231 Reportedly, 80 percent of the financial professionals: Chris Otts, "Who to Trust for Financial Advice?," *Courier-Journal*, http://www.courier-journal.com/article/20130413/BetterLife05/304130024/229656267, (April 14, 2013); quote is by Helaine Olen; Martin Smith, *The Retirement Gamble*, Frontline documentary, (April 23, 2013); the narrator stated: "But the vast majority of so-called advisors— around 85 percent—are not fiduciaries."

231 A survey released in 2010 by the Consumer Federation: Alexis Leondis, "Clueless U.S. Investors Believe Brokers have Fiduciary Duty, Survey Says," http://www.bloomberg.com/news/2010-09-15/-clueless-u-s-investors-believe-brokers-have-fiduciary-duty-survey-says.html, (September 15, 2010).

232 However, broker-dealers are excluded from the definition: "SEC Study Recommends Uniform Fiduciary Standard for Investment Advisers and Broker-Dealers," Baker Hostetler, http://www.bakerlaw.com/alerts/sec-study-recommends-uniform-fiduciary-standard-for-investment-advisers-and-broker-dealers-2-8-2011, (February 8, 2011).

232 Section 913 of the Dodd-Frank Wall Street Reform: "SEC Requests Input for a Potential Uniform Fiduciary Standard of Conduct," www.bingham.com/Alerts/2013/03/SEC-Requests-Input-on-a-Uniform-Fiduciary, (March 12, 2013).

232 Second, financial advisors would likely need: Helaine Olen, *Pound Foolish*, Portfolio, (2012), 110.

233 In a *New York Times* article by Tara Siegel Bernard: Tara Siegel Bernard, "Will You Be My Fiduciary?" *New York Times*, (February 16, 2010).

233 The Fiduciary Pledge: Ibid.

241 According to a report issued by J.P. Morgan Asset Management: Jasper Berens, "Adviser Charging: Putting a Price on Financial Advice," (May 2011), 5.

241 Australia is implementing a similar (no commission) policy: Jason Zweig, "Going Dutch: Could Fee Hurdles Come Down Everywhere?" *Wall Street Journal*, (June 21, 2013).

243 The large firms have traditionally directed: Susanne Craig and Jessica Silver-Greenberg, "Selling the Home Brand: A Look Inside an Elite JPMorgan Unit," *New York Times*, (March 3, 2013).

245 Below is a list of potential services: Portions of this list are from a special report by Bob Veres, *Inside Information*, (May 10, 2013).

Chapter Ten: Investment Strategies

256 This mistake was apparent in the 2008 financial crisis: Data is from S&P 500 Financials (Sector), June 1, 2007 = $508.86, March 6, 2009 = $81.74; decline = 83.9 percent, rounded to 84 percent, http://www.google.com/finance?cid = 10634625, accessed on August 8, 2013.

257 When dividends were reinvested, the average annual return: Morningstar, Inc., "Power of Reinvesting: 1993–2012," chart from presentation "Principles of Investing," (March 1, 2013).

258 Heavy selling of ETFs spread losses to other parts: Scott Patterson, "How the 'Flash Crash' Echoed Black Monday," *Wall Street Journal*, (May 18, 2010).

258 However, he warns that ETFs can be dangerous: Jeff Sommer, "A Mutual Fund Master, Too Worried to Rest," *New York Times*, (August 12, 2012).

259 In 2012, the size of stocks categorized as large-cap: "Market Capitalization; Categorization of Companies by Capitalization," http://en.wikipedia.org/wiki/Market_capitalization, accessed July 13, 2012.

259 Typically, value stocks trade at low prices: "Value Stocks vs. Growth Stocks: Timing Counts," http://knowledge.wharton.upenn.edu/article.cfm?articleid = 890, (March 25, 2004).

261 Barclays purchased most of the assets of Lehman Brothers: "Agreed Lehman Settlement Will Give Bondholders 21 Percent Recovery," http://www.creditflux.com/Investing/2011-06-30/Agreed-Lehman-settlement-will-give-bondholders-21-recovery/, (June 30, 2011).

262 This was evident during the five years ending: Data is from *2013 Ibbotson Classic Yearbook, Large Company Stocks and Intermediate Term Government Bonds*, (2013) 37–38. Source: © 2013 Morningstar. All rights reserved. Used with permission.

262 FINRA (the Financial Industry Regulatory Authority) defines: "Smart Bond Investing— Bond Basics," http://www.finra.org/Investors/InvestmentChoices/Bonds/SmartBondInvesting/bondbasics/, accessed on August 13, 2013.

266 In 2011 Daniel Goldie and Gordon Murray reported: Daniel C. Goldie and Gordon S. Murray, *The Investment Answer*, Hachette Book Group, (2011), 61.

266 An article in *The Economist* reported "The S&P 500 has now": "Hedge Funds: Going Nowhere Fast," http://www.economist.com/news/finance-and-economics/21568741-hedge-funds-have-had-another-lousy-year-cap-disappointing-decade-going, (December 22, 2012).

266 This is shortened to "2 and 20" in investment parlance: Simon Lack, "Hedge Funds Benefit Insiders Only," *Investment News*, (February 4, 2013).

267 Morningstar defines risk as "the extent to which an investment": Definition is from *2013 Ibbotson Classic Yearbook*, Morningstar, Inc., (2013), 294.

267 A good measure is to look at how you reacted: Dow Jones Industrial Average (DJIA) historical data is from www.bigcharts.com, accessed on March 1, 2013.

268 Goldie and Murray, authors of the book: Goldie and Murray, *The Investment Answer*, 25.

271 However, for investors who can stomach the risk and volatility: Data is from *2013 Ibbotson Classic Yearbook, Large Company Stocks and Intermediate Term Government Bonds,* (2013), 37–38. Source: © 2013 Morningstar. All rights reserved. Used with permission.

271 The average annual return over the 25 years: Ibid.

271 Over the 25-year period, the average annual return for the 50–50 portfolio: Ibid.

275 "The best investments for you depend on personal factors": Carl Richards, "Searching for the Best Investment," *Behavior Gap*, email dated June 21, 2012.

280 Sometimes investors have trailed the benchmark: Dalbar, Inc. "2013 Quantitative Analysis of Investor Behavior," report, (April 2013).

281 They hold stock mutual funds for an average: Ibid.

281 This is similar to the "Lake Wobegon" effect: www.brainyquote.com, accessed on August 8, 2013.

281 Research has shown we feel losses: Daniel Kahneman, *Thinking, Fast and Slow*, Farrar, Straus and Giroux, (2011), 284.

284 For a couple aged 65, there is a 25 percent chance: Morningstar, Inc., "Retirees Should Plan for a Long Retirement," slide from presentation "Retirement Income," (March 1, 2013).

288 Average Annual Return for Portfolios with Different Asset Allocations (1926–2012): Data is from *2013 Ibbotson Classic Yearbook, Large Company Stocks and Intermediate Term Government Bonds*, (2013) 37–38. Source: © 2013 Morningstar. All rights reserved. Used with permission.

288 Average Annual Return for Portfolios with Different Asset Allocations (2000–2012): Ibid.

288 A classic 1986 study within the financial industry estimated: Gary Brinson, Brian Singer, and Gilbert Beebower, "Determinants of Portfolio Performance," *Financial Analysts Journal*, (1986) 42(4): 39–48.

288 A study by Daniel Wallick and colleagues at Vanguard: Vanguard Group, Inc. "Vanguard's Principles for Investing Success, Principle 2: Develop a Suitable Asset Allocation Using Broadly Diversified Funds," (2013), 9.

289 Stocks and Bonds: Risk Versus Return: Morningstar, Inc. Source: © 2013 Morningstar. All rights reserved. Used with permission. Stocks in this example are represented by the S&P 500 and bonds are represented by the 20-year U.S. government bond. Risk and return are based on annual data over the period 1970–2012 and are measured by

standard deviation and arithmetic mean. The data assumes reinvestment of all income and does not account for taxes or transaction costs.

292 "Intelligent investors should feel free to fish": Don Phillips, "A Twisted Debate," *Morningstar Advisor*, (February-March 2013).

298 According to research from Morningstar, during the 15-year period: Morningstar, Inc., "Asset-Class Winners and Losers," slide from presentation "Portfolio Diversification and Performance," March 1, 2013. Small stocks are represented by the Ibbotson* Small Company Stock Index. Large company stocks are represented by the S&P 500*, government bonds by the 20-year U.S. government bond, Treasury bills by the 30-day U.S. Treasury bill, and international stocks by the Morgan Stanley Capital EAFE* index. The data assumes reinvestment of all income and does not account for taxes or transaction costs. The diversified portfolio is equally weighted among all five asset classes.

Chapter Eleven: Retirement Strategies

304 "We want to be able to sit out once in a while": Mitch Anthony, *The New Retirementality*, Dearborn Trade, (2001), 5–6.

304 *New York Times* journalist Joe Nocera wrote an article: Joe Nocera, "My Faith-Based Retirement," *New York Times*, (April 27, 2012).

305 According to the Employee Benefit Research Institute's: Ruth Helman, Mathew Greenwald & Assoc.; and Craig Copeland and Jack VanDerhei, "The 2012 Retirement Confidence Survey: Job Insecurity, Debt Weigh on Retirement Confidence, Savings," Employee Benefit Research Institute, report, (March 2012), 32.

305 "Ninety percent identify at least one financial reason"; Ibid, 26.

311 This shortcut came from statistical analysis conducted by: William P. Bengen, "Determining Withdrawal Rates Using Historical Data," *Journal of Financial Planning*, (October 1994), 171–180.

311 Using stock market returns from 1926 until 1993, he determined: Ibid.

311 Bengen later released additional analysis: William Bengen, "How Much is Enough?," *Financial Advisor Magazine*, (May 2012).

311 although he warned against using the higher rate: from email correspondence to author in July 2013, William Bengen explained that using the 4.5 percent withdrawal rate has some strict requirements. One is that all sources of retirement income (outside the investments) and all expenses must grow at the same inflation rate. He explained that this is rarely the case, which is why he warned against using the 4.5 percent rate. When I asked for clarification, he provided the following formula: withdrawals from investment portfolio = retirement income minus retirement spending. He explained that all sources of income outside of the investments (such as social security, pensions, etc.) must increase at least as quickly as the expenses increase. Bill applies an inflation factor such as the consumer price index from the prior year to the expenses. If the CPI is 3 percent, then the retirement income side of the equation (social security, pensions, etc.) must also increase 3 percent. Because pensions often do not have a cost-of-living adjustment, the requirement is rarely met.

311 It requires that the portfolio contain at least 50 percent equities: Bengen, "Determining Withdrawal Rates Using Historical Data," 171–180.

315 In 2004, financial planner Jonathon Guyton added decision rules: Ron Lieber, "How Retirees Can Spend Enough, but Not Too Much," *New York Times*, (August 28, 2009).

316 In fact, his research suggests that a withdrawal rate as high as 6 percent: Ibid.

316 Another financial planner, Michael Kitces, researched withdrawal rates: Ibid.

316 If the P/E ratio is below 12, he surmised that the stock market: Ibid.

317 David Blanchett, head of retirement research for Morningstar: David M. Blanchett, Michael Finke, and Wade D. Pfau, "Low Bond Yields and Safe Portfolio Withdrawal Rates," *The Journal of Wealth Management*, abstract, (Fall 2013), 16.2: 55–62.

317 A 2013 article summarizing their research suggests a much lower withdrawal rate: Ibid.; Darla Mercado, "Low-rate Environment Means Slower Withdrawal Pace: Study," *Investment News*, (February 11, 2013), 4.

324 If you have a mortgage rate of 4 percent, your *after-tax* mortgage interest rate: (4.0 percent x 0.67 = 2.68 percent). The 0.67 is derived by subtracting the marginal tax rate from 1.0; (1.0 − 0.33 percent tax rate = 0.67).

325 Corporations are doing this to reduce their long-term liabilities: "Sears, New York Times Take Pension Action After IRS Guidance," *CFO Journal*, (September 17, 2012); Ellen Schultz, "Trading in Your Pension," *Wall Street Journal*, (September 21, 2012).

325 How do you decide between a lump sum or the traditional: Ibid.; Paul Sullivan, "When Your Pension Offers a Choice," *New York Times*, (July 28, 2012); Shefali Anand, "Retirees Face Tough Choice on Pensions," *Wall Street Journal*, (August 6, 2012); Walter Updegrave, "Your Pension: Lump Sum or Lifetime Payments?," CNN Money, (November 21, 2012); Walter Updegrave, "Pension: Lump Sum or Monthly Payments for Life?," CNN Money, (June 11, 2009).

326 Ellen Schultz, journalist for the *Wall Street Journal* writes: Ellen Schultz, "Trading in Your Pension," *Wall Street Journal*, (September 21, 2012).

Chapter Twelve: Time for a Change

339 Neuroscientists are finding that we each have distinct: Richard J. Davidson and Sharon Begley, *The Emotional Life of Your Brain*, Hudson Street Press, (2012), 2.

345 Stages Three and Four in the Stages of Change Model: James Prochaska, "Six Steps That Can Change Your Life," WebMD, http://www.webmd.com/fitness-exercise/features/six-steps-that-can-change-your-life, (May 22, 2000).

346 Researchers discovered that "hypoglycemic were more likely": Roy F. Baumeister, *Willpower*, Penguin Group, (2011), 44–46.

348 When you check your progress at month's end: Ibid., 247–248.

348 Jim Loehr and Tony Schwartz, in their book: Jim Loehr and Tony Schwartz, *The Power of Full Engagement*, Simon and Schuster, (2003).

350 Debbie Macomber wrote a book titled *Twenty Wishes*: Debbie Macomber, *Twenty Wishes*, MIRA Books, (2008).

360 Research has shown that when dieters write down: Charles Duhigg, "The Power of Habit," *Experience Life*, (January–February 2013).

360 "Resilient people are like trees bending in the wind" Steven Southwick, *AARP Magazine*, (November–December 2009), 24.

360 Another definition of resilience is: Hara Estroff Marano, "The Art of Resilience," *Psychology Today*, http://www.psychologytoday.com/print/24760, (May 1, 2003).

363 She explained that taking charge of your own happiness: Karl Pillemer, *30 Lessons for Living*, Hudson Street Press, (2011), 206–207.

INDEX

■ ■ ■ ■ ■